Communications in Computer and Information Science 2298

Series Editors

Rationale

The CCIS series is devoted to the publication of proceedings of computer science conferences. Its aim is to efficiently disseminate original research results in informatics in printed and electronic form. While the focus is on publication of peer-reviewed full papers presenting mature work, inclusion of reviewed short papers reporting on work in progress is welcome, too. Besides globally relevant meetings with internationally representative program committees guaranteeing a strict peer-reviewing and paper selection process, conferences run by societies or of high regional or national relevance are also considered for publication.

Topics

The topical scope of CCIS spans the entire spectrum of informatics ranging from foundational topics in the theory of computing to information and communications science and technology and a broad variety of interdisciplinary application fields.

Information for Volume Editors and Authors

Publication in CCIS is free of charge. No royalties are paid, however, we offer registered conference participants temporary free access to the online version of the conference proceedings on SpringerLink (http://link.springer.com) by means of an http referrer from the conference website and/or a number of complimentary printed copies, as specified in the official acceptance email of the event.

CCIS proceedings can be published in time for distribution at conferences or as post-proceedings, and delivered in the form of printed books and/or electronically as USBs and/or e-content licenses for accessing proceedings at SpringerLink. Furthermore, CCIS proceedings are included in the CCIS electronic book series hosted in the SpringerLink digital library at http://link.springer.com/bookseries/7899. Conferences publishing in CCIS are allowed to use Online Conference Service (OCS) for managing the whole proceedings lifecycle (from submission and reviewing to preparing for publication) free of charge.

Publication process

The language of publication is exclusively English. Authors publishing in CCIS have to sign the Springer CCIS copyright transfer form, however, they are free to use their material published in CCIS for substantially changed, more elaborate subsequent publications elsewhere. For the preparation of the camera-ready papers/files, authors have to strictly adhere to the Springer CCIS Authors' Instructions and are strongly encouraged to use the CCIS LaTeX style files or templates.

Abstracting/Indexing

CCIS is abstracted/indexed in DBLP, Google Scholar, EI-Compendex, Mathematical Reviews, SCImago, Scopus. CCIS volumes are also submitted for the inclusion in ISI Proceedings.

How to start

To start the evaluation of your proposal for inclusion in the CCIS series, please send an e-mail to ccis@springer.com.

Miguel Félix Mata-Rivera ·
Roberto Zagal-Flores · Daniela Elisabeth Ballari ·
José Antonio León-Borges
Editors

Geographical Information Systems

5th Latin American Conference, GIS-LATAM 2024
Mexico City, Mexico, September 2–6, 2024
Proceedings

Springer

Editors
Miguel Félix Mata-Rivera
UPIITA - Instituto Politécnico Nacional
Mexico City, Mexico

Roberto Zagal-Flores
ESCOM - Instituto Politécnico Nacional
Mexico City, Mexico

Daniela Elisabeth Ballari
Universidad del Azuay
Azuay, Ecuador

José Antonio León-Borges
Universidad de Quintana Roo
Cancún, Mexico

ISSN 1865-0929 ISSN 1865-0937 (electronic)
Communications in Computer and Information Science
ISBN 978-3-031-80016-0 ISBN 978-3-031-80017-7 (eBook)
https://doi.org/10.1007/978-3-031-80017-7

This Springer imprint is published by the registered company Springer Nature Switzerland AG
The registered company address is: Gewerbestrasse 11, 6330 Cham, Switzerland

Preface

In this edition, the 5th GIS-LATAM conference continued to be a vital platform for addressing the challenges faced by our communities and the planet. This year, we are pleased to report a successful return to primarily in-person presentations, complemented by hybrid sessions that allowed broader participation from around the globe. The exchange of ideas and research has never been more essential as we are looking for innovative solutions through geospatial technologies.

The vision of GIS-LATAM is to provide a forum for researchers to share significant findings that advance our understanding of Earth's processes and the interconnected systems that shape our world. This edition showcased a diverse array of peer-reviewed research papers grouped into key thematic areas: Sustainable Energy and Resource Management, Environmental Monitoring and Management, Public Health and Social Issues, Education and Technology in GIS, Climatic Patterns and Natural Disasters

This year, we received 35 submissions, reviewed by three members of the program committee, achieving an acceptance rate of approximately 40%.

The conference program featured a rich lineup of discussions and keynote presentations that reflected the innovative research included in these proceedings. We invite readers to explore the complete conference program at www.gislatam.org.

We extend our appreciation to the many colleagues who devoted their time and expertise to the research featured in this edition, as well as to the reviewers who ensured the quality of the submissions.

Our sincere thanks also go to those who helped organize the conference, ensuring the inclusion of the most relevant topics and the participation of key researchers, educators, and practitioners. Special thanks to ANTACOM A.C., the Laboratory of Geospatial Intelligence and Mobile Computing at UPIITA-IPN, Urban Data lab, GeoDataX Laboratory, the UPIITA staff, and our sponsors. GIS LATAM 2024 shows our strong commitment to advancing GIS education and research in universities across Latin America.

September 2024

Roberto Zagal-Flores
Daniela Elisabeth Ballari
José Antonio León-Borges
Miguel Félix Mata-Rivera

Organization

Organizing Committee

General Chair

Miguel Félix Mata-Rivera	UPIITA-IPN, Mexico

Co-chairs

Roberto Zagal-Flores	ESCOM-IPN, Mexico
Daniela Elisabeth Ballari	Universidad del Azuay, Ecuador
Jose Antonio Léon-Borges	Universidad de Quintana Roo, Campus Cancún, Mexico
Miriam Olivares	Yale University, USA

Local Manager

Jairo Zagal-Flores	UNADM, Mexico

Staff Chair

Carlos Hernandez Nava	UPIITA-IPN, Mexico

Program Committee (Research Papers)

Christophe Claramunt	Naval Academy Research Institute, France
Carlos Di Bella	INTA, Argentina
Christopher Jones	Cardiff University, UK
Diana Castro	ENCB-IPN, Mexico
Didier Leibovici	University of Nottingham, UK
Farid Karimipour	University of Tehran, Iran
Felipe O. Tapia Silva	UAM, Mexico
Gavin McArdle	University College Dublin, Ireland
Georg Gartner	TU Vienna, Austria
Gloria Faus Landeros	ITESM-Campus Guadalajara, Mexico
Hassan Karimi	University of Pittsburgh, USA

Ki-Joune Li	Pusan University, South Korea
Kyoung-Sook Kim	AIST, Japan
Manuel Enrique Puebla Martínez	Universidad de las Ciencias Informáticas, Cuba
María Elena Torres Olave	UACJ, Mexico
Mauro Gaio	LIUPPA - UFR S&T de PAU (UPPA), France
Roberto Zagal	ESCOM – IPN, Mexico
Sergio Ilarri	University of Zaragoza, Spain
Shoko Wakamiya	Nara Institute of Science and Technology, Japan
Willington Siabato	Universidad Nacional, Colombia
Xiang Li	East China Normal University, China
Zakaria Abdelmoiz Dahi	Constantine University, Algeria
Kamel Zeltni	Constantine University, Algeria
Christian Cintrano	University of Málaga, Spain
Francisco Aragón	Universidad de Granada, Spain
Ricardo Garcia	CIBNOR, Mexico
R. Weibel	University of Zurich, Switzerland
S. Carlos Di Bella	INTA, Argentina
S. Winter	University of Melbourne, Australia
S. Yokoyama	Tokyo Metropolitan University, Japan
J. Zarazaga	University of Zaragoza, Spain
D. Ziebelin	Université Grenoble Alpes, France
Daniela Elisabeth Ballari	Universidad del Azuay, Ecuador

Sponsors

SIP-IPN
ANTACOM A.C.
UPIITA-IPN

Collaborators

FES ACATLAN
ESCOM-IPN
TECNOLÓGICO DE MONTERREY, Campus Estado de México

Contents

Geographics Aspects and LOPA Methodology: A Comprehensive Approach to Biogas Generation Plants

Elizabeth Velázquez Morales[1](✉) and Vladimir Avalos-Bravo[2]

[1] Instituto Politécnico Nacional, SEPI-ESIQIE, Mexico City, Mexico
evelazquezm1302@alumno.ipn.mx
[2] Instituto Politécnico Nacional, CIITEC, SEPI-ESIQIE, SARACS Research Group ESIME Zacatenco, Mexico City, Mexico
ravalos@ipn.mx

Abstract. This paper focuses on carrying out a risk analysis methodology for the hydrocarbon sector in the context of clean and renewable energies to evaluate the risk associated with biogas plants all over Mexico. This methodology allows us to identify the necessary protection measures to guarantee the safe and reliable operation of the biogas plants by using a solid and reliable tool that will enable us to evaluate and manage the generation and storage equipment in terms of design, using the SIL, PFD, and LOPA indicators by providing effectiveness of independent layers such as instrumented safety equipment and additional technical, operational and management safeguards that work together to reduce risks and ensure safe and reliable operation of the plants. It is essential to highlight that the layer of protection analysis is not a static process but is regularly reviewed and updated as changes are made to the process, equipment, or applicable regulations in the biogas plants and how the risk could change depending on the place the plants are located.

Keywords: Risk analysis · LOPA · Biogas · SIL · PFD · Mexico City

1 Introduction

The gas industry is one of the most dangerous industries in the world, with more deaths from fires and explosions than any other industry. Injuries and death occur despite extensive regulation by Occupational Safety and Health (OSHA). When an explosion occurs, it is often discovered that the root cause is a lack of compliance with OSHA safety regulations [10]. An explosion can also occur due to improper handling or maintenance of containers and other equipment. Biogas plants are complex process engineering systems in which a whole range of different hazards can occur. Hazards can be divided into human health and environmental risks; for this reason, it is essential to know more about the biogas industry. The value chain of biogas production is divided into four major stages: the collection of raw materials, pretreatment for processing, conversion, and conditioning.

M. F. Mata-Rivera et al. (Eds.): GIS-LATAM 2024, CCIS 2298, pp. 1–13, 2025.
https://doi.org/10.1007/978-3-031-80017-7_1

- Raw material collection: This stage includes identifying the type of substrate and its characterization, as well as collection and storage.
- Pretreatment refers to the elimination of impurities that may affect the performance of anaerobic digestion. These impurities can be physical, chemical, thermal, or biological.
- Conversion: Conversion refers to the digestion of the substrate in the absence of oxygen. The process is divided into four stages: hydrolysis, acidogenic, acetogenic, and methanogenic.
- Conditioning: In the last stage of the substrate conversion (methanogenic), biogas is obtained, and depending on its final use, it will be required to be conditioned to obtain biomethane and eliminate compounds that affect the properties of the biogas, which include water, carbon dioxide, hydrogen sulfide, and some siloxanes.

1.1 Substrates and Composition

The substrate refers to the biomass type used for biogas production, which must consider its properties depending on the desired characteristics of the biofuel. The substrate must have a prior preparation in which crushing and mixing with water are essential without leaving out the solids content within the anaerobic digester, which can be between 3% and 6%, depending on the reactor design and whether it has internal mixing.

Furthermore, each substrate's performance depends on the substrate and the digester's environmental conditions, particularly the temperature and pH [13]. Different substrates and their performance in the production of biogas and methane depend on the percentage of dry matter (DM) and dry organic matter (DOM), as can be seen in the table below (Table 1).

Table 1. Properties of the different substrates and their biogas yield [13].

Substrate	DM % of fresh matter	DOM % of fresh matter	Biogas m^3/kg DOM	Methane % m^3CH_4/m^3 Biogas
Wet cattle manure	7.5–13	6.4–10	0.17–0.63	53–62
Pig manure in wet base	2.3–11	1.3–7.1	0.–0.88	47–68
Dry cattle manure with straw	25	21	(0.45)	55
Dry solid horse manure with straw	27	23	0.3–0.44	52
Broiler	25	22	0.15–0.53	42–68
chicken manure	–		0.4–0.5	50–60
Dried sheep manure with straw	15–25	12–20	0.45	
Pig manure with straw			0.25–0.4	52

(continued)

Table 1. (*continued*)

Substrate	DM % of fresh matter	DOM % of fresh matter	Biogas m^3/kg DOM	Methane % m^3CH_4/m^3 Biogas
wheat straw			0.5	
corn grass	5		0.75	53
buttermilk			0.5–0.6	52
Potato crop leaf	27–57	25–46	0.21–0.7	52–56
grass silage	14–35	12–31	0.55–0.8	55
Lucerne	25–37	24–36	0.3–1.13	47–69
corn silage	7.5–13	6.4–10	0.17–0.63	53–62
Cereal silage (rye)	25–61	23–58	0.49–0.68	59–62
Sudan Grass	33–46	14–36	0.33–0.38	54–62
Beet silage	10–11	9.3–9.9	0.7–1.13	52
Trap-derived grease	48	85	0.2–0.4	60–77
tripe content	11–19	9–16	0.45–0.55	60
Rumen content			0.5–0.8	44–55
animal meal			0.85	
Glycerin	100		0.42–0.85	50
malt eye	21–25	20–24	0.39–0.72	55
Ethanol production waste (wheat origin)	4.6–76	4.3–71	0.61	53–55
Potato peel	25		0.68	50
Molasses	5		0.15–0.68	54
Canteen waste	14–19	12–16	0.874	43–77
Used frying oil	95			68

The composition of biogas shares physicochemical characteristics with some gases used mostly as fuels, the most determining factor being the calorific value and methane content. The properties and attributes of gases used as an energy source are shown below. Biogas can be compared to natural gas and synthesis gas [12] (Table 2).

The theoretical production of biogas can be known from the substrate to be used, thanks to the Buswell equation, only if the elemental chemical composition of the input organic matter is known. The Buswell equation represents a balanced reduction reaction in which the products of anaerobic digestion are methane, carbon dioxide, and ammonia [1] as observed in Eq. 1 "a, b, c and d are the stoichiometric coefficients of the biodegradable molecules. This analysis assumes that all donated electrons are exclusively used for metabolic energy, so cellular synthesis is not considered, as can be seen in the Buswell and Symons relation [1].

Table 2. Physicochemical characteristics of combustible gases [14].

Parameter	Units	Natural Gas	Synthesis Gas	Biogas (60% CH_4)
Lower Heating Value Density	MJ/m^3	31.8	16.1	21.5
	$Kcal/m^3$	7600	3846	5134
	Kg/m^3	0.82	0.51	1.21
Wobbe index (lower)	MJ/m^3	39.9	22.5	19.5
Maximum Flame Speed	m/s	0.39	0.7	0.25
Theoretical Air Requirement	m^3aire/m^3 gas	9.53	3.83	5.71
Maximum CO_2 Concentration After Combustion	% volumen	11.9	13.1	17.8
Dew Point	°C	59	60	60–160

$$C_cH_hN_nS_s + \frac{1}{4} * (4_c - h - 2_o + 3_n + 2_s) * H_2O \rightarrow \frac{1}{8} * (4_c - h - 2_o + 3_n + 2_s) * CO_2 + \frac{1}{8} * (4_c - h - 2_o + 3_n + 2_s) * CH_4 + nNH_3 + sH_2S \quad (1)$$

1.2 Uses and Applications of Biogas

In its noblest use and exploitation, it is to be used as a source of mechanical, electrical, thermal, and chemical energy. Although the best option must be chosen considering certain aspects such as economic, technical, and environmental, below is a diagram that shows the different uses of biogas and the type of energy generated [5] (Fig. 1).

Fig. 1. Biogas production value chain [15].

Currently, biogas is increasingly used in European countries, China, and Latin American countries. According to the Biogas Handbook, In China, up to 18 million rural domestic biogas digesters are estimated to be operating in 2006, and the total Chinese biogas potential is estimated at 145 billion cubic meters, while in India There are approximately 5 million small-scale biogas plants currently in operation. Countries such as Nepal and Vietnam also have many small-scale, family-owned biogas facilities. Most biogas plants in Asia use simple technologies and are, therefore, easy to design and reproduce. On the other side of the Atlantic, the United States, Canada, and many Latin American countries are on the path to developing modern biogas sectors, and, in parallel, favorable policy frameworks are being implemented to support this development [16].

Furthermore, the trend of fuels used in transportation, this being one of the uses where thousands of tons of greenhouse gases are emitted annually, shows a trend from 2020 in a scenario of established policies and until 2050 an increase in its use in fuels mainly in biofuels, hydrogen and natural gas that according to Illustration 4, petroleum products by the year 2050 will be limited to around 50 million barrels of oil per day, while for natural gas they are estimated around of 70 million barrels of oil equivalent per day (mbe/d) by 2050 [8]. Regarding infrastructure for 2030, it is reported that in 2021 investments in clean energy reached 1.3 trillion dollars, equivalent to 700 billion dollars in investment in energy, 400 billion dollars in efficiency and final use. It is estimated that 2030 will grow more than 50% in a scenario of established STEPS policies equivalent to 2.0 trillion dollars, where an investment of 1,100 trillion dollars is estimated in energy, around 50 trillion dollars in low-emission fuels, and around 750 trillion dollars in efficiency and end-use [8].

The demand for gaseous fuels by the year 2050 will increase in a STEPS scenario. Where natural gas plays an important role, increasing by an average of 0.4% per year between 2021 and 2030; on the other hand, the demand for global biogas in a scenario of established policies will increase from 22 million cubic meters equivalent (mcme) for 2021 at 224 mcme [8]. Currently, Mexico has optimistic scenarios for 2030; according to the "Technological Road Map," an installed capacity of 800 Mm3/year is estimated (in millions of annual cubic meters of biomethane equivalent to normal conditions). Temperature and pressure) for the generation of energy belonging to the public sector [5]; on the other hand, in Mexico, there are currently 15 biogas plants operating in the private sector, so it is considered that the industry is still not consolidated. Likewise, Mexico has established commitments to reduce greenhouse gas emissions, primarily in the energy transition law where it was implemented that 25% of electrical energy must come from renewable energies by 2018 and 30% by 2021. And 35% by 2024. Additionally, the Mexican government made another commitment by 2030 to reduce the national greenhouse gas emissions by 22% [15], and some of them have adopted measures for the use of biogas for electricity generation, with the state of Nuevo León being the state that provides the most electricity through biogas.

2 Biogas Plants

A biogas plant includes everything from collecting the substrate to its final disposal and the use of the biogas, according to the biogas value, and this can be as complex as required, according to the value needed for the biogas.

The process includes several stages and simplified biogas production in a typical agricultural co-digestion plant [16].

1. First stage of the process: storage, conditioning, transportation, and feed insertion.
2. The process's second stage includes biogas production in the reactor or digester.

3. The third stage of the process includes the substrate storage tank and conditioning for use as fertilizer.
4. The fourth stage of the process includes biogas storage, conditioning, and use.

2.1 Design

The design of a biogas plant can vary from environmental protection and waste reduction to renewable energy production and can include financial and non-financial incentives. Local farmers and farmer organizations, organic waste producers and collectors, municipalities, energy producers, and other involved actors are the usual initiators of biogas projects. From the vital spark of the idea of a biogas project until the end of its useful life, the process goes through the following steps [15]:

1. Project idea
2. Pre-feasibility study
3. Feasibility study
4. Detailed planning of biogas plant
5. Authorization procedure
6. Construction of the biogas plant
7. Operation and maintenance
8. Reinvestment, renewal, and replacement of components
9. Demolition or rehabilitation

There are various models for configuring biogas projects, which depend on the availability of food and the financial capacity of investors.

2.2 Anaerobic Digestion

Anaerobic digestion refers to the process of decomposition of high-molecular-weight solids in the absence of oxygen, reducing organic matter and stabilizing it. In a facility, the result of anaerobic digestion is biogas plus a digestate. Suppose the digestion of organic matter is carried out through mixtures of substrates (for example, animal manure or organic waste from the food industry). In that case, the process is called co-digestion.

The process of obtaining biogas through anaerobic digestion depends on the type of substrate to be used. The biochemical process of anaerobic digestion includes several steps of matter decomposition: hydrolysis, acidogenesis, acetogenesis, and methanogenesis.

2.3 Biomethane Obtaining

Upgrading, better known as cleaning biogas from anaerobic digestion, does not have the properties to be called biomethane. However, there are biochemical processes that allow biogas to reach the desired purity according to the expected use. Among the impurity removal treatments is the elimination of water vapor, hydrogen sulfides, siloxanes, and carbon dioxide, as seen below (Fig. 2).

The gases present in biogas, due to their chemical and physicochemical composition, generate a danger for humans due to their properties. They are present in the process and

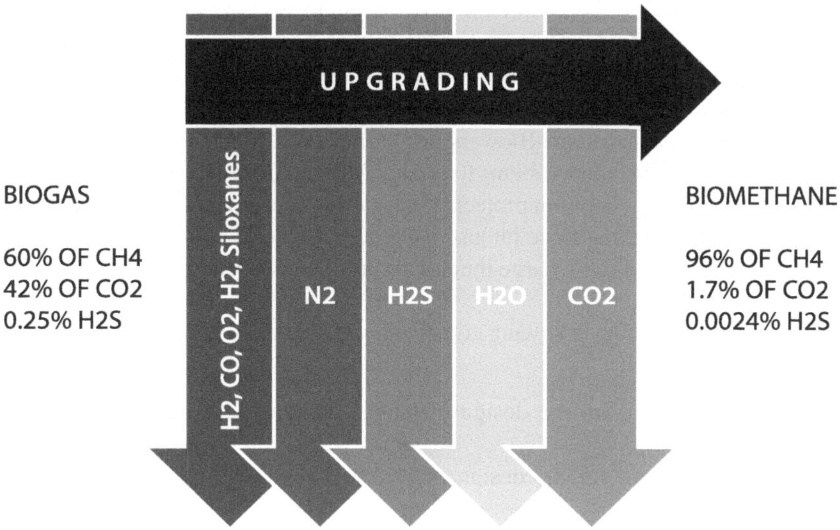

Fig. 2. Upgrading Process Description [2].

can affect humans since cases of death due to asphyxiation have been reported [12]. It is important to mention that explosion and fire risks can occur under certain conditions and in combination with air, which can form a mixture of explosive gases (Fig. 3).

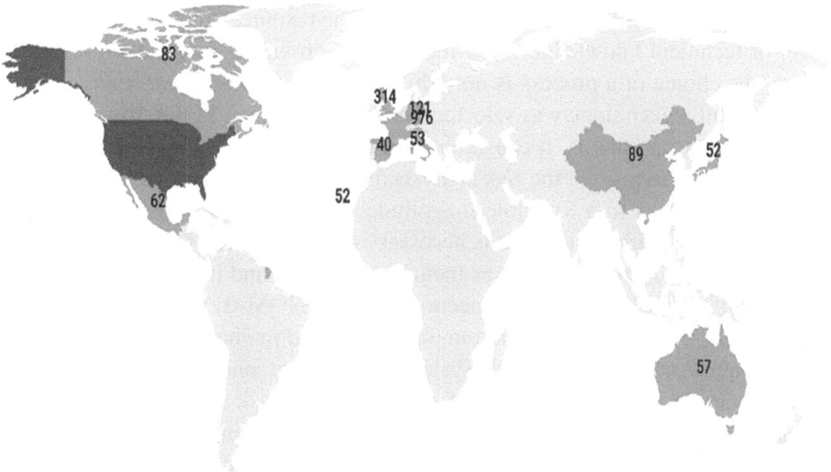

Fig. 3. Total number of Biogas Explosions Map [9].

Currently, Mexico still needs to develop a standard that allows the proper use of biogas, so there are areas of opportunity to improve measurement, regulation, sanction, and support methods for biogas production [12]. It is essential to mention that in Mexico, biogas plants have been growing too much; for example, Nopalimex, with its location in Zitacuaro, Michoacan, is the first biogas plant in Mexico that generates electricity and biogas from the cactus. It also produces ethanol, nopal for human consumption, organic humus, and nitrogen water, which can be used as fertilizer. In addition, wastewater treatment plants such as Mapro-Blowers and Products of Mexico (BPM) in Ecatepec State of Mexico have installed systems to produce biogas in wastewater treatment plants in Mexico. The biogas generation project at the Atotonilco wastewater treatment plant is one of the largest in Mexico since biogas plants can also be used in rural homes, where a daily routine is needed to recharge them. Gas production is constant and greater than in discontinuous plants.

The development of the following competency standards is suggested, which can be broken down if required:

- Competence standard for the design of biogas facilities (conduction, storage, and burning).
- Competency standard for the design of H_2S and moisture removal systems from biogas.
- Competence standard for operating electrical and thermal energy generation systems from biogas.
- Competency standard for safety verification in biogas handling and use facilities.

3 LOPA Methodology Applied to a Biogas Plant

The selection of the technique contains a series of decision-making, which means that it is chosen depending on the results to be obtained, the complexity, nature, and degree of uncertainty of the risk assessment, the extent of the resources required based on time and level of technical knowledge if the method can provide a quantitative result [11]. Therefore, the choice of a process is not arbitrary, and, in this case, a semiquantitative and semiqualitative technique was selected for risk assessment. LOPA allows an appreciation of the controls; that is, it can evaluate the controls and their effectiveness. The analysis is intended to present the risk analysis of a plant and determine if its protection layers reduce the risks to a tolerable magnitude. The ASEA establishes that for risk analysis in the hydrocarbon sector, it is necessary to know the risks of operating a natural gas plant, LP gas, among others; as mentioned, biogas and its similarities with fuel gases are similar for what is required according to the NOM-013-SECRE-2012 Safety requirements for the design, construction, operation, and maintenance of liquefied natural gas storage terminals that include systems, equipment, and facilities for reception, conduction, vaporization and delivery of natural gas). A risk analysis that establishes a "Regulated in the Facility Design stage; Layers of Protection Analysis (LOPA) must include the identification of safety functions, including emergency stop, and define the safety integrity level (SIL) of the possible resulting functions. Both studies must be carried out by personnel specialized in the subject [7].

LOPA is a methodology used for simplified risk analysis; LOPA generally uses the order of magnitude categories to initialize the frequency of the event, the severity of the consequence, and the probability of failure of independent protection layers (IPL) to approximate the risk of a stage. LOPA is typically implemented after a qualitative hazard assessment, such as a process hazard analysis (PHA). As its name implies, LOPA is an analysis that determines whether there are sufficient layers of protection and whether the risk against an accident scenario can be tolerated [3].

According to the ISO 31000 standard, some of its limitations and strengths are listed below:

- It requires less time and resources than a fault tree analysis or a fully quantitative risk assessment, but it is more rigorous than qualitative, subjective judgments.
- Helps identify and direct resources on the most critical layers of protection.
- Identifies operations, systems, and processes for insufficient protection.
- It is focused on the most severe consequences.
- Limitations include:
- LOPA focuses on a cause-consequence pair and a scenario at a given time. Complex interactions between risks or between controls are not covered.
- Quantified risks may not account for common mode failures.
- LOPA does not apply to complex scenarios with many cause-consequence pairs or where various consequences affect stakeholders.

LOPA is used to understand how a process deviation can lead to a dangerous consequence if not interrupted by the successful operation of an independent protection layer (IPL) safeguard. An IPL is a protection that can prevent a scenario from propagating to a consequence of concern without being negatively affected by the initiating event or inaction of any other protection layer on the same scenario [6].

There are at least eight independent protections (IPL), and normally, these are applied starting at the center of the diagram:

- Layer 1: Process design (e.g., inherently safer designs).
- Layer 2: Basic controls, process alarms, and operator supervision.
- Layer 3: Critical alarms, operator monitoring, and manual intervention.
- Layer 4: Automatic action (e.g., SIS or ESD).
- Layer 5: Physical protection (e.g., relief devices).
- Layer 6: Physical protection (e.g., dikes).
- Layer 7: Plant emergency response; and it doesn't show
- Layer 8: Community emergency response.

LOPA can be represented by diagrams and mathematically by a computational equation, where the frequency of an initiating event is multiplied by the probabilities of each IPL.

$$f_i^C = IEF_i * PFD_{i1} * PFD_{i2} * \ldots * PFD_{ij} \tag{2}$$

where:

f_i^C = Frequency of occurrence of the consequence for scenario i. Typical units are per year ("Low Demand") or per hour ("High Demand").

IEF_i = The frequency of the initiating event (IE) per scenario. Typical units are per year.

PFD_{ij} = Probability of failure on demand of an independent protection layer (IPL) j for scenario i.

Part of the evaluation consists of determining when a protection layer is independent. For example, if one or several layers depend on an operator's operation and are not considered independent, this simultaneous failure mode is known as common cause failure. However, each independent layer of protection must be auditable, meaning it must be placed in a demand situation and proven to be reliable [6].

Like any risk assessment method, LOPA has rules, which can be divided into steps to be shown in more detail.

Step 1: Identify the consequence of filtering the scenarios. Since LOPA typically evaluates scenarios developed in a previous study, the first step by LOPA analysts is to assess these scenarios, and the most common evaluation method is consequence-based. The consequence is usually identified during a qualitative hazard review (such as a HAZOP study). The analyst then evaluates the result (including the impact) and estimates its magnitude. Some companies stop at the magnitude of a release (of material or energy), which implies, but does not explicitly state, the impact on people, the environment, and the production system. Other companies will model the release and, more explicitly, estimate the risk to people, the environment, and production, considering the probability of harm resulting from a specific scenario, such as the probability that operators are in danger during a release scenario.

Step 2: Select an accident scenario. LOPA is applied to one scenario at a time. The scenario can come from other analyses (such as qualitative analyses), but the scenario describes a single cause-consequence pair.

Step 3: Identify the scenario-initiating event and determine its frequency (events per year). The initiating event must lead to the consequence (given the failure of all safeguards). The frequency should consider background aspects of the scenario, such as the frequency of the mode of operation for which the scenario is valid. Most companies provide guidance on how to estimate frequency to achieve consistency in LOPA results.

Step 4: Identify the IPLs and calculate the on-demand failure probability of each IPL. Some accident scenarios require only one IPL, while others may require many IPLs or a low likelihood of failure on-demand IPLs to achieve a tolerable risk. Recognizing existing safeguards that meet IPL requirements for a given scenario is at the heart of LOPA. Most companies provide a predetermined set of IPL values for the analyst to use to choose the values that best fit the scenario being analyzed.

Step 5: Estimate the scenario's risk by mathematically combining the consequence, initiating event, and IPL data. Depending on the definition of consequence (impact event), other factors may be included during the calculation. Approaches include arithmetic formulas and graphical methods.

Regardless of the methods, most companies provide a standard form to document results and describe how to use LOPA data to estimate risk, using the initiating event frequency, IPL values, and consequence values.

Step 6: Assess the risk to decide on the scenario and make risk decisions with LOPA. This includes comparing the risk of a scenario with a company's tolerable risk criteria and related objectives.

Derived from the application of the Layers of Protection Analysis (LOPA), verification is obtained of the independent layers of protection that are considered, and that will be implemented for each of the Risk Scenarios of interest and, where applicable, the need to apply some Security Instrumented System (SIS) or other additional Layer of Protection to guarantee Risk management at Tolerable Risk levels.

An independent layer of protection will be understood as the device, system, or action that can prevent a scenario from producing the undesired consequence, regardless of the initiating event or the action of any other Protection Layer associated with the scenario [4]. Independent means that the performance of the Protection Layer is not affected by the initiating event and is not affected by failures of other Protection Layers. The security integrity level (SIL) selection is based on evaluating the probability of failure on demand (PFD) of the different protection devices and systems. In the context of this book, comments and ranges of PFDs used as preliminary selection criteria for the various protective elements are provided. It is important to note that these ranges are for screening purposes only and do not specify a specific SIL. Some examples of protective elements and their PFD ranges cited in the literature and industry are the following:

Relief valve: This device prevents the system from exceeding the specified pressure. Its effectiveness may vary depending on service and experience.
Rupture Disc: This disc prevents the system from exceeding the specified pressure. Its effectiveness can be very sensitive to service and experience.
Basic Process Control System: It may be credited as an Independent Protection Layer (IPL) if it is not associated with the considered initiating event. For additional requirements and discussions, refer to IEC 61508 and IEC 61511.
Safety Instrumented Functions (Interlocks): Reference is made to IEC 61508 and IEC 61511 for life cycle requirements and additional discussions. A specific SIL level is not specified in this book.
SIL 1: Typically consists of a single sensor (redundant for fault tolerance), a single logical processor (redundant for fault tolerance), and a single final element (redundant for fault tolerance).
SIL 2: Typically consists of "multiple" sensors (for fault tolerance), "multiple" logic processor channels (for fault tolerance), and "multiple" final elements (for fault tolerance).
SIL 3 Typically consists of multiple sensors, logic processor channels, and end elements.

It is important to note that these PFD ranges and SIL levels may vary based on specific regulations and industry practices. The calculation of a PFD required for a particular safety instrumented function (SIF) is performed in continuous examples, and a particular SIL level is not specified in this book. SIL selection is based on the PFD evaluation of protective elements such as relief valves, rupture discs, process control systems, and safety instrumented functions.

4 Discussion and Results

After carrying out the risk analysis by layers of protection, recommendations must be made based on the results obtained. These recommendations are derived from the risk assessments designed to mitigate or reduce the risks identified in the process. Recommendations may include preventive or mitigating measures that should be implemented to improve safety and reduce the probability of unwanted events. Some possible recommendations could be:

Improvement of control systems: Improvements can be proposed in existing control systems, such as implementing redundant or more sophisticated control systems that allow early detection of abnormal situations.

Updating operating procedures: Standard operating procedures can be reviewed and updated to ensure that security best practices are followed, thereby minimizing the possibility of human error.

Staff training: It is important to provide additional training to staff involved in operating and maintaining the biogas plant. This may include safety courses, training in properly handling equipment, and emergency procedures.

Implementation of additional safeguards: If significant risks are identified, installation of new independent protection layers (IPL) or enhancement of existing ones may be recommended. These safeguards may include alarm systems, additional security devices, or enhanced emergency procedures.

Regular inspection and maintenance: Establishing a regular inspection and maintenance program is essential to ensuring that all equipment is in good working order and meets established safety standards.

Continuous monitoring: Continuous monitoring systems may be recommended to detect anomalies or deviations in the operation of the biogas plant. This allows a quick response to risky situations.

It is important to note that recommendations may vary depending on the circumstances and specific risks identified in the risk analysis by layers of protection. Furthermore, security experts must evaluate and apply these recommendations and comply with the corresponding regulations and standards.

5 Conclusions

The implementation of a protection layer risk analysis approach, using concepts such as SIL (safety integrity level), PFD (probability of failure on demand), and LOPA (independent protection layer analysis), is essential to guarantee safety in a biogas generation plant. The SIL provides a quantitative measure of the effectiveness of independent layers of protection, such as safety instrumented systems and additional safeguards. The lower the PFD value, the greater the reduction in the frequency of undesirable consequences, which implies greater reliability and safety in the process.

Risk analysis by layers of protection allows for identifying and evaluating initiating events, causes, and associated consequences. Through the LOPA, the layers of security necessary to prevent or mitigate the identified risks can be determined. These layers may include control systems, safety devices, operating procedures, and training and training measures. The conclusion derived from this risk analysis approach is that specific measures and recommendations must be implemented to improve safety in a biogas generation plant. This involves a combination of technical, operational, and management safeguards to reduce risks and ensure safe and reliable plant operation.

It is essential to highlight that the risk analysis by layers of protection is not a static process but must be reviewed and updated regularly as changes are introduced in the process, equipment, or applicable regulations. Furthermore, successfully implementing these recommendations requires the commitment and participation of everyone involved, from operators and maintenance personnel to decision-makers and safety management.

In summary, the layered risk analysis approach, based on SIL, PFD, and LOPA, provides a practical framework for assessing and managing risks in a biogas generation plant. By implementing the recommendations derived from this analysis, a safer work environment can be achieved, minimizing risks to personnel, the environment, and plant assets.

Acknowledgments. This project was funded under the following grant: SIP-IPN: No-20241201, and the support of CIITEC-IPN Instituto Politecnico Nacional., and special thanks to Hernan Abraham Pérez Flores for the image edition.

References

1. Baquerizo, R.P.: Revista Virtual (2016). Obtenido de https://www.researchgate.net/publication/292159125_El_modelo_de_Buswell_Aplicacion_y_comparacion_Principales_factores_que_influyen_en_su_aplicacion
2. Begiristain, I.: Universidad de León (2021). Obtenido de https://buleria.unileon.es/bitstream/handle/10612/14959/TFG_CC.AA_BegiristainIgoa_Ixabel.pdf?sequence=1&isAllowed=y
3. Bridges, W., Dowell , A., Gollin, M., Greenfield, W., Poulson, J., Turesky, W. (2001). Layer of protection analysis
4. Casal, J., Montiel, H., Planas, E., Vílchez, J. (1999). Análisis del riesgo en instalaciones industriales
5. Codwell, P.J., Beltran, L., Zendejas, F., Flores, A., Brasdefer, G., Ortiz, C.R.: Secretaría de Energía Docuemntos (2017). Obtenido de Mapa de Ruta Tecnológica: https://www.gob.mx/sener/documentos/mapas-de-ruta-tecnologica-de-energias-renovables
6. Departamento de Ingeniería Química: Layer of Protection Analysis. ScienceDirect (2014)
7. Diario Oficial de la Federación: Secretaría de Gobernación (2021). Obtenido de https://www.dof.gob.mx/nota_detalle.php?codigo=5636594&fecha=29/11/2021#gsc.tab=0
8. Energía, A.I.: World Energy Outlook (2022). Obtenido de https://www.iea.org/reports/world-energy-outlook-2022
9. Fábrega, C.: Up Commons (1999). Obtenido de https://upcommons.upc.edu/bitstream/handle/2099.1/3142/50084-2.pdf
10. IPCC: (2008). Obtenido de https://www.ipcc.ch/site/assets/uploads/2018/02/ar4_syr_sp.pdf
11. ISO 31000: Gestión del Riesgo (2013)
12. López., J.R.: Secretaría de Energía (2017). Obtenido de https://www.gob.mx/cms/uploads/attachment/file/265430/Guia_lodos_2017.pdf
13. Red Mexicana de Bioenergía, A.: Obtenido de Red Mexicana de Bioenergía (2012). https://rembio.org.mx/
14. SENER: Biocombustibles gaseosos (2017). Obtenido de Reporte de Inteligencia tecnológica: https://www.gob.mx/sener/documentos/mapas-de-ruta-tecnologica-de-energias-renovables
15. SENER: Mapas de Ruta Tecnológica de Energías Renovables (2018). Obtenido de https://www.gob.mx/cms/uploads/attachment/file/329895/Mapa_Ruta_Tecnologica_BIOGAS_Final-Red.pdf
16. Teodorita, A., Rutz, D., Prassl, H., Kottner, M., Finsterwalder, T., Volk, S., Janssen, R.: Biogas Handbook (2008). Obtenido de chrome-extension://efaidnbmnnnibpcajpcglclefindmkaj/https://www.lemvigbiogas.com/BiogasHandbook.pdf

Google Earth Engine Based Forest Monitoring and Decision Support: Evidence from Elrawashdah Forest, Sudan

Mohamed B. O. Osman[1,2(✉)] and Kornel Czimber[1]

[1] Institute of Geomatics and Civil Engineering, University of Sopron, 9400 Sopron, Hungary
mohamedbabekir95@gmail.com

[2] Department of GIS and Cartography, University of Khartoum, 11115 Khartoum, Sudan

Abstract. Sustainable forest management in Sudan is objected by several administrative and technical obstacles such as weakened governance, lack of funds and personnel, and the acute gap in spatio-temporal data coverage. Data unavailability stems from unsystematic inventories, limited baseline studies and minimal reliance on advanced geospatial technologies. Provision of a forest monitoring system will empower a mechanism to collect and analyze data to gain insights on the state of the forest and will enable constant updates and continuous monitoring for informing decisions. With reference to Elrawashdah forest, eastern Sudan, this paper intends to introduce and set an example for google earth engine-based forest monitoring system that will measure various forest integrity indices, multi-temporal forest analysis, and leverage forest up-to-date data availability to raise to the level of the challenges of informing decision making for forest sustainable management. The paper assessed the forest integrity by the NDVI, EVI and RVI indices from 1990 up to 2023. And multitemporal change detection analysis. It was revealed that, the forest had grown during the decade 1990–2000s by 115 sq. km; approximately 28% of the forest total size; as bare lands had naturally regenerated due to rainfall increases after drought strikes in seventies and earlier eighties. However, the forest had then drastically shrunken during the last two decades, i.e. throughout 2000 and 2010 more than 10% of the forested lands had disappeared; nearly 33 sq. km. Then, throughout the period between 2010 and 2020 the forested land had declined more; nearly 42 sq. km of the forest cover had vanished, approximately 14% of the forest total size, consequently, bare and agricultural lands prevailed instead. In conclusion, the study showed that the forest ecosystem had been destructed and hurriedly overwhelmed by agricultural lands that are expanding rapidly and the average annual loss of the forest has exceeded 1% which is an alarming rate. The study recommends that, the agricultural expansion into the forest must immediately be stopped and tree logging to be controlled and governed by rotational forest cultivation.

Keywords: Deforestation · Monitoring · Decision support · Forest sustainable management

M. F. Mata-Rivera et al. (Eds.): GIS-LATAM 2024, CCIS 2298, pp. 14–26, 2025.
https://doi.org/10.1007/978-3-031-80017-7_2

1 Introduction

Sudan's fragile arid and semi-arid ecosystems are constantly deteriorating due to natural forces like ongoing desertification and frequent drought strikes. However, the excessive pressure of anthropogenic activities on the environment and natural resources such as forests, soil, and rangelands, which are stimulated by rapid growth in human and animal populations, are responsible for the most significant part of environmental deprivation.

This grabs attention to studying the environmental changes; especially Land Use Land Cover change, in Sudan and its counterparts of developing countries, since environmental change, will significantly influence their natural resources and vital economic and productive sectors of agriculture and pastoralism in addition to the pressing challenges of addressing the national development priorities of food security, water supply, public health, and others (Eltayeb, 2011).

Forests and vegetation resources, in general, are renewable resources that could endure persistence while being yielded and economically exploited yet remain intact and conserved. In case they have not been destructed by excessive pressure and poor management. Nonetheless, deforestation and vegetation removal prevailed in Sudan and became the underlying environmental problem.

Due to uncontrolled and poorly planned land use land cover transformations all over the country. However, the forests and ranges were affected the most, the reports of (FAO, 2010; FAO, 2015) stated that Sudan is among the top ten deforested countries. Sudan forests are remarkably decreased at the rate of 1% annually. Approximately one-third of the country's forest disappeared in the last three decades.

As it is well known in developing countries like Sudan, livelihoods and productive sectors are predominantly primary economic activities of farming and pastoralism that exclusively depend on the physical environment and natural resources, indicating strong interchangeable and mutual influences among environmental status and socioeconomic aspects (Eltayeb, 2011). This gives sustainability and resources conservation a vital developmental and economic dimension.

Despite the aforementioned socioeconomic importance, land resources of Sudan, especially the forests, are confronted by complicated and manifold exploitation problems, which led to degradation, even depletion at times, of those resources, this is reflected in lessened food availability, decreased incomes, and increased relevant conflict (Egemi, 2017a). The production maximization, resource utilization, and socioeconomic development plans should therefore consider environmental protection and resource conservation as one of the utmost development priorities to achieve sustainability and improvement. ElHassan (2006) noted absence of strategic planning for land resources management and land use map that guides well-defined and planned resources allocation in Sudan.

Sustaining forests and land resources while exploiting them, requires a profound understanding of the dynamics of land use land cover structures, climatic and environmental conditions, and human-natural interactions. For this, it is imperative to monitor and constantly study and update information of the state of the land use land cover categories and their transformations over time, to formulate informed policies and build decision support systems that guide proper resources management, especially in Sudan, where the studies and inventories for land resources and forests are infrequent and unsystematic, with no innovative and informative "geo-information-based" monitoring system.

Therefore, as an efficient solution, an information system that serves as monitoring and spatial decision support system (SDSS) leading to development of an integrated geodatabase should be built to alleviate acute deficit in data, baseline studies, and inventories. Likewise, massive and various data volumes are critically required for sustainable management of the environment and resources. This necessitates needs for adoption and utilization of automated technology.

This research's endeavor will be, therefore, concentrated on providing SDSS that monitors LULC dynamics and accumulates a geo-database to facilitate policy making in the study area and to enable addressing proper environmental and resources management, via taking advantages of the massive ICT and digital data analytics advancements.

2 Problem Statement

In this swiftly changing world, where there are massive and rapid changes in land use land cover patterns and structures, population growth, and climate change. Management of renewable resources is a manifold and challenging issue. Unplanned LULC dynamics have adverse impacts and cause land degradation. LULC transformations are widely used to denote the environmental and natural resources degradation.

Land, according to the economists, is one of tringle productive factors along with labor (work) and capital. Despite this, In Sudan remarkable and large-scale land use land cover changes were witnessed and have influenced natural resources and environmental integrity (Egemi, 2017b; Egemi, 2017a). Forests, rangelands and fertile soils received the greater part of adverse consequences of LULC transformations.

Deforestation was, therefore, highlighted as the most serious environmental threats in Sudan along with desertification and land degradation. Forests sector in Sudan confronts various challenges that hinders the quest of achieving conservation and prevent deforestation. Therefore, according to the FAO, Sudan is among the world's top 10 countries of highest deforestation percentage, estimated at rate of 1% annually.

Similarly, a disastrous development status prevailed in Sudan, i.e. the contradictory state of production intensification endeavors without considering environmental and resources conservation and sustainability. For instance, in Gadaref state, where the study area is located, the inappropriate expansion of mechanized agriculture schemas contributed to the extensive deforestation, natural vegetation clearance, and other environmental degradation forms. Literature indicate the study area has experienced a profound and extensive transformations in its LULC structure over the few past decades, the mainstream recorded change indicates of vanishing forest to cover to the growing croplands and bare lands.

Sustainable forest management, efficient LULC control and resources exploitation, in Sudan, are generally confronted with several challenges of data availability, funding, and others i.e. the quantitative, qualitative, spatial coverage inadequacy of the data brought adverse impacts. Likewise, the used traditional ground inventory methods resulted in some hindrances to data accuracy and integrity assessment, as the non-unified sampling techniques and changing sample locations and sizes affected data consistency and integrity.

Better understanding and efficient management of forest LULC change require timely monitoring and systematic assessment in the light of legal framework regulating forest management and exploitation. In Sudan, regrettably forest inventory is carried out once or twice a decade, depending on the budget. However, there are other non-budgetary challenges i.e. lack of utilization and dependence on recent technologies provided by ICT, GIS and RS.

3 Necessity of Forests' SDSS

The lack of spatio-temporal data coverage significantly hampers sustainable forest management in Sudan, generally, as it limits the knowledge of the transformations and their patterns and over time and space, hence, the ability to monitor and assess forest resources effectively over time. Spatio-temporal data is thus critical for understanding the dynamics of forest ecosystems, including changes in forest cover, health, and biodiversity. Without adequate data coverage, it becomes challenging to track deforestation rates, forest degradation, and the impact of human activities, such as agriculture and urbanization, on forested areas. This gap hinders the development of evidence-based policies and strategies for conservation and sustainable use of forest resources, which are essential for maintaining ecosystem services and supporting the livelihoods of communities dependent on forests.

Data availability will facilitate and boost forest resources and ecosystem management; likewise, it will enable building and operating early warning and decision support systems to enhance management. Several studies elaborated the pressing necessity to build geo-information systems and critical roles of developing a geodatabase of natural resources in Sudan (Eltayeb, 2011; Alhadary, 2007; Ganawa, 2017). Continuous monitoring and assessment will ensure spatio-temporal data availability that will help in updating management practices, guide strategic planning and waning system.

Moreover, in Sudan, where conflicts and socio-political instability further complicate environmental governance, the lack of reliable data exacerbates the challenges in enforcing forest protection laws and in implementing reforestation or afforestation initiatives. Inaccurate or outdated information can lead to mismanagement of forest resources, resulting in increased deforestation, loss of biodiversity, and degradation of ecosystem services, all of which contribute to climate change and reduce the resilience of local communities to environmental changes. Many of the previous studies stressed on the necessity of effective knowledge management in forest and natural resources sectors in general (Kadoda & Abu Asha, 2016; Holi, 2016). Likewise, unanimous consensus on the findings of the literature in Elrawashdah forest that proved the remarkable trending deterioration in the forest cover density and area (Sulieman, 2018; Sulieman, 2013; Kobbail et al., 2013; Yagoub et al., 2015; Abdalla, 2016), increased fragmentation (Sulieman, 2018) and land use land cover change (Sulieman, 2018; Abdalla, 2016).

4 Objectives

The overall objective of this research is to foster more effective and efficient management of the forest LULC, by provisioning a GIS-based decision support system. To do so, the research endeavors:

1. To model and map forest LULC
2. To investigate the environmental variable indicators and forest trends,
3. To guide suitable LULC and sustainable forest Management
4. To constantly Assess and monitor the forest LULC
5. To facilitate forest decision support and early warning

5 Methodology

5.1 Study Area

Elrawashdah forest is located in the northern east of El-Gedaref city El-Gedaref state, which lies in semi-arid climatic zone between latitude (12–17) N and longitude (34–36). Elrawashdah forest size is estimated at 52080 square hectare (520.8 Km^2). In its physical geography, Elrawashdah forest is characterized by its extended flat surface, fertisole soils, monsoon rainfalls between 400–500 mm annually. While the human geography map y shows that it is an area for residential, range, logging, charcoal, farming, etc. of activities. See Figs. 1 and 2.

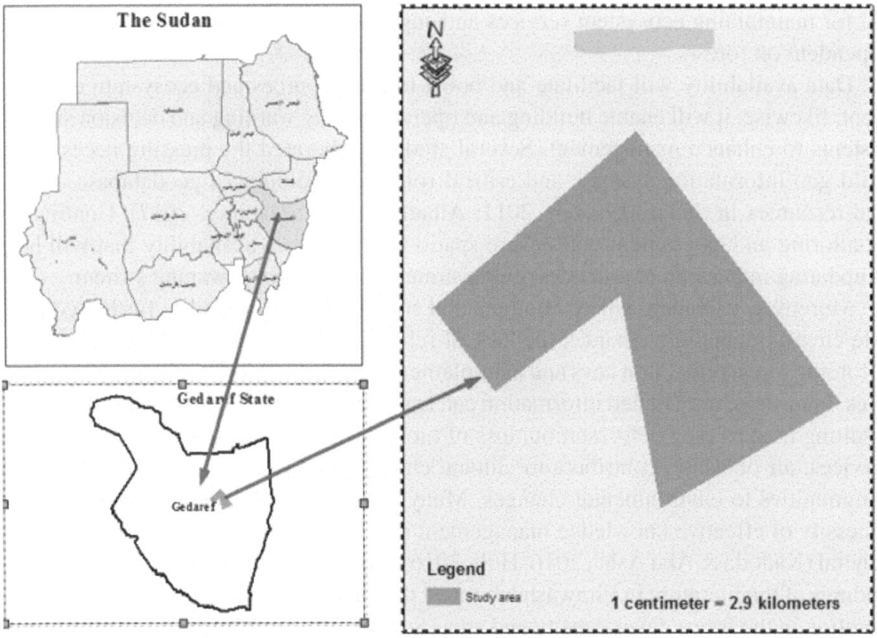

Fig. 1. Shows the location of the study area

5.2 Data Collection

This study has principally been based on the remotely sensed data, four multi-temporal Landsat images were acquired as follows; Landsat thematic mapper (TM) for the year

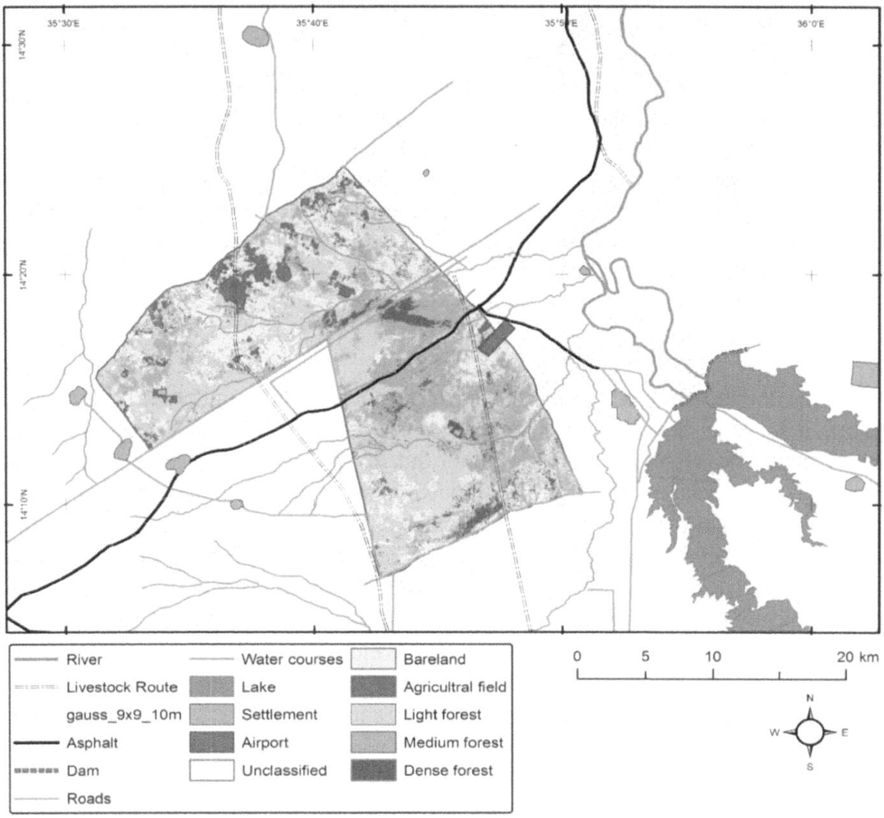

Fig. 2. Shows the geography of the study area. Source (Sulieman, 2018)

1990, Landsat enhanced thematic mapper (ETM+) for the year 2000, Landsat (TM) for the year 2010 and eventually Landsat operational land imager (OLI) for the year of 2020, respectively. It worth mentioning, Google earth data has been utilized to verify the accuracy and correctness of the classified imageries.

This paper, furthermore, adopted google earth engine assessment and monitoring system, given to the fact that GEE is very efficient environment that enable users to access and process massive datasets, with no need to download and preprocess that enormous data. Likewise, GEE is reproduced and repeatable analysis that will be able to be continued and updated to cover the monitor the ongoing changes in the preset time.

5.3 Data Analysis

GIS and RS technologies offer an abundant opportunity to monitor and manage natural resources, such as forests, in a multi-temporal, multi-spatial and multi-spectral resolutions and scales (Kumar et al., 2015). Therefore, this study adopted and utilized remote sensing-based change detection methodology, namely maximum likelihood and post-classification change detection techniques aided with visual image interpretation.

Multi-temporal Landsat images were utilized to assess changes in the Elrawashdah forest. Monthly median for three indices of EVI, RVI and NDVI respectively, median was chosen rather than the average, due to the remarkable seasonal variance in the state of forest and general green mass, that is caused by the monsoon rain regime that happens between July-September, while the rest of year is dry with no rains.

Images for the years 1980, 1990, 2000, 2010 and 2020 were classified by maximum likelihood classifier to use the to figure out the inter-decadal change in the forest. Accuracy assessment has been done by taking sample points and compare them to the google earth at different times, to verify accuracy and reliability of the classified images.

5.3.1 Multi-Temporal Changes Detection

Maximum likelihood classification has been operated to the remotely sensed data, to prepare it for post classification change detection analysis, this technique of change detection analysis is built on subtraction algorithm that processes the classes or categories of the classified images. Viz, the two input images would be handled as the initial state; for the image of earlier date and the final state is represented by later date, thus, the initial image classes would be subtracted; individually, from their counterparts in the final image, this would result on the actual changes that occurred for each class in the respective time interval. Ultimately, the results would either be expressed by number of cells for each class or percentages, which would allow quantification and determination of the size and amounts of the occurring changes and express them on easily comprehendible manner using the usual size units.

Post classification change detection analysis was applied to discern the variations of each interval periods, in other words, the occurred changes were calculated through subtracting the classified imageries for periods between1990 up to 2000, 2000 up to 2010 and 2010 up to 2020, respectively. The below flow chart shows briefly the analytical procedures that were followed in this study, see Fig. 3.

5.3.2 Forest Indices Timeseries

This research developed an integrated programming and coding environment that is concentrated on google earth engine might use different programming languages, as a methodologic and instrumental tools to achieve its ultimate goal of developing a monitoring and information system that leverage forest management and boost enhanced practices for sustainability insights in that forest.

DSSs are typically designed and developed to efficiently deal with a complex system such as ecology, and the observed climate change impacts of the last decades motivated us to develop a strategic and dynamic DSS. (Czimber & Gálos, 2016) Google earth engine is an integrated environmental data archive that includes, not limited to, land cover socioeconomic data, geophysical and climate forecasts. GEE is designed to enable the researchers to easily distribute their results to academia, policy makers, non-governmental bodies, fieldworkers and even the general public (Gorelick et al. 2017).

Google Earth Engine API allows the users to develop and employ web apps to make their datasets and results easily queried and explored. Additionally, it enables to control

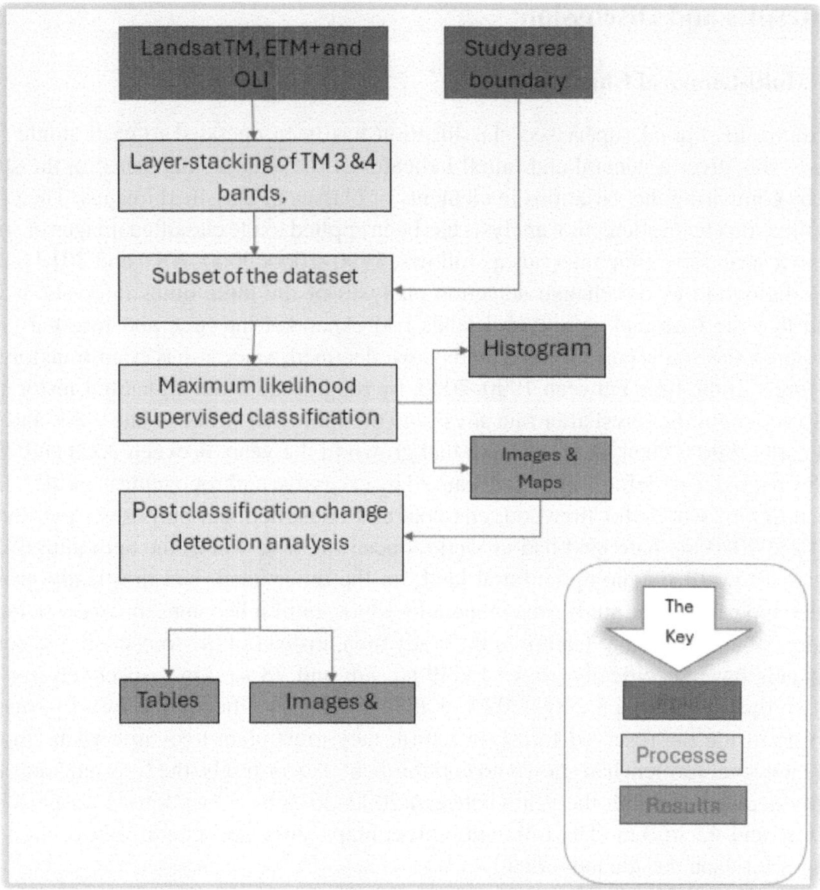

Fig. 3. Illustrates the methodology workflow. Source: designed by the author

how other users interact with the data, this lets individuals without GEE full access and programming experience to explore data without having to code or edit. For this GEE is a tremendously suitable to be a home and environment for forest monitoring SDSS.

GEE will facilitate overcoming the drawbacks of the traditional forest data management "file system" through ensuring easy and less-time consuming analysis and graphical summarization, combating data loss along with enabling replicability and verification of data analysis, all in reduced cost that will mitigate and overcome the ill-effects of funding and personnel lack.

6 Results and Discussion

6.1 Multi-temporal Change

Maximum likelihood supervised classification has been operated to each single four images, this gives a general and initial indicator of the changes happened in the study area by comparing the variations in elements or classes of classified images. Then post classification change detection analysis has been applied to the classified images of study area in a successive time intervals as follows, 1990–2000, 2000–2010 and 2010–2020. From the output of the change detection analyses of the three times intervals, it was found that the bare and agricultural lands had expanded into tree and forested lands throughout the study period. Bare lands have declined, since it has been transformed into forest in the time between 1990–2000, by roughly 28% due to natural restoration of 115 sq. km of the forest after rain stress and droughts that stroke in late1980s and last until early 1990s. Then, the bare land; had grown in the years between 2000 and 2010 by 48 sq. km due to deforestation that caused by excessive anthropogenic activities, like, overcutting of woods for firewood, charcoal and constructional purposes. And during 2010 and 2020 the bare land had as well reduced to 36 sq. km as the agricultural land expanded toward it. The agricultural land, on the other hand, had drastically grown, since it appeared in the study area in the mid-1990s, until it becomes the overwhelming component and dominant feature in the study area, instead of the forest and tree cover. Croplands have specifically grown by 39 sq. km and 78 sq. km respectively for the last two decades between 2000–2020, as the local forest office has allowed farmer to cultivate inside the reserved forest, in return, they must plant trees in certain amount acres, however farmers had shown no commitment. Accordingly, the forested lands had vividly declined through the years between 2000–2010 by 33 sq. km and over 2010–2020 by and 42 sq. km. The following three, maps show and graphically discern the changes for each decade individually.

Climatic variability is also perceived to be a causative factor for Elrawashdah forest deterioration, as it negatively affects the restoration and regeneration of the forest resources, especially in the context of the pressing anthropogenic forest products demand, especially the grazing shrubs. Likewise, the increased variability in climate that is characterized by increased heat and fluctuated rains will adversely influence the healthiness of the vegetations in general.

6.2 Forest Indices Time Series

From the findings, on can notice the variability in the state of forest greenness and integrity. Not only the seasonal variability. But also the trending deterioration that is taking place as the intensity and the size of the forest is getting reduce by the pressing anthropogenic activities of cropping, herding and tree logging. Likewise, the climatic variability is also evident, number of previous studies in the study area associated the climatic change and unfavorable conditions with the integrity and healthiness of the forest ecosystem. The findings of these time series indices support that. See Figs. 4, 5 and 6.

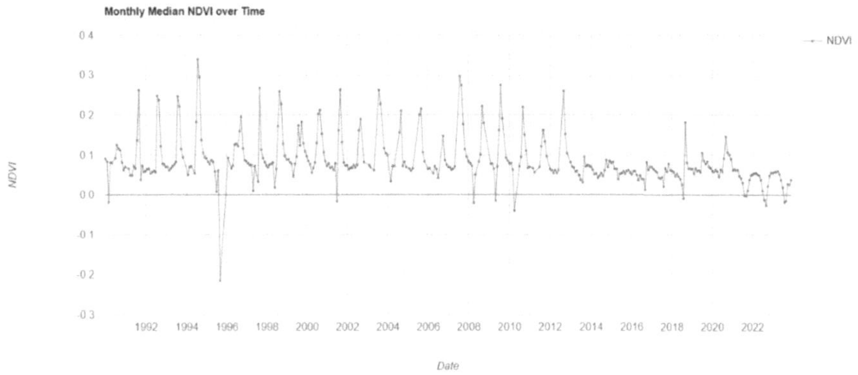

Fig. 4. Shows the NDVI trend over Elrawshdah forest between 1990–2023

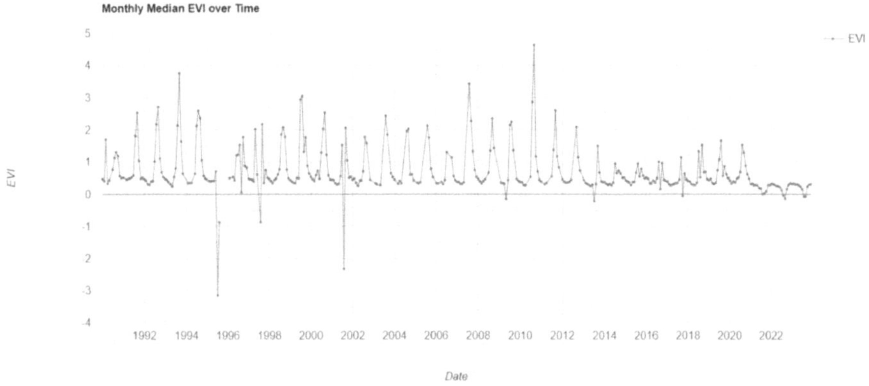

Fig. 5. Shows the EVI trend over Elrawshdah forest between 1990–2023

Considering lack of baseline data and studies, unsystematic inventories and poor traditionally archiving data, remote sensing-based change detection and timeseries analysis will not only enrich data availability and pave the way for forest knowledge management infrastructure, it will further facilitate the policy and decision making, through summarizing and providing insights for policy makers through highlighting the trends on the forest to inform forest management roadmap, accordingly.

This paper through revealing the timeseries indices and trends of RVI and EVI, it is investigating the greenness and biomass that indicate the quantitative indicator if the forest size and mass, as well as the healthiness and greenness of forests vegetations that is indicated by the NDVI timeseries.

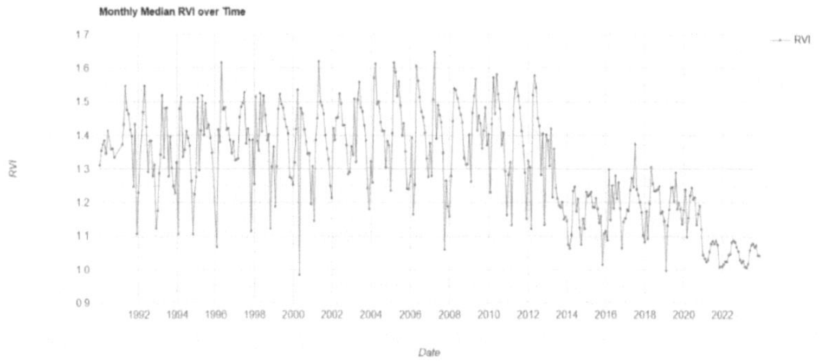

Fig. 6. Shows the RVI trend over Elrawshdah forest between 1990–2023

7 Conclusion

This research seeks to set an example that can be re-used in the other Sudan forest to overcome the forest management hurdles data unavailability, lack of fund and trained personnel, cost-effective monitoring of the extensive forest expanses, which will enrich and revolutionize the forest management practices in the country, and its similar ones of other developing nations.

The previous studies tackled the forests in terms of detecting the changes occurred in certain period of time, this enabled figuring the quantitative reduction in the forest, yet timeseries analysis gives more information and indicators on the patterns of changes and reduction ratios over long term and the intra-annual forest status.

The potential limitations or challenges associated with the implementation of the proposed forest monitoring system is the trained cadre and provisioning of geospatial technologies infrastructure, software and hardware, and integrated environment that entice more reliance on those technologies.

It is remarkably observed that agricultural and bare lands had enormously grown and overwhelmed over the forest, thus, the forest has rapidly deteriorated, within the course of twenty years; as stated above, the forest had lost vast areas which had been transformed into bare lands and agricultural lands. The annual average of forest loss has exceeded 1% of the forest's total size, and exceeded the average (0.8%), which was estimated by FAO in 2010. This, furthermore, gives an indicator that the forest has not been managed in a sustainable manner. Taking into consideration the escorting population growth, the forest would be further susceptible to be deforestation in future, hence it would; expectedly, disappear in a very soon future. This paper, thus, recommends that the agricultural expansion must immediately be prohibited, and the degraded areas of the forest should be afforested, additionally, the overcutting must be controlled and restricted by rotational reforestation plans to sustain the forest. Likewise, the paper suggests regular and extensive inventories are to be carried out alongside assessment of local communities needs from the woods to specify where and how much to be used and where to be reforested.

References

Abdalla, S.O.: Vegetation Cover Change Assessment in El-feel forest Using Remote Sensing. Unpublished master dissertation, University of Khartoum (2016)

Alhadary, Y.A.: Pastoral adaptation and socioeconomic transformation in African Sahel: Case Study of Gadaref State, Unpublished PhD thesis. University of Khartoum (2007)

Czimber, K., Gálos, B.: A new decision support system to analyse the impacts of climate change on the Hungarian forestry and agricultural sectors. Scand. J. For. Res. (2016). https://doi.org/10.1080/02827581.2016.1212088

Egemi, O.A.: Land use transformation, conflict and rural poverty in the rain lands of Sudan. Sudan Geogr. J. **1**(1), (2017a)

Egemi, O.A.: Land Use in Sudan; Study Report, Reducing Emissions from Deforestation and Forest Degradation, , REDD+. Readiness Program. Ministry of Agriculture and Forests National Corporation (2017b)

Elhassan, H.M.: The Dinder National Park: an example of resource-based conflict resolution. In: ElTayeb, G. (ed.) Land Issues and Peace in Sudan, (A book). (SECS) Sudanese Environmental Conservation Society and UNDP, Khartoum, Sudan (2006)

Eltayeb, G.: Climate change and its impacts on the living mechanisms of farmers and pastoralists in Gadaref State. (SECS) Sudanese Environmental Conservation Society and Gadaref University, Khartoum, Sudan (2011)

FAO.: Country Programming Framework for Sudan. Plan of Action (2015–2019): Resilient Livelihoods for Sustainable Agriculture, Food Security and Nutrition. FAO representation in Sudan. (2015). Retrieved from: http://www.fao.org/3/a-i4785e.pdf

FAO.: Global Forest Resources Assessment 2010, Country Report, Sudan. FRA2010/198. FAO, Rome. Italy (2010). Retrieved from: http://www.fao.org/3/al633E/al633E.pdf

Ganawa, E.: Sudan Natural Resources Database and Threats of Desertification. National Symposium of Sustainable Agricultural Development, University of Khartoum (2017)

Gorelick, N., Hancher, M., Dixon, M., Ilyushchenko, S., Thau, D., Moore, R.: Google earth engine: planetary-scale geospatial analysis for everyone. Remote Sens. Environ. **202**, 18–27 (2017). https://doi.org/10.1016/j.rse.2017.06.031

Holi, Y.: Knowledge management for sustainable development. Graduate college Conference, University of Khartoum, Khartoum, Sudan (2016)

Sulieman, H.M.: Exploring divers of forest degradation and fragmentation in Sudan:the case of Erawashda Forest and its surrounding community. Sci. Total. Environ. **621**, 895–904 (2018a). https://doi.org/10.1016/j.scitotenv.2017.11.210

Kadoda, G.F., Abu Asha, F.A.: A Knowledge sharing platform for Sudan's forest inventories investigating portal technology, Graduate college Conference, University of Khartoum, Khartoum, Sudan (2016)

Kobbail, A.A., Elmadina, A.M., Sulieman, M.S.: Management of natural forest reserves in collaboration with vilagers: a case study of El-Rawashedah and El-ain natural forests. Sudan J. Desert. Res. **4**(1), 23 (2013)

Kumar, N., Yamaç, S.S., Velmurugan, A.: Applications of remote sensing and GIS in natural resource management. J. Andaman Sci. Assoc. **20**(1), 1–6 (2015)

Sulieman, H.M.: Exploring drivers of forest degradation and fragmentation in Sudan: the case of Erawashda Forest and its surrounding community. Sci. Total. Environ. **621**, 895–904 (2018b). https://doi.org/10.1016/j.scitotenv.2017.11.210

Sulieman, H.M.: Natural regeneration potential of abandoned agricultural land in the southern Gadarif Region, Sudan: implications for conservation. Afr. J. Ecol. **52**(2), 217–227 (2013). https://doi.org/10.1111/aje.12108

Yagoub, Y., Bo, Z., Ding-min, J., Jahelnabi, A., Fadoul, S.: Land use and land cover change in northeast Gadarif State: case of El Rawashda Forest, Sudan. J. Geogr. Inf. Syst.Geogr. Inf. Syst. **7**, 140–157 (2015). https://doi.org/10.4236/jgis.2015.72013

Geospatial Intelligence for Circular Economy in Mexico City

E. Marquez-Salas Yailyn and Diana Castro-Frontana(✉)

National Polytechnic Institute-ENCB, 07738 Mexico City, Mexico
ymarquezs1600@alumno.ipn.mx, dgcastro@ipn.mx

Abstract. The Circular Economy is a proposal for a new economic model based on three principles:

1) Eliminate waste and pollution
2) Circulate products and materials (at their highest value) and
3) Regenerate nature

So, in a circular economy, products and materials remain in use through maintenance, reuse, refurbishment, remanufacturing, recycling, etc. We wanted to set a baseline of companies that perform circular economy activities in México City and map the results. We found a way to relate these activities with officially recognized economic activities in the North American Industrial Classification System (NAICS). Then, we used its coding system to locate companies in the National Statistical Directory of Economic Units geodatabase (DENUE-2023).

Of the 1086 economic activities recognized in the NAICS, 97 are related to the circular economy activities (that fit primarily with the second and third principles). The 97 codes were reorganized into six new categories: reuse, repair, refurbish, repurpose, recycle, and recover. Then, these codes were used to filter DENUE-2023 and map micro, small, and medium-sized companies in each R-category in Mexico City.

Of 475,331 records in Mexico City, only 47,339 could be located in an R-category. The repair category is the largest, with more than 50% of businesses (25,197). There are 10,276 economic units dedicated to refurbishing (21.7%), followed by reusing companies with 9,482 establishments (20%); 2,196 businesses dedicated to recycling (4.6%), 138 economic units in the "repurpose" category (0.3%), and only 50 establishments (0.1%) in the recovery category. Maps show the spatial distribution of these companies.

Keywords: circular economy · economic units · reuse · repair · refurbish · repurpose · recycle · recover · MSMEs · NAICS · SCIAN · DENUE · Mexico City · GIS

1 Introduction

The circular economy (CE) is a new economic model, a new development paradigm of a system where materials never become waste and nature is regenerated [1]. Our current economic model operates as a linear model in which natural resources are extracted,

M. F. Mata-Rivera et al. (Eds.): GIS-LATAM 2024, CCIS 2298, pp. 27–52, 2025.
https://doi.org/10.1007/978-3-031-80017-7_3

transformed into millions of different products and then discarded, at the end of their life cycle (or even before) in the form of waste and emissions to the soil, water and air, with little return to industrial processes. The linear economy is hugely wasteful: most of the value in materials we use is lost to landfills, and the things we create, and produce are consistently under-utilized. For example, in Europe, the average car is parked 92% of the time, 31% of food is wasted along the value chain, and the average office is used only 35–50% of the time, even during working hours [2]. Other negative externalities of this linear model include noise pollution, the release of toxic substances, and greenhouse gas emissions.

In contrast to the disruptive linear economy and as a response to it, the so-called circular economy offers an approach to economic development that seeks to separate growth from the consumption of finite resources. The Ellen McArthur Foundation, the pioneer organization that promotes the circular economy worldwide, has created three principles to make the transition from linear to circular economy [3]:

- Eliminate waste and pollution
- Circulate products and materials (at their highest value)
- Regenerate nature

These principles are intended to benefit businesses, society, and the environment and should be applied by countries, by companies, and by all the people. To facilitate this transition the Ellen McArthur Foundation has identify a set of six actions that businesses and governments can take. This framework is known as the RESOLVE framework, an acronym formed from the following actions: Regenerate, Share, Optimize, Loop, Virtualize, and Exchange [3]. These actions have been translated for public communication into specific activities. For example, the term Loop includes activities like remanufacture products or components, recycle materials. Share means "reuse or use secondhand stuff", prolong life through maintenance, design for durability, upgradability, etc.

1.1 Circular Economy and the Era of R

Walter Stahel in his book The Circular Economy, defines "the era of R" as: "*techno commercial strategies to keep goods and components at highest value level through the following actions*" [4]:

- Reuse
- Repair
- Remarket
- Re-refine and
- Reprograme goods, and
- Spread the circular industrial economy knowledge to class and boardrooms, to academia and to new R professions

As per Stahel definition, the circular industrial economy (CIE) manages stocks of manufactured assets (such as infrastructure, buildings, vehicles, equipment and consumer goods) to maintain their value and utility as high as possible for as long as possible, and stocks of resources at their highest purity and value [4]. As one can see, this definition was incorporated as the second principle of the circular economy (CE). So, in a circular economy, products and materials remain in use through maintenance, reuse, refurbishment, remanufacturing, recycling, and composting. This approach addresses climate change and other global issues, such as biodiversity loss, waste, and pollution, by separating economic growth from the consumption of limited resources [4].

The initial "era of R" proposed by Stahel has since evolved into different R-frameworks [5, 6], one of which is informally known as the "R ladder". This R ladder was first introduced during the "What Design Can Do" (WDCD) contest. WDCD is an international organization founded in 2011 and based in Amsterdam, aiming to accelerate the transition to a sustainable, fair, and just society through the power of redesign [6]. They created this ladder to guide contestants in placing their projects within one of the Rs and to visualize how their creations align with one or more circular economy models. This ladder adds new Rs to the original proposed by Stahel and connects it with the three circular economy principles (See the Fig. 1). The activities shown in Fig. 1 have in common that most of them (except remanufacturing) are oriented to selling services instead of goods. In 2010, Walther Stahel wrote the book "The Performance Economy" where he pointed out that the trend of buying services instead of goods may become the biggest driver of the transition from industrial to a performance or functional service economy [7]. This idea of the performance economy is implicit in the second principle of circular economy: to preserve and extend life of products.

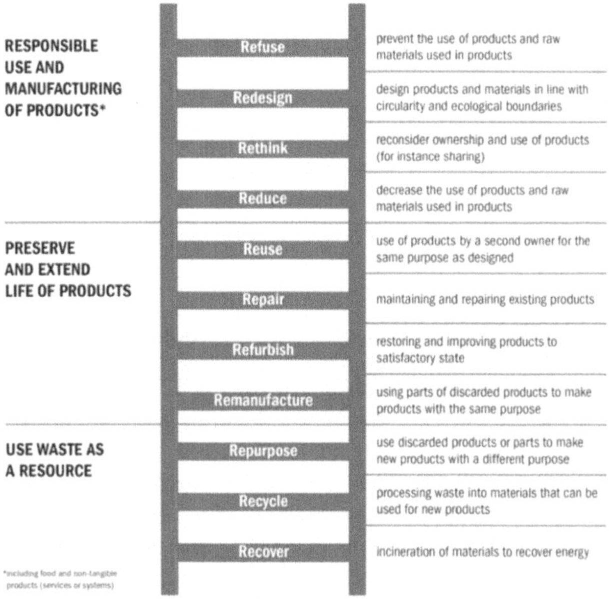

Fig. 1. The R-Ladder proposed by the WDCD organization (Source: WDCD Homepage)

The R-ladder was created to prioritize strategies and actions so that the higher R up on the ladder, the more impact a solution has in the circular economy.

1.2 Cities and Circular Economy

More than half of the current world's population lives in urban areas, Cities represent 85% of global GDP generation but are also massive users of material and energy resources. They account for 75% of natural resource consumption, 50% of global waste production, and 60–80% of greenhouse gas emissions [2]. There are almost 2,000 metropolitan areas around the world with more than 300,000 inhabitants. ONU-Habitat predicts that by 2035 almost a billion people will dwell in metropolitan areas in the next 15 years and there will be 429 new metropolises by 2035 [8].

Circular economy principles can also be applied to cities. In the report "Circular economy in cities: project guide" the Ellen MacArthur Foundations gives these steps to make the transition: 1) designing out waste and pollution from cities, 2) keeping products and materials in use and maintaining their value, and regenerating systems in and around cities [9].

Cities are characterized by a dense concentration of resources, capital, data and talent within a limited geographic area. This closeness can facilitate the implementation of a circular economy in several ways. For instance, reverse logistics and material collection processes can become more efficient due to the geographical proximity of users and producers, opening up more opportunities for reuse and collection-based businesses [10]. If a high number of people support sharing and reuse models (where products or assets are used by multiple users in a city), then these businesses will flourish. Additionally, the environmental impact of cities is mitigated by these actions. A study of seven European nations found that a shift to a circular economy would reduce each nation's greenhouse gas emissions by up to 70% and grow its workforce by about 4%, thus contributing to a low-carbon economy [11].

Therefore, a circular city integrates the CE principles throughout all its operations, creating an urban system that is inherently regenerative, accessible, and abundant. The goal of a circular city is to generate prosperity, enhance livability, and boost resilience for both the city and its citizens, all while separating value creation from the consumption of finite resources [2].

1.3 Circular Economy Law and Mexico City's Circular Economy Program

Mexico City faces a critical waste problem, producing 12,404 tons/day of solid waste. Of this, 6,014.9 tons/day (48.49%) are sent to landfills in neighboring municipalities [12]. This percentage falls significantly short of achieving the primary goal of Mexico City's "Zero Waste Action Plan," which aims to make it a Zero-Waste city by 2030 [13]. It also faces an air pollution problem, as do many other cities in the world.

On February 28, 2023, Mexico City's Congress approved the first Circular Economy Law in Mexico. The law aims for responsible production and consumption habits through reuse, restoration, remanufacturing, and recycling. Some specific goals of this law include [14]:

- Encouraging a circular economy for sustainable and regenerative development.
- Promoting responsible consumption habits among residents.
- Incentivizing sustainable production actions such as redesign and repair.
- Fostering sustainable business models to minimize environmental impacts.

- Facilitating collaboration between companies to enhance resource efficiency and utilization.

Article 16, Section I and II of the law highlights that the municipalities of Mexico City are required to "promote actions to develop projects in the field of circular economy to enhance the productive capacities of workers and job seekers" and to "promote responsible production and consumption throughout the value chain of products and services, in close collaboration with society."

Furthermore, the Circular Economy Program consists of 11 action areas, some to point out are Axis 5: "*Zero Waste*," which aims to reduce waste generation; Axis 6: "*Reuse*" and Axis 7: "*Right to Repair*" focused on encouraging businesses centered on product reuse and repair towards sustainable practices and reduce waste [15].

The circular economy activities also contribute to sustainable development goals (SDG), particularly to the following: SDG 8: decent work and economic growth; SDG 9: industry innovation and infrastructure; SDG 11: sustainable cities and communities; SDG 12: responsible consumption and production [16]. This project is a continuation of an effort to 1) find a systematic way to map circular economic activities in cities, and 2) perform quantitative spatial analyses that can be applied to calculate future circular economy indicators in cities.

1.4 The North America Industry Classification System (NAICS)

The North American Industry Classification System (NAICS) is the standard used by Federal statistical agencies in classifying business establishments for the purpose of collecting, analyzing, and publishing statistical data related to the economy [17]. The NAICS is designed to provide a consistent framework for economic data collection and analysis across the North American countries: United States of America, Canada and Mexico.

In Mexico, NAICS is translated as "*Sistema de Clasificación Industrial de América del Norte (SCIAN)*". The SCIAN (or NAICS from now on) reflects the structure of the Mexican economy and serves as the foundation for the generation, presentation, and dissemination of all statistics on economic activities in the country. This system allows the standardization of economic information, making it comparable within the North American region (USA, Canada and Mexico) [18]. In Mexico, the NAICS comprises 1,086 economic activities, each with a unique code.

To be able to link an official economic activity in the NAICS with the circular economy framework (shown in Fig. 1), we had to come up with a new R-ladder proposal (See Fig. 2). Activities like "rethink", "redesign" or "refuse" are nonexistent in the NAICS. By reading each of the 1086 code descriptions we figured out whose circular activities can be truly identified and located with a NAICS code and therefore be considered as official economic activities. Then, we also wanted to know the spatial location of businesses in Mexico City with officially recognized NAICS code and know which of them are related to circular economy.

A proposal for a "NAICS-Circular Economy framework" had to be created and is shown in Fig. 2. In this framework only 7R remained: reuse, repair, refurbish, remanufacture, repurpose, recycle, and recover.

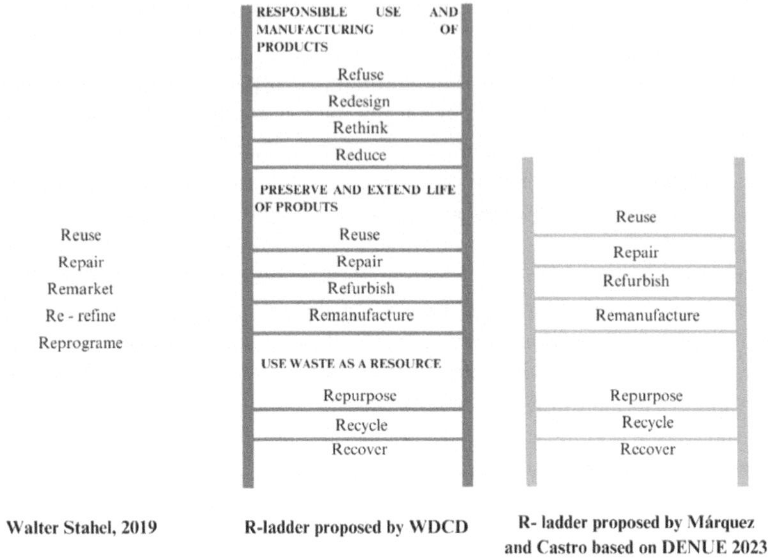

Fig. 2. R categories of activities related to circular economy

For this paper, it is important to define each term because several NAICS codes were grouped in an R category.

- Reuse: the act of using something again [7]
- Repair: to fix something that is broken, damaged or torn [7]
- Refurbish: improving something (furniture, buildings, etc.) by cleaning and decorating it. In IT devices it refers to repairing and cleaning equipment so that its condition is as new [7]
- Repurpose (includes renew and repurpose): changing something to make it suitable for a new purpose. To find a new use for an idea, product, or building [7]
- Recycle: to use a special industrial process to make materials and products ready to be used again [7]
- Recover: in the circular economy "recover" means to obtain some form of energy from waste. So, any business that converts waste to energy is classified in this category [3].

1.5 Directory of Economic Units (DENUE)

The National Statistical Directory of Economic Units (DENUE) is a census of all commercial establishments (economic units) in the country. It is conducted by the National Institute of Geography and Statistics (INEGI). It is published as a directory offering identification, location, economic activity, and size data for more than 5 million active economic units nationwide. The DENUE is continuously updated by authorized informants, who can update or supplement their business data and incorporate commercial information online through an application created for this purpose. Prior to publication, the information is validated by INEGI according to its standards [20]. The information is made available to the public in various formats. The 2023 version contains 5,564,612 registered businesses in the whole country. Each one is also marked with the NAICS code it belongs to. The DENUE was the main input for this project, as the vector layer with the location of all economic units in the country was obtained from this database (updated to 2023) and filtered to include only those in Mexico City. The original database contains 475,331 records. This means a total of 475,331 businesses were registered only in Mexico City.

1.6 Micro, Small and Medium Business (MSMEs)

INEGI classifies economic units with NAICS code into micro, small and medium-sized enterprises (MSMEs) according to their number of employees. In a study about the 2023 Business Demography (EDN) and Economic Censuses, INEGI estimated that 99.8% of establishments in Mexico fall into the micro, small, or medium-sized category and significantly contribute to job creation [21]. However, MSMEs are more vulnerable to changes (income, personnel, location, among others) than large companies. For every 10,000 registered MSMEs, 61 establishments open, and 71 close each month [22]. Implementing new strategies, such as operational and business models, is crucial for the survival of MSMEs. Table 1 shows MSMEs' classification according to their number of employees:

Table 1. Classification of economic units according to their number of employees (Source: INEGI, Comunicado de prensa 285/20)

Size	Number of employees	Percentage
Micro	0–10	95%
Small	11–50	4.0%
Medium	51–250	0.8%
Large	> 251	0.2%

The predominance of micro and small enterprises highlights their crucial role in the Mexican economy, particularly in the service sector. This underscores the need to strengthen and support micro, small, and medium-sized enterprises to promote sustainable and balanced economic growth in the country. MSMEs are considered key to accelerating the cities transition to a circular economy. As an example, the city of London has launched a support program called "ReLondon's SME" that helps companies either adopt circular practices, or -if they already have a circular business model- mainstream and scale their business [10]. There is a complete section of examples of circular economy in cities (case studies) at the EllenMacArthur webpage [10].

1.7 Promoting and Mapping R-ladder Activities

There is an example of mapping circular economy activities in Mexico. The Ecolana website was created to map recycling spots in Mexico City and later in the country.

The website started mapping small and medium waste collection centers and it has evolved to establish alliances with large companies with circular economy goals that want their products to have less environmental impact [23]. However, the focus is mostly on recycling, they do not map other R-ladder activities and still rely on personnel (on-site mapping) to update their website.

Another platform is Latitud R. It was created in 2011 as an initiative of the InterAmerican Development Bank and large companies as Coca Cola-LatinAmerica, PepsiCo and the Latin American and Caribbean Network of Waste Recyclers and Avina Foundation. In 2020 and 2021, two large companies, Dow Chemical and Nestlé joined the platform. The main goal is to support the development of the recycling chain in Latin America and the Caribbean, promote the formalization and improvement of working conditions for grassroots recyclers within integrated waste management systems, and foster the growth of an inclusive circular economy in the region [24].

In 2024, Carrera et al., performed a systematic review of literature on how Portuguese SMEs are addressing the challenge of circular economy. The results revealed that Portuguese legislation does not effectively support the implementation of the circular economy. Consumers are not fully engaged with the issue, companies struggle to communicate their practices, and there is a perceived lack of credibility among consumers. Additionally, the cost-benefit ratio of such practices is not always favorable [25].

In Mexico CE legislations at national and subnational levels are underway, the Circular Economy Law of Mexico City is an example. Other Mexican states as Quintana Roo, Chihuahua and Baja California have also promoted their own circular economy laws. Nevertheless, there are still no publications that provide information on mapping the geographical location of enterprises involved in circular economy in Mexico.

2 Research Objectives

To establish a baseline of businesses dedicated to circular economy activities, especially those focused on the second and third principle of CE: reuse, repair, remanufacture, etcetera, in Mexico City through geodatabase analyses.

2.1 Specific Objectives

- To find a way to connect officially recognized economic activities in the North American Industry Classification System (NAICS) with businesses related to circular economy using geographic data.
- To classify and refine the Mexican Directory of Economic Units (DENUE) in micro, small, and medium-sized enterprises actively involved in the second and third principles of the circular economy (reusing, repairing, remanufacturing, repurposing, recycling, recovering).
- To perform spatial analyses and find the spatial distribution of micro, small, and medium-sized companies involved in the circular economy in Mexico City.

3 Materials and Method

The materials used for this project are:

- North American Industry Classification System (NAICS) database, version 2023.
- National Directory of Economic Units (DENUE) database, version (2023/11), in shapefile (shp) and csv formats.
- Excel
- QGIS software version 3.34.1
- ArcGIS Pro

The development of this research included the following steps:

3.1 Downloading the 2023 NAICS Database

A detailed review of the NAICS and identification of economic activity codes related to any activities associated with the circular economy. We achieved this by reading and analyzing the 1086 NAIC code descriptions. Then, we selected the codes whose descriptions corresponded to activities related to circular economy (R-ladder) and put them apart. Finally, all the identified NAICS codes were grouped into any of the following categories. Table 2 shows some NAICS codes included in each R category created:

- Reuse
- Repair
- Refurbish
- Repurpose
- Recycle
- Recover

Table 2. Some SCIAN codes included in each R category

R category	Total SCIAN codes	Examples of SCIAN codes included in this category:
Reuse	38	532110, 532420, 532491
Repair	21	811115, 811430, 811211
Refurbish	6	811121, 811122, 812210
Repurpose	5	562112, 562111, 562122
Recycle	17	211312, 434313, 434314
Recover	10	562922, 562912, 562221
Total	97	

3.2 Downloading the DENUE 2023 Mexico City Database in SHP Format

Within this database, the NAICS code is expressed originally in the "codigos act" field, allowing us to link NAICS and DENUE information. This database field was renamed to CVE_SCIAN. The same was done for the CSV file.

3.3 Editing the DENUE CDMX CSV File

The attribute table was edited in Excel. Only records with selected SCIAN codes were filtered, and a new database was generated, excluding irrelevant fields.

3.4 Adding New Fields: Two New Fields were Added to the Database

The field "R_ladder" for establishment classification and "Size" for company size (micro, small, or medium based on the number of employees per INEGI, as shown in Table 1). These fields were filled in, and the file was exported to SHP and GeoPackage (gpkg) for use in QGIS and ArcGIS Pro (Fig. 3).

	S_NAME	CVE_SCIAN	ACT_NAME	EMPLOYEES	SIZE	R_LADDER	STREE_TYPE
1	)S Y PURI...	237111	Construccion d...	11 a 30 personas	Small	Recycle	CALLE
2	ΛA DE AG...	221312	Captacion, trata...	0 a 5 personas	Micro	Recycle	CALLE
3	ΛA DE AG...	221312	Captacion, trata...	11 a 30 personas	Small	Recycle	CALLE
4	ΛA DE AG...	221312	Captacion trata...	51 a 100 perso...	Medium	Recycle	EJE VIAL
5	ΛA DE AG...	221312	Captacion trata...	11 a 30 personas	Small	Recycle	AVENIDA
6	ΛA DE AG...	221312	Captacion trata...	0 a 5 personas	Micro	Recycle	AVENIDA
7	ΛA DE AG...	221312	Captacion trata...	51 a 100 perso...	Medium	Recycle	CALLE
8	ΛA DE AG...	221312	Captacion trata...	11 a 30 personas	Small	Recycle	EJE VIAL
9	ΛA DE AG...	221312	Captacion trata...	0 a 5 personas	Micro	Recycle	CALLE
10	CI◆N GE...	221312	Captacion trata...	0 a 5 personas	Micro	Recycle	PERIFERICO
11	ΛA DE AG...	221312	Captacion trata...	101 a 250 pers...	Medium	Recycle	AVENIDA
12	CI◆N GE...	221312	Captacion trata...	11 a 30 personas	Small	Recycle	CALLE

Fig. 3. New fields modified/created in the CDMX geodatabase

In QGIS, maps were created for each R category and company size, maintaining the geolocation of each establishment. Six maps were made (one for each R category). Finally, statistical analysis and charts were produced using Excel to complement the map information. They can be found in the results section.

4 Results

From the activities with official codes in NAICS (1086), 97 codes relate to activities in our R-framework. It represents 8.93% of activities under the NAICS code. Table 3 shows the NAICS codes related to the six R categories of the circular economy:

Table 3. NAICS codes (97) related to circular economy activities

Code	Code	Code	Code
221311	519212	562121	811121
221312	531111	562122	811122
222111	531112	562211	811129
222112	531113	562212	811191
237111	551114	562221	811192
325310	531115	562222	811199
326212	531116	562911	811211
331310	531119	562912	811219
331411	532110	562921	811311
331412	532121	562922	811312
331419	532122	562998	811313
331510	532210	562999	811314
331520	532220	721111	811410
434311	532230	721112	811420
434312	532291	721190	811430
434313	532292	721210	811491
434314	532299	721311	811492
434319	532310	721312	811493
466410	532411	811111	811499
468212	532412	811112	812120
484210	532420	811113	812130
485320	532491	811114	812210
485510	532492	811115	
519211	532493	811116	
562111	562112	811119	

4.1 Economic Units with R Category Activities in Mexico City

On the other hand, Mexico City's DENUE 2023 has a total of 475,331 records. From these, 47,339 economic units were subclassified with an R. Table 4 shows these numbers:

Table 4. Economic units before and after the reclassification process.

Mexican State	Economic Units in Denue 2023	Economic units (MSMEs) after filtering DENUE using our NAICS-circular economy framework
Mexico City	475,331	47,339

The following figures (Figs. 4, 5, 6, 7, 8, and 9) show business details (records) that fall into each category:

Reuse: it Includes economic units shown if Fig. 4

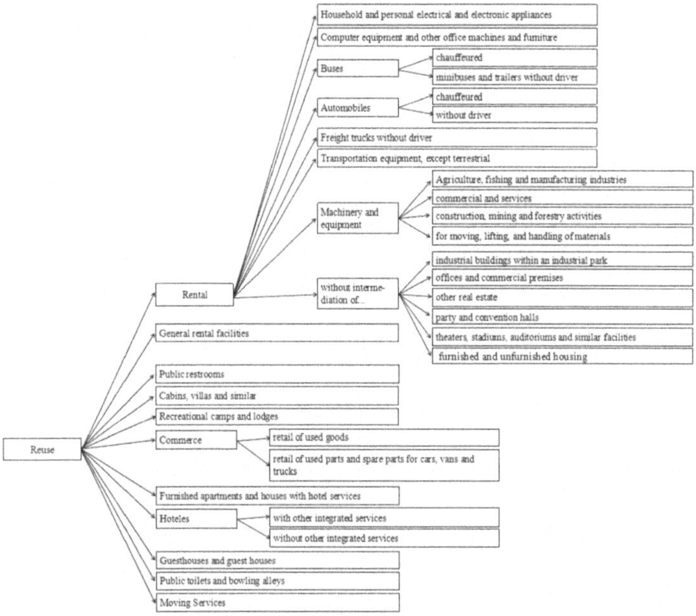

Fig. 4. Economic units (database records) included in the Reuse category.

Repair: it includes economic units shown if Fig. 5.

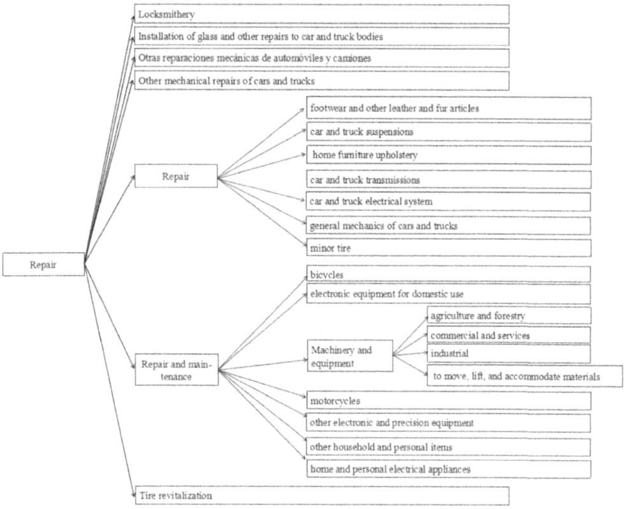

Fig. 5. Economic units included in the Repair category

Refurbish: it includes economic units shown if Fig. 6.

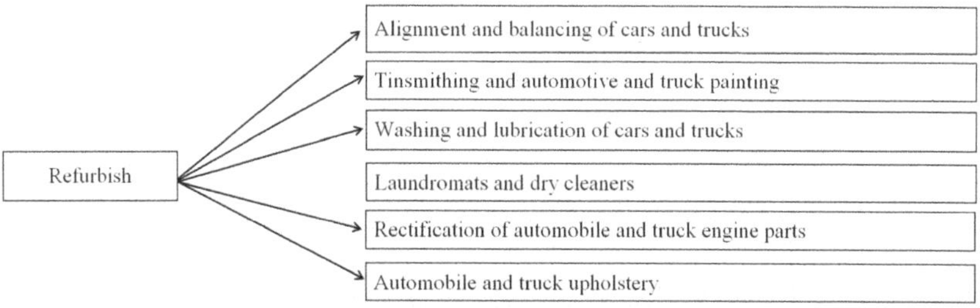

Fig. 6. Economic units included in the Refurbish category

Repurpose: it includes economic units shown if Fig. 7.

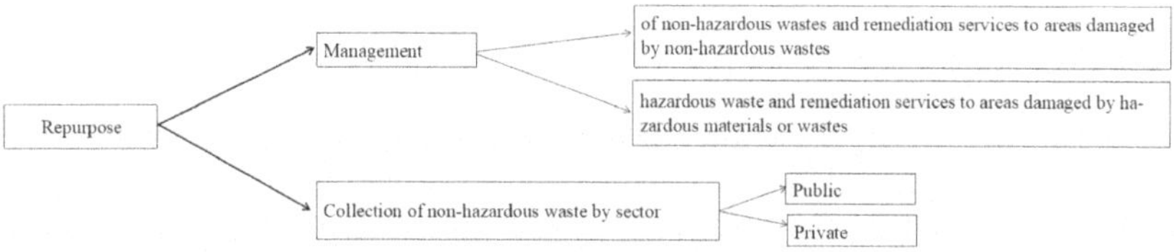

Fig. 7. Economic units included in the Repurpose category

Recycle: it includes economic units shown if Fig. 8.

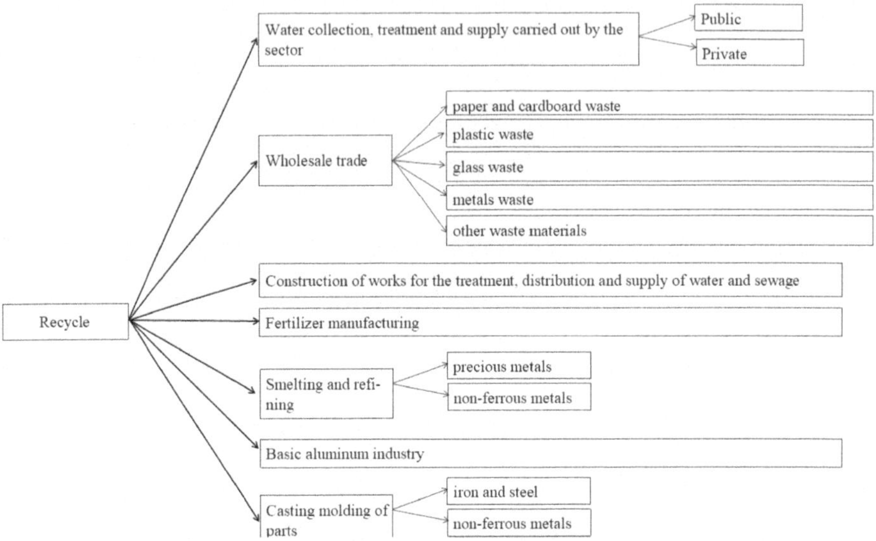

Fig. 8. Economic units included in the Recycle category

Recover: it includes economic units shown if Fig. 9.

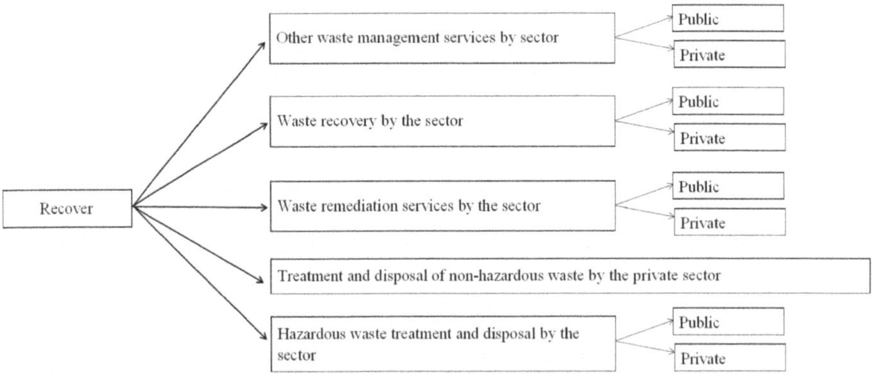

Fig. 9. Economic units included in the Recover category

From the reclassification and filtering of the DENUE we found that, in Mexico City, there is a trend of establishments specialized in repairing products, which represent more than 50% of the businesses (25,197). In addition, there are 10,276 economic units dedicated to refurbishing stuff (21.7%), followed by reusing activities with a total of 9,482 establishments (20%); 2,196 establishments dedicated to recycling (4.6%), 138 economic units in the "repurpose" category (0.3%), and only 50 establishments (0.1%), within the category of recovery (energy from waste) as shown in Fig. 10.

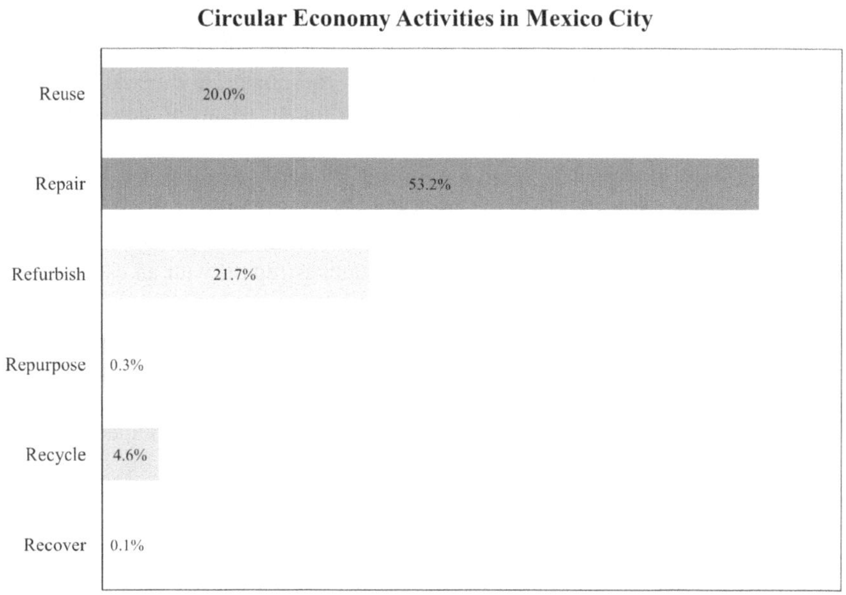

Fig. 10. Percentage of businesses with circular economy activities (by R-ladder category) in Mexico City

Regarding the size of these establishments, we found that 96% of the companies that carry out activities related to the second and third principles of the circular economy are micro-enterprises (with a maximum of 10 employees). On the other hand, small enterprises (those employing between 11 and 50 people) total 1,560 economic units. Medium-sized companies (between 51 and 250 employees) are 264 units (0.6%) and finally, large companies (more than 250 employees) are represented by only 75 establishments (0.15%) as shown in Table 5.

Table 5. Economic units' classification by size, in Mexico City.

Business size	Number of companies	Percentage
Micro	45,440	96%
Small	1,560	3.3%
Medium	264	0.6%
Large	75	0.1%
Total	47,339	

Figure 11 shows a combination of company size, and the percentage of each R category performed by each group. Micro-sized companies represent the vast majority in Mexico City (Table 5) and, from them, 54.5% contribute to repairing activities (Fig. 11). This means that micro-enterprises are mainly focused on repairing products to good conditions to keep their value. The repair category includes restoring, airing or replacing components, updating specifications, and improving the cosmetic appearance of multiple goods (such as automobiles, machinery, electronic equipment, household appliances, bicycles, among others), summing up 24,770 establishments (many of them focusing on automobile repair.

Economic units classified as small-enterprises primarily engage in activities associated with product reuse (57.2%), meaning they keep products in their original use, form, and purpose. This category includes activities as rental (822 economic units). The second frequent R category in small-sized companies is repair, with an estimated 373 units which represents 23.9% (see Fig. 11).

Continuing with the medium-sized businesses, we can highlight that those dedicated to reusing stuff represent 61.4% (164 economic units), followed by repairing companies with 17.8% (47 economic units).

As for companies classified as large businesses, there is higher participation in reuse activities, with 49 companies (65.3%), followed by 15 economic units dedicated to recycling (20%). As we can see, recycling activities are performed mostly by large companies probably, probably because they require higher investments.

Repurpose and recover (energy from waste) companies are almost nonexistent in Mexico City. Actually, it is difficult to find companies that convert end of life products into completely different goods. So, there is a gap here for new businesses in this category. The same happens with recovering energy from discarded products. There are no Waste-to-Energy (WtE) plants in Mexico City and since 48.49% of solid waste goes to landfill [12], recovering energy from it would be a much better option than landfills.

4.2 Spatial Distribution of Economic Units with Circular Economy Activities, by Size, in Mexico City

The following figures show the spatial distribution of businesses in Mexico City, by R-category and their size (Figs. 12, 13, 14, 15, 16, and 17). Based on the results, we found that business models likely to grow are those dedicated to product reuse and recycling, as these activities tend to become large enterprises. On the other hand, businesses focused on repairs rarely scale up to larger-sized companies. There are opportunities for new companies dedicated to refurbishing products, recovering materials, and repurposing products.

Large companies engaged in activities like renting construction machinery, offices, and hotels significantly contribute to economic growth, requiring substantial capital investment due to the nature of their operations. Conversely, establishments with lower initial investments, such as retail stores, dominate the city's economy. These stores, particularly those focused on goods exchange, are crucial for local economic dynamism, with the automotive and truck goods sector being especially relevant due to the city's heavy reliance on these transportation means. High demand for vehicles and related services significantly boosts economic activity in the city.

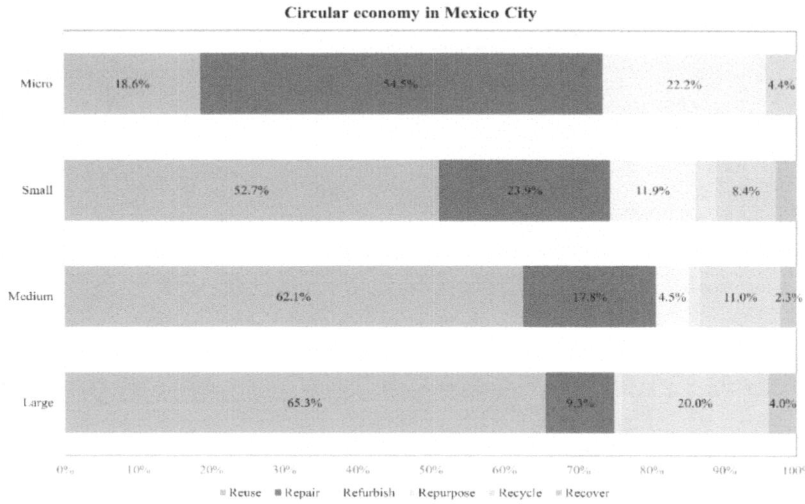

Fig. 11. Circular economy activities performed by micro, small, medium, and large-sized companies in Mexico City

Figure 12 shows the map of the Reuse category. The reuse activities include the direct leasing of offices and commercial spaces, furnished apartments/houses, trucks, buses, and machinery, public libraries, hotels, public toilets as well as the sale of used goods. These business models reduce the need to manufacture new items and prevent unwanted goods from being wasted, thus extending their useful life. The "Retail of used goods" standouts and accounts for and estimated of 1,766 economic units.

Repair: this category includes 21 NAICS codes, which sum up 25,197 economic units, of which 24,770 are microenterprises, many of them in the automotive repair sector. The most frequent economic activity in Mexico City within the repair category is "general mechanical repair of automobiles and trucks," with 5,214 establishments, followed by "repair and maintenance of other household and personal items," estimated at 3,217 businesses (Fig. 13). The seven larger companies in this category specialize in "repair and maintenance of other electronic and precision equipment," highlighting new business opportunities in the electronics sector, reflecting a trend towards diversification and specialization in high-tech areas.

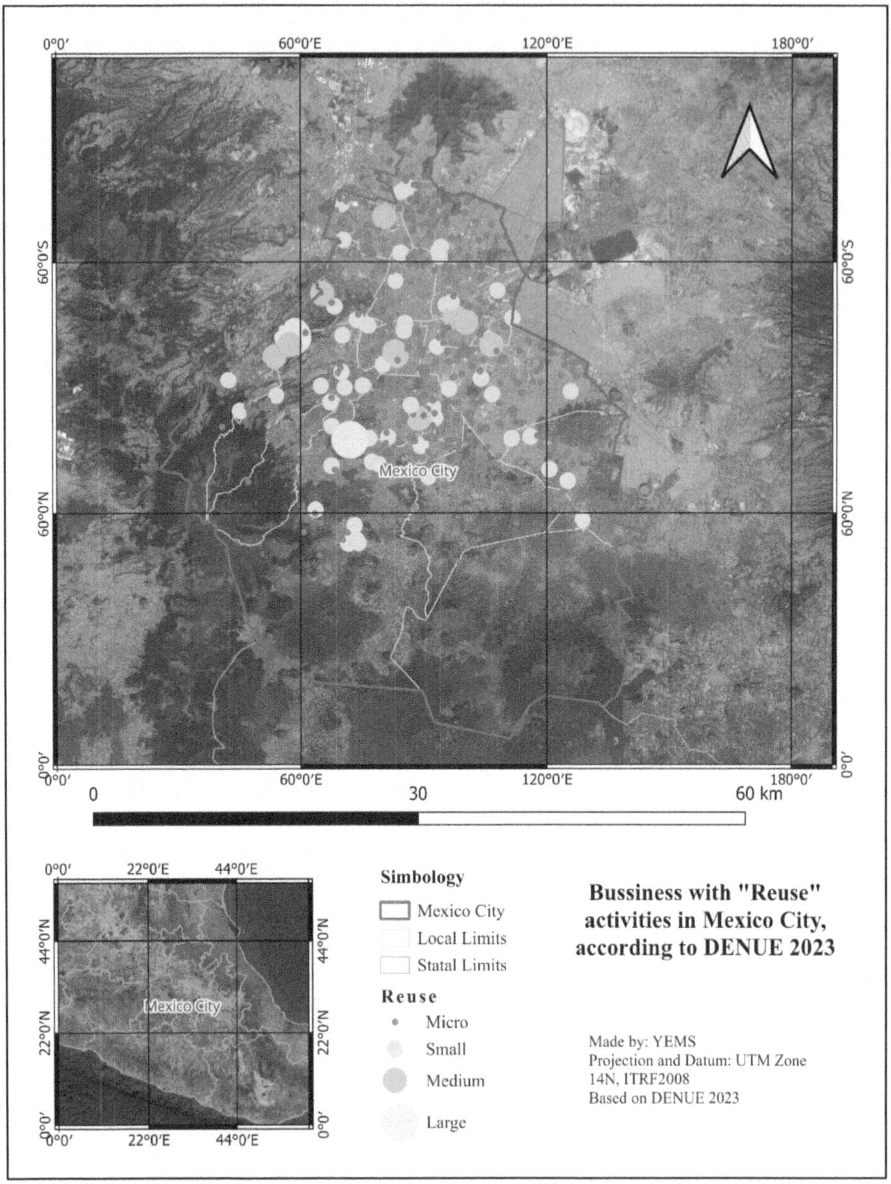

Fig. 12. Businesses with Reuse activities in Mexico City

Refurbish: There are 10,276 economic units in this category with 98% being microenterprises. Many provide laundry and dry-cleaning services, accounting for 6,307 businesses, followed by "automobile and truck bodywork and painting," with 2,083 establishments. This activity tends to be done by small-sized companies (Fig. 14).

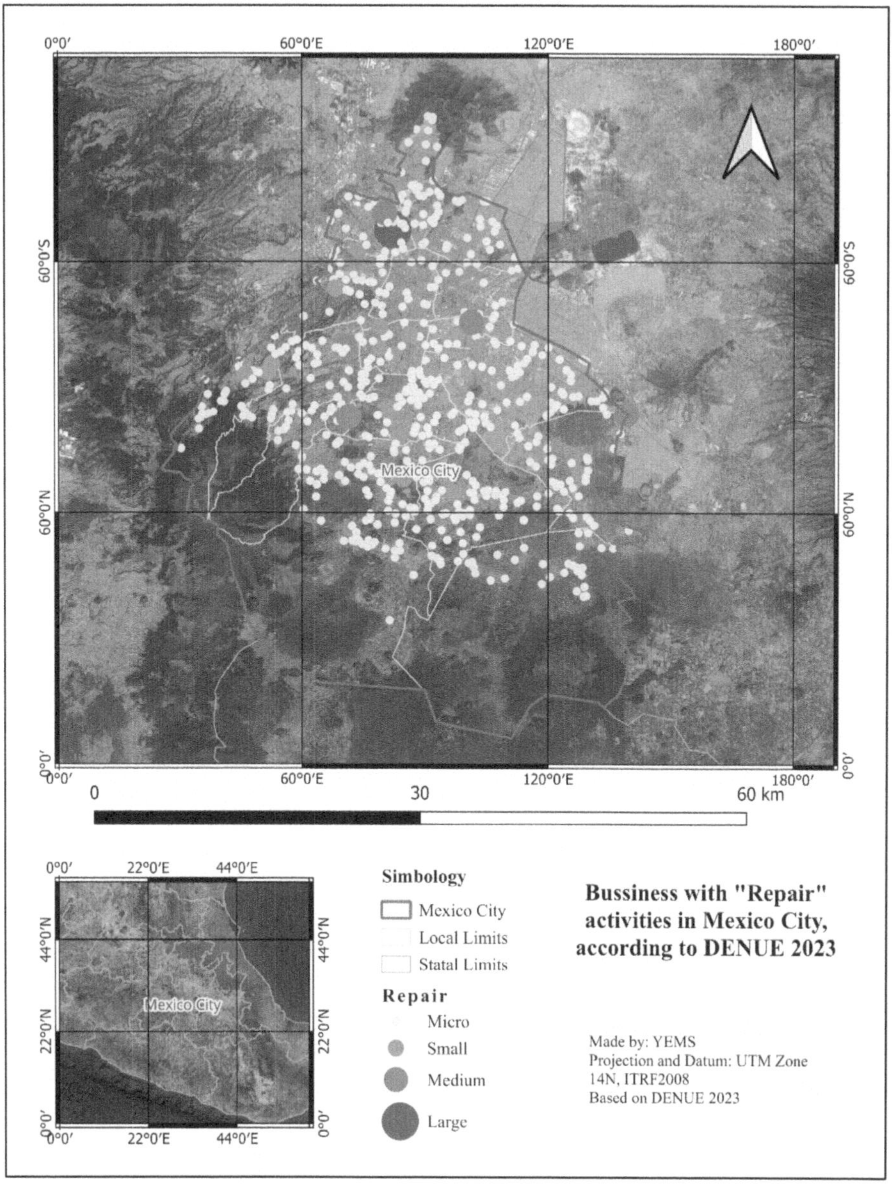

Fig. 13. Businesses with Repair activities in Mexico City

Repurpose: activities such as waste collection, hazardous waste treatment, and remediation of damaged areas (due to anthropogenic activities) are included in this classification (see Fig. 7 for more details). There are 138 businesses, 75% of which are microenterprises (Fig. 15). Although they currently represent a small proportion of the total, there are opportunities for growing new companies in these emerging activities

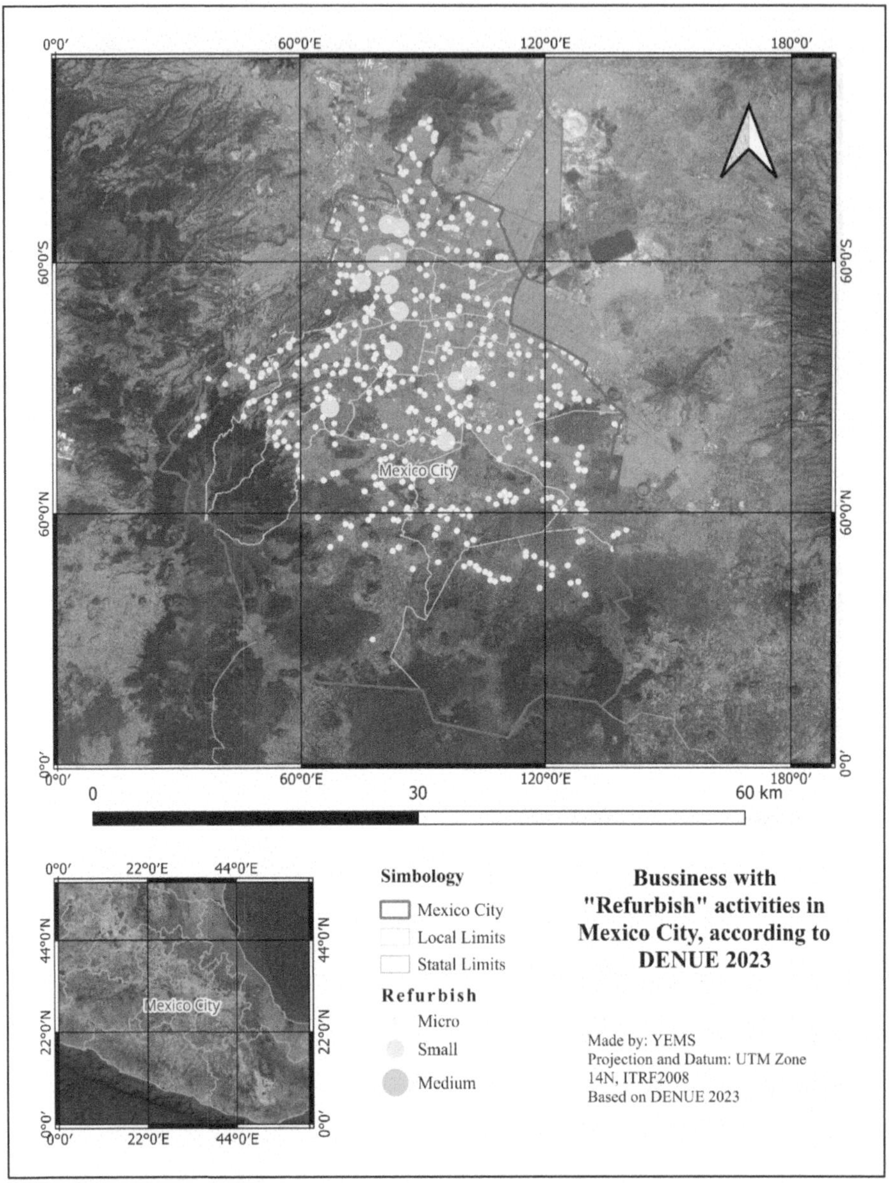

Fig. 14. Businesses with Refurbish activities in Mexico City

necessary in any city. The high proportion of microenterprises in this sector suggests that this service is required and that there is a market for expansion. At the same time, companies that provide services such as waste management are necessary in any city.

Recycle: recycling companies represent only 4.6% of the R activities in Mexico City. Numerically they account for 2,196 economic units, with 2,021 being microenterprises

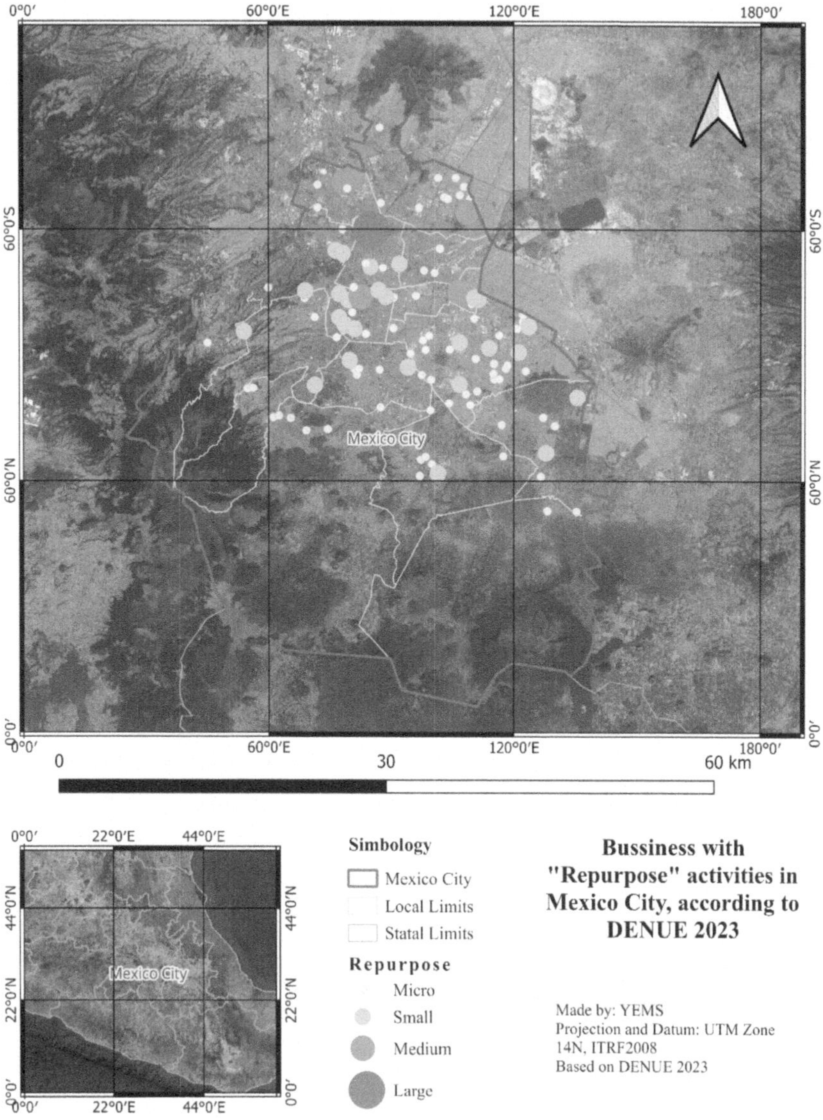

Fig. 15. Businesses with Repurpose activities in Mexico City

and only 15 large companies. Key activities include "water collection, treatment, and supply," both by the public and private sectors, which is crucial for Mexico City (See Fig. 16). Despite the relatively low participation in recycling activities compared to other categories, the significant number of microenterprises in this field highlights its growth potential and economic contribution. The low representation of large companies indicates an opportunity for investment and expansion in recycling. Water and solid waste management activities are essential for urban sustainability.

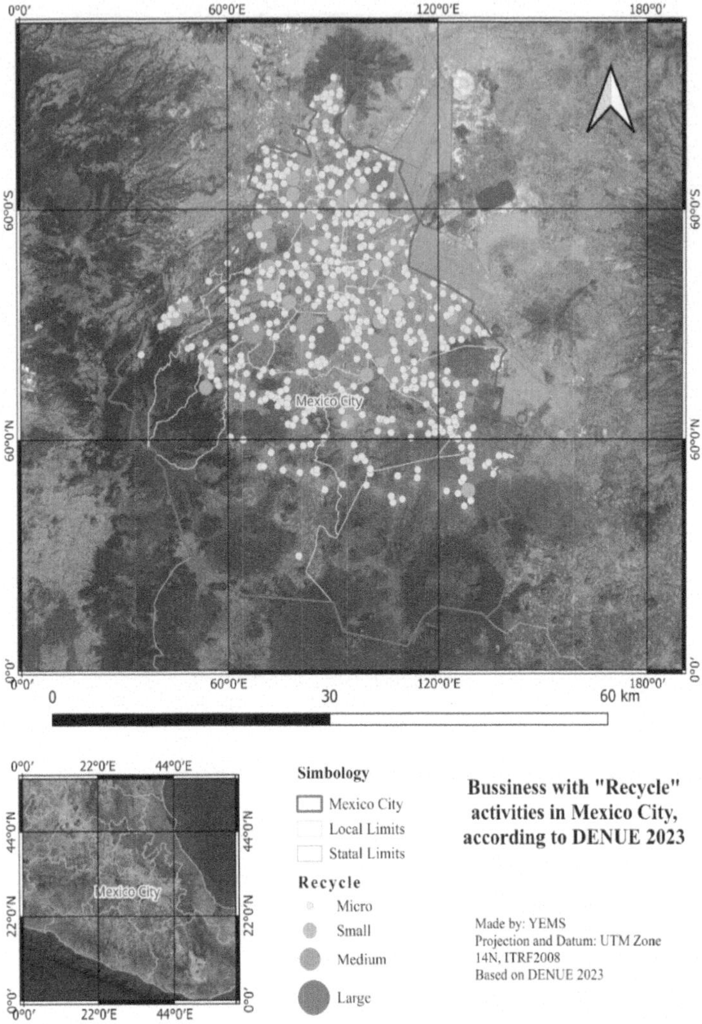

Fig. 16. Businesses with Recycle activities in Mexico City

Recover: there are approximately 50 businesses dedicated to material recovery, including activities related to remediation. “Private sector waste remediation services” comprises 12 establishments. The details are shown in Fig. 17.

Recovery businesses in Mexico City are low, with only 50 identified businesses. However, private-sector waste remediation services stand out as a significant activity. The small number of companies in this sector suggests there is an opportunity for growth and development, particularly in remediation and waste management activities, and also for industries treating biowaste, biorefineries or converting waste into energy. Expanding recovery businesses could improve environmental management and offer long-term economic and social benefits for people in Mexico City.

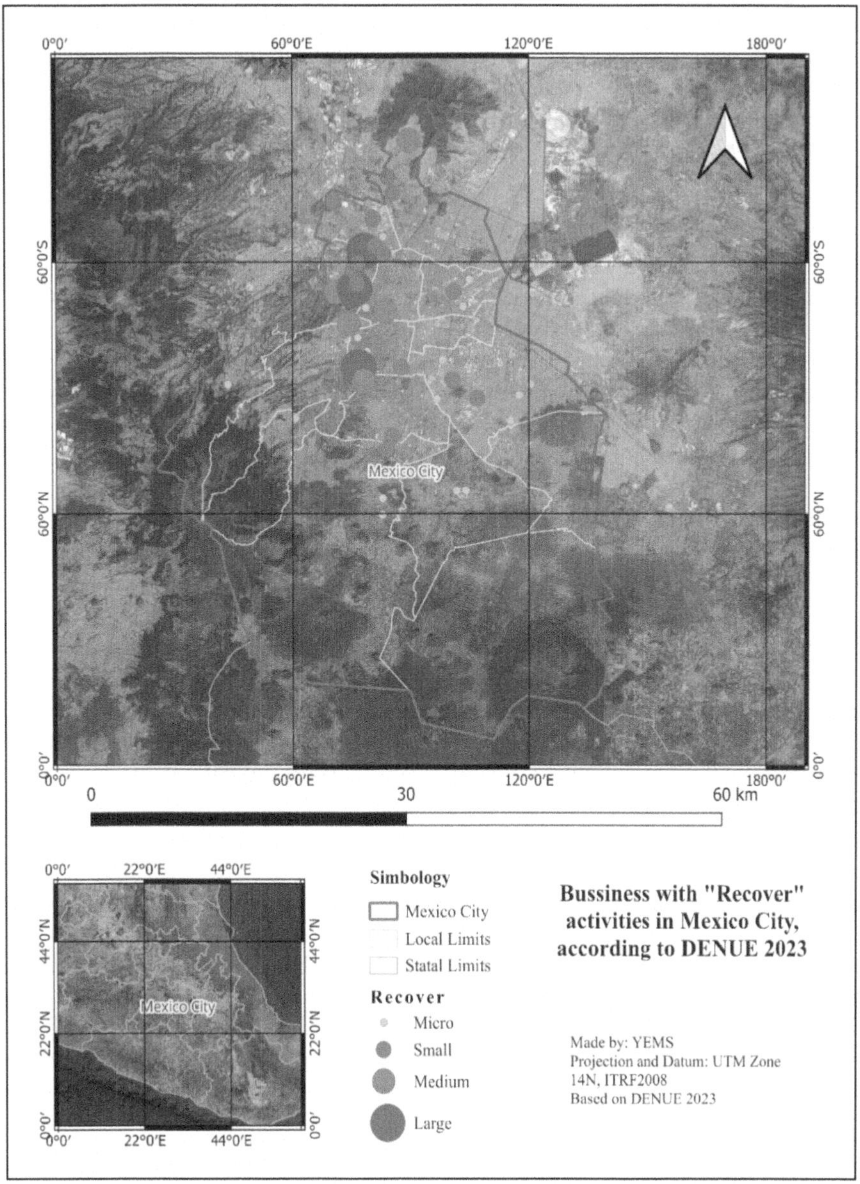

Fig. 17. Businesses with Recover activities in Mexico City

Many other spatial analyses can be done from these data. More inquiries are needed to discover quantitative information to calculate circular indicators for Mexico City (some could be the number of people employed in all these activities by age, gender, scholarly, or the flux of material in repairing businesses). Although more analyses are needed, there are potential jobs in all these fields due to the promotion of CE in Mexico City.

A study on the city of London estimated that by 2036, a circular economy could create 12,000 net new jobs in the fields of reuse, remanufacturing, and materials innovation [26]. Another study made by the Green Alliance and Wrap in 2015 suggests that by 2030, the circular economy could create over 200,000 gross jobs and reduce unemployment by about 54,000 in Britain [27].

5 Conclusions

Activities that are important in the framework of circular economy such as “rethink”, “redesign” or “refuse” are nonexistent in the NAICS. This means they are not yet recognized as official economic activities in Mexico, USA or Canada. Of the 1086 economic activities in the NAICS, we found 97 codes that are related to the circular economy (they align primarily with the second and third CE principles). The 97 codes were reorganized into six new categories: reuse, repair, refurbish, repurpose, recycle, and recover. Then, these codes were used to link the NAICS with the National Statistical Directory of Economic Units geodatabase (DENUE-2023) and reclassify it to map micro, small, and medium-sized companies in Mexico City that perform activities within the circular economy model.

Of 475,331 records in Mexico City, only 47,339 could be located in an R-category. The repair category is the largest, with more than 50% of businesses (25,197). In addition, there are 10,276 economic units dedicated to refurbishing (21.7%), followed by reusing related businesses with 9,482 establishments (20%); 2,196 establishments dedicated to recycling (4.6%), 138 economic units in the “repurpose” category (0.3%), and only 50 establishments (0.1%) within the recovery category. Maps show the spatial distribution of these companies.

The economic landscape of Mexico City shows a significant prevalence of microenterprises across various activities related to circular economy, especially in the repairing area (“automobile and truck repair” and “repair and maintenance of other household and personal items” being the most common). These microenterprises play a crucial role in the city’s economic and environmental sustainability. The automotive and household maintenance sectors stand out for their numbers, while large companies that focus on repairing electronic and precision equipment, represent new business opportunities in high-tech areas. In another step of this project, we aim to find spatial distribution patterns of these businesses and more “hidden” information by using geographical information systems.

Cities, like Mexico City, could be uniquely positioned to drive a global transition towards a circular economy, with their high concentration of resources, capital, data, and talent over a small geographic territory, and could greatly benefit from the outcomes of this transition. The benefits of supporting circular economy activities in cities include reduced carbon emissions, increased liveability, increased economic activity related to reverse logistics business models (to keep materials in use) thus reducing waste and relieving pressures on municipal services budgets [2].

This is a pioneer project whose main contribution is the creation of a geographic baseline database for circular economy businesses in Mexico City, recognized in the NAICS code. The identification of NAICS codes related to circular economy is important because it represents the basis for future treatment of more recent DENUE versions and the circular business geodatabase update using more advance technologies like big data and machine learning.

Acknowledgments. This work was supported by the Secretariat of Research and Graduate Studies (SIP) of the National Polytechnic Institute. The research was conducted at the National School of Biological Sciences (projects SIP20242319 and SIP20241067). The authors also thank the Commission for the Operation and Promotion of Academic Activities (COFAA) for the support in carrying out this project.

References

1. EllenMacarthur Homepage. https://www.ellenmacarthurfoundation.org/about-us/what-we-do. Last Accessed 10 Aug 2024
2. Ellen MacArthur Foundation.: Cities in the circular economy: An initial exploration, (2017)
3. Ellen MacArthur Foundation.: Towards a circular economy: business rationale for an accelerated transition, (2015)
4. Stahel, W.: The Circular Economy: a User's Guide. Routledge, Taylor & Francis, London and New York (2019)
5. WDCD Homepage. https://www.whatdesigncando.com/mission/. Last Accessed 07 Aug 2024
6. Tewary, A., Upadhyay, P.: Proposing a 6R framework promoting circular strategies for platform organizations. Digital Policy, Regulation and Governance (2024)
7. Stahel, W.: The Performance Economy, 2nd edn. Palgrave Macmillan, Basingstoke, England (2010)
8. UN-Habitat.: The new urban agenda. UN-Habitat, Nairobi (2020)
9. Ellen MacArthur Foundation.: Circular economy in cities: project guide, (2019)
10. Ellen Macarthur Homepage. https://www.ellenmacarthurfoundation.org/topics/cities/overview. Last Accessed 12 Aug 2024
11. Stahel, W.: The circular economy. Nature **531**, 435–438 (2016)
12. SEDEMA.: Inventario de residuos sólidos de la Ciudad de México 2022. SEDEMA, Mexico City (2022)
13. SEDEMA Homepage. https://www.sedema.cdmx.gob.mx/programas/programa/basura-cero. Last Accessed 15 Aug 2024
14. Gobierno de la Ciudad de México.: Ley de Economía Circular de la Ciudad de México. In: Gaceta Oficial de la Ciudad de México, Mexico City (2024)
15. Consejería Ciudad de México Homepage. https://data.consejeria.cdmx.gob.mx/portal_old/uploads/gacetas/502a580cc6886e0689492f3c07e97604.pdf. Last Accessed 28 June 2024
16. Castro, D.: WEB-GIS platform to visualize small and medium enterprises with circular business models in Mexico. In: Sidorov, G., Ritter, G.(eds.) Research in Computing Science. GISLATAM 2023, vol. 152, no. 1, pp 6–21, Mexico City (2023)
17. Census Bureau Homepage. https://www.census.gov/naics/. Last Accessed 24 May 2024
18. INEGI.: Síntesis metodológica del sistema de clasificación industrial de América del Norte: SCIAN 2023, Mexico (2023)
19. Oxford dictionary Homepage. https://www.oed.com/?tl=true. Last Accessed 16 May 2024
20. INEGI Homepage. https://www.inegi.org.mx/app/descarga/?ti=6. Last Accessed 24 Jan 2024
21. INEGI.: Comunicado de prensa 285/20. INEGI, Mexico (2020)
22. INEGI.: Comunicado de prensa 383/24. INEGI, Mexico (2024)

23. Ecolana Homepage. https://ecolana.com.mx/. Last Accessed 05 Aug 2024
24. LatitudR Homepage. https://latitudr.org/. Last Accessed 05 Aug 2024
25. Carreira, R.J., Ferreira, J., Ramos, A.L.: Mapping circular economy in Portuguese SMEs. Sustainsssability **16**(16), 7009 (2024). https://doi.org/10.3390/su16167009
26. IISD Homepage, https://www.iisd.org/system/files/publications/employment-effects-circular-economy.pdf?q=sites/default/files/publications/employment-effects-circular-economy.pdf. Last accessed 15 Aug 2024
27. Morgan, J., Mitchell, P.: Employment and the Circular Economy: Job Creation in a More Resource Efficient Britain. Green Alliance, London (2015)

Integrating a GIS Enhanced Security System in Wireless Sensor Networks (WSN): A Geospatial Deployment Approach

Alfredo Antonio Aguilar-Cristo, Daniel Sergio Martínez-Ramírez, Tanya Gabriela Makita-Balcorta, Homero Toral-Cruz, David Ernesto Troncoso-Romero, and José Antonio León-Borges(✉)

Universidad Autónoma del Estado de Quintana Roo, Campus Cancún, Av. Chetumal SM 260, Cancún, México

jleon@uqroo.edu.mx

Abstract. Nowadays, the gathered information from in-situ Wireless Sensor Networks (WSNs) over embedded systems is a crucial issue because WSNs offer details on the variables of interest for field researchers. These WSNs have been integrated into a Geographic Information System (GIS) to measure PH, temperature, light, and ultraviolet rays inside the cavern and the water in urban Cenotes in Cancun, Quintana Roo. It is important to consider the integrity of the information obtained from WSNs, and the security and protection of the WSN system. As mentioned, any WSN connects to different networking devices such as mobile users, central computers, remote database servers, and the Cloud. WSN uses the mobile technology GSM/GPRS to send information about research variables of interest to these devices. Because of the WSN connectivity to the Internet is possible by a mobile telephony module to send data sensor data into a remote database manager server, typically based on a Raspberry Pi 3 computer. This experimental Embedded Network Security System (ENSS) offers a cybersecurity solution to protect mobile users, central computers, remote database servers, and the Cloud from any direct attack against the WSN, especially the Rasp-berry Pi 3 computer. Therefore, as a scope, we present the deployment of a real-time ENSS on a Raspberry Pi 3 computer using security protocols through a Virtual Private Network (VPN), Secure Shell (SSH), and a Firewall as well to protect in-situ data from potential cybernetic attacks.

Keywords: Firewall · Global System for Mobile Communications (GSM) · General Packet Radio Service (GPRS) · Raspberry Pi 3 model B · Secure Shell (SSH), · Virtual Private Network (VPN) · Wireless Sensor Network (WSN)

1 Introduction

In practice, the use of gathered information from environmental in-situ Wireless Sensor Networks (WSNs) is a crucial security issue for field researchers because this kind of information represents the traffic among different computing devices: in-situ and remote

M. F. Mata-Rivera et al. (Eds.): GIS-LATAM 2024, CCIS 2298, pp. 53–72, 2025.
https://doi.org/10.1007/978-3-031-80017-7_4

Cloud-connecting computers. Moreover, other network components consist of remote databases which also contain information of many monitoring devices that represent connected users to the Cloud. Besides connectivity, WSNs are also vulnerable to potential security threats because the *measured information* is important for back-end remote users.

In the case of the Quintana Roo state, there is a developing real-time monitoring system of water cenotes [1–6]. Therefore, this present research work now focuses on an experimental embedded security system for further use in a previous developed WSN prototype, deployed by the University of Quintana Roo (UQRoo) not only at Cancun city but also some other locations in the Mexican Caribbean coast. This environmental WSN uses interconnected sensor nodes which use mobile network technologies such as Global System for Mobile (GSM) and/or General Packet Radio Service (GPRS) communications to connect with a remote database server platform which contains the environmental data from the WSN [7, 8].

As presented in [7], the real-time WSN monitoring prototype uses an Arduino Uno-based microcontroller which gathers data from sensor nodes to monitor the incident light intensity, the pH, the temperature, and the UV index to determine the cenote quality water whereas a configured centralised server database is based on a Raspberry Pi 3 model B computer. Analogously, a built-in Arduino Uno GSM/GPRS module provides the network connectivity between the WSN and a remote monitoring mobile phone. However, the implementation scenes are located in two populated areas in the Cancun urban zone.

However, there is a permanent risk of the integrity and reliability of the collected data by the WSN because of potential threats against the Cloud-connecting back-end remote computing devices. These user devices consist of mobile phones, remote computers, remote databases and among other networking devices. Moreover, a non-protected WSN always represents a potential risk of security. In previous environmental works [8, 9], the obtained information by different node locations lacks of any network security system.

In terms of cyberattacks, possible impacts of a potential threads, such as remote and/or in-situ types, would be a link blocking between our homemade WSN with other connected remote devices such as mobile phones, computers, and environmental databases from the WSN. Therefore, the integrity and the reliability of any WSN data is crucial security issue to be considered in this research.

As research scope, this work is towards the development of an Embedded Network Security System (ENSS) as a further security deployment of the current environmental WSN architecture in the Mexican Caribbean zone. However, the key cenote locations of study are as follow: Cancun urban zone, Puerto Morelos, Riviera Maya, Cozumel, Chetumal, and Holbox [8, 9].

The relevance of these key locations in the Mexican Caribbean lies on their both economical and tourism activities and its environmental consequences in cenotes. Therefore, a security system is a crucial issue to be considered because a more protected environmental information guarantees a better monitoring of the deployed WSN. As environmental information types, the deployed WSN measurements consider these pollutant concentrations such as: hydrocarbon and total and faecal coliforms [8, 9]. Moreover, environmental cenote parameters such as incident light intensity, pH, temperature, and

UV radiation [7] in the Cancun urban zone but for further deployment in the other mentioned locations in the Mexican Caribbean.

As presented in [7–9], the core of the used environmental WSN in the Cancun urban zone consists of a Raspberry Pi 3 model B architecture. Therefore, this central computer of the WSN is compatible with other Raspberry Pi 3 computers. Then, this implemented ENSS works over a Raspberry Pi 3 B+ architecture.

For this current deployment, the proposed Embedded Network Security System (ENSS) consists of these security protocol implementations: a firewall, a Secure Shell (SSH), and a Virtual Private Network (VPN) because our homemade WSN is exposed to potential threats because of its connectivity with the university network. As another scope of this deployment, the used Raspberry Pi 3 B+ computer will implement these protocols for evaluation only.

2 WSN Preliminaries

2.1 Wireless Sensor Networks (WSNs) for Environmental Measurements

As preliminary topic, Wireless Sensor Networks (WSNs) have many diverse deployments and these networks yield a gradual decreasing cost. Therefore, WSN solutions are being more accessible in terms of costs because of the advances in wireless technologies and WSN offer a proper industrial solution in many applications [8, 9]. As mentioned by Mehra and Kathri [8, 10], a WSN design depends on their application and demand and a crucial stage is the connectivity and infrastructure issues. Moreover, some other monitoring activities of WSNs can be found in automotive, entertainment, environmental, and among other applications [11].

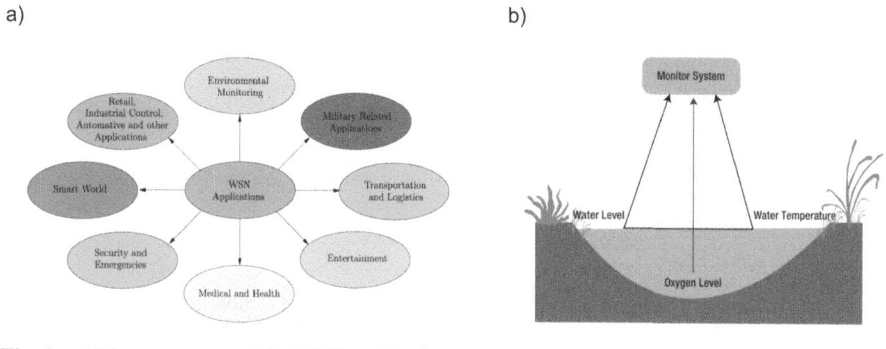

Fig. 1. a) The taxonomy of the WSN applications [11]. b) A typical fishpond monitoring system, as viewed in [9], to define the topology scene for deploying environmental WSNs.

Despite the wide range of applications of WSN, there are some critical issues to consider for a WSN deployment. Mehra summarises these issues in terms of:

- Hardware Infrastructure of the WSN.
- Energy Management Schemes for Wireless Sensor Networks (WSNs).

- Networking Methodologies.
- Wireless Sensor Node Energy Consumption.
- Major Application of Wireless Sensor (WS)

In addition, Yetgin presents a clear depiction of the taxonomy of WSN applications [11] in Fig. 1a). In Cancun, the major application for our homemade WSN [7] is towards environmental purposes for local cenotes [7].

For an environmental WSN implementation, the location scene determines how the topology of the installation of the WSN network. In Fig. 1b), Bell presents an interesting example how to deploy a fish bond application which defines the monitoring topology the level and temperature of water including the oxygen level to keep fish in healthy conditions. In our case, the selected sector of Cancun is the region 510 [7, 9, 12–17]. In [7], our WSN considers the measurement of the *incident light intensity* besides the *UV index*, the *pH* and the *temperature of water* as four variables of interest in a pair of cenotes in different urban areas at Cancun. However, there is a security concern in terms of the gathered information by our homemade WSN. In Fig. 2, we represent the current topology of the network.

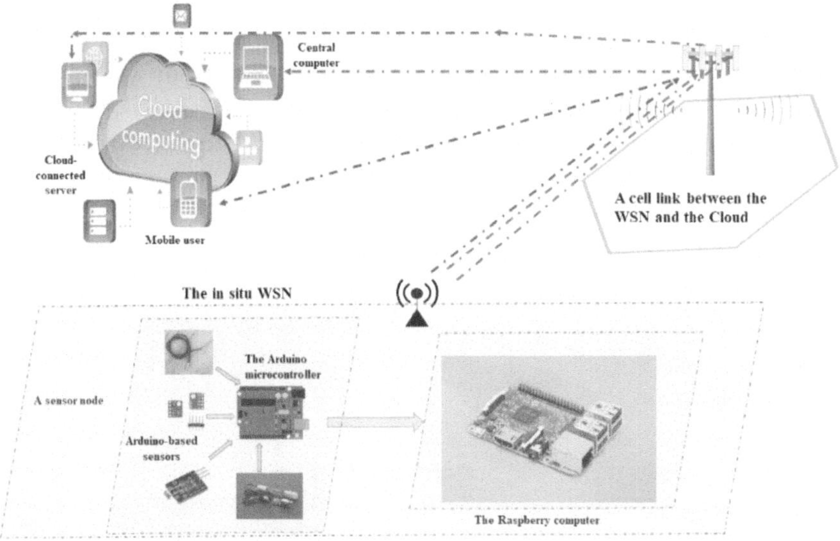

Fig. 2. The current WSN links with the key users: a mobile user, a remote central computer, and a remote server. All users connected with the Cloud [7, 9, 16, 17].In next section, we present a summarised description of our environmental WSN in the Mexican Caribbean coast.

2.2 The WSN Integration into a GIS

As previously mentioned, the current WSN implementation in the Mexican Caribbean region lies on the cenote locations as measurement nodes as presented below in Table 1.

Table 1. The WSN node locations in the Mexican Caribbean, see [8, 9] for details.

Zone Location	Geographical Coordinates
Cancun urban area	21° 11′ 25.5″N, 86° 50′ 14.9″W 21° 9.0′ 41.3″ N, 86° 51′ 0.81″W 21° 8.0′ 19.0″N, 86° 51′ 39.35″W
Puerto Morelos	20° 50′ 53.7″N, 86° 52′ 33.98″W
Riviera Maya	20° 39′ 43.59″N, 87° 4′ 7.25″W; 20° 12′ 31.26″N, 87° 28′ 21.81″W
Cozumel	20° 26′ 35″ N, 86° 59′ 40″W
Chetumal	18° 46′ 2.37″N, 88° 18′ 24.92″W 18° 30′ 50.98″N, 88° 25′ 27.29″W
Holbox	21° 32′ 16.0″N, 87° 13′ 12.0″W

In [8], the implemented WSN presents the hydrocarbon pollution in cenotes during two vocational seasons, summer and autumn, during the months of July and October as "High" and "Low" pollution concentration, respectively. The sort of hydrocarbon involved in the environmental WSN node pollution levels are as follow: Anthracene, Benzo[a]pyrene and Pyrene including the relationship with annual asphalting because of the fuel runoff from vehicles besides the tourism. In Fig. 3, the study zones, indicated as nodes, are presented in a map of the Quintana Roo state.

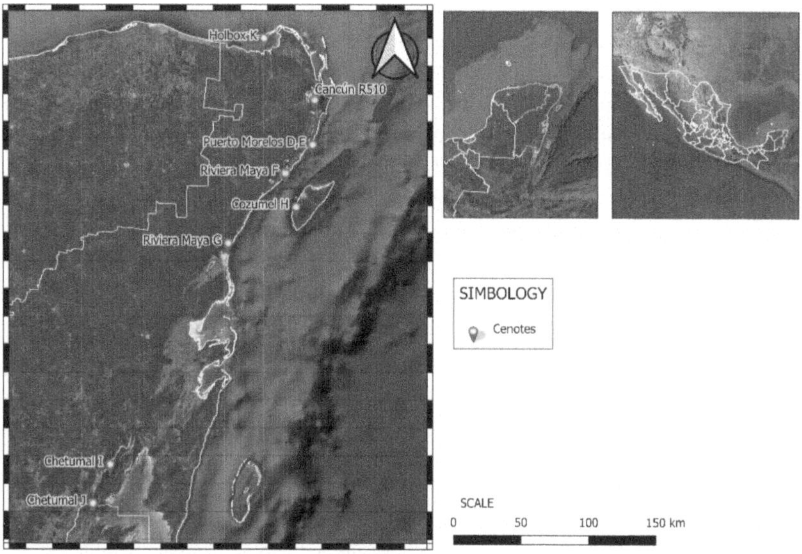

Fig. 3. The actual location of the cenotes along the Mexican Caribbean zone for the current WSN: Cancun urban zone, Puerto Morelos, Riviera Maya, Cozumel, Chetumal, and Holbox [8, 9].

On the other hand, there is a more recent environmental study to determine the hydrocarbon contamination patterns in a period from 2016 to 2017, in the same locations as [8], to evaluate the Polycyclic Aromatic Hydrocarbon (PAH) concentrations. PAH hydrocarbon substances are presented in detail [9] as indicated: fluoranthene, anthracene, phenanthrene and naphthalene which present a raise of 7% for these contaminating substances.

In next subsection, we present the security requirements a brief description of the Embedded Network Security System (ENSS), based on a Raspberry Pi 3B platform, to be deployed in a our environmental WSN which will be integrated into a Geographic Information System (GIS). However, as scope, the security stage is crucial to ensure any further external cybernetic threat against the GIS, deployed in a remote computer. In the case of our network, the ENSS stands for an early security stage because the proposed ENSS can cease the connectivity access between the remote computer and the ENSS, and the ENSS itself.

2.3 The ENSS Requirements for the WSN

As previously mentioned, our current homemade environmental network does not integrate any security protocol. As viewed in Fig. 2, the WSN computer implements web connectivity applications to receive/transmit data from any built-in data sensor node within the in-situ WSN because the Raspberry Pi 3B platform can act as the local database server. Based on its physical characteristics, this computer was selected because of its credit card size, providing to our database server a compact size to make an easier installation.

According to Fig. 2, the Raspberry Pi 3B card basically has three links with these remote users: a mobile phone user, a central computer, and a database server. Each link is presented as follows. First, the red dotted-discontinuous line represents the link between the WSN and the mobile phone user to gather real-time measurements, then, the green dotted-discontinuous line shows the connection between our network and the central computer to collect real-time in-situ data. Whilst the connective blue dotted-discontinuous line illustrates the joint between the network and the cloud-connected server.

Considering this potential security issue, our team consider these security protocols as mentioned: Firewall, Secure SHell (SSH), and the Virtual Private Network (VPN). The reason to deploy these protocols obeys to functionality because it is easier to deploy them on the WSN Raspberry Pi 3B computer rather than installing extra software on each remote user but for the central computer.

To justify the use of these protocols, is to define the type of potential threats to our WSN such as intrusion (IP and port scanning); denial of service; weakness in network infrastructure and communication protocols, and among other further both hardware and software risks [18–20]. Even though this research work is not focused towards cybersecurity, our team applied a wireless firewall as a restriction between the wireless private network and the Internet to prevent external attacks by any intruder to the WSN link between the Raspberry computer and the mobile phone user. For the case of the VPN protocol, VPN consists of a Point-to-Point Tunnelling Protocol (PPTP), Layer 2 Tunneling Protocol (L2TP), and IPSec that carries Point-to-Point Protocol (PPP) layers across the Internet to provide multiple links with additional security. In practice, VPNs consist of a trusted session between the remote central computer and the WSN via the Raspberry module as PPTP ends, then, a VPN can be also used as firewall server [20]. Besides extra security components, VPN needs an additional structure by an application protocol, SSH whose use is highly recommended as a part of the best security practices to deal with threats and vulnerabilities between a remote user access and the WSN to intercept and monitor attacks such as session hijacking, broadcast monitoring, and Arp spoof monitoring. As a desirable feature of SSH is a Linux-based protocol because the Operating System (OS) to evaluate our in-situ embedded security system is the Raspbian OS version, implemented as the OS over the Raspberry Pi 3B+ computer.

The next section, we present the key computing equipment to deploy our embedded security system.

3 The Embedded Network Security System (ENSS): Hardware Requirements

3.1 A Summary of the Raspberry Pi 3 Model B Computer

Because of its centrality on our homemade ENSS, the Raspberry Pi 3 Model B computer implements web connectivity applications to receive/transmit data from any built-in data sensor node within the in-situ WSN because this computer can act as the local database server. Based on its physical characteristics, this computer was selected because of its credit card size, providing to our database server a compact size to make an easier installation.

According to the Raspberry site, the chosen database server used in this implementation is the Raspberry Pi 3 Model B. Table 2 describes the technical specifications of the Raspberry Pi 3 Model B computer and it is shown in Fig. 4 below.

In next subsection, we present brief definitions of security protocols: firewall, SSH, and the VPN to de deployed on the Raspberry Pi 3 model B computer.

3.2 The Remote Central Computer

As the remote central computer, the authors selected a SONY® VAIO SVF14211CLB model which consists of a 64-bit OS with these features.

Table 2. Technical specifications of the Raspberry Pi 3 Model B computer, see [21].

Specification	
Processor:	Quad Core 1.2 GHz Broadcom BCM2837 64bit CPU
Memory:	1 GB RAM
Connectivity:	BCM43438 wireless LAN and Bluetooth Low Energy (BLE) on board 100 Base Ethernet
GPIO:	40-pin extended GPIO
Video & sound:	4 USB 2 ports 4 Pole stereo output and composite video port Full size HDMI®
Multimedia:	CSI camera port for connecting a Raspberry Pi camera DSI display port for connecting a Raspberry Pi touchscreen display
SD card support:	Micro SD port for loading your operating system and storing data
Input power:	Upgraded switched Micro USB power source up to 2.5 A
Production lifetime:	Raspberry Pi 3 Model B will remain in production until at least January 2028

Fig. 4. The Raspberry Pi 3 model B computer.

The Table 3 indicates the technical specifications for the Arduino Uno R3 model.

The next section presents configuration of the WSN security system for the firewall, the SSH, and the VPN protocols on the Raspberry Pi 3 model B+ computer.

Table 3. Technical specifications for the Arduino Uno R3 model.

	Arduino UNO R3
Processor	Intel Pentium 2117U (2 cores/2 threads @ 1800 MHz)
RAM	4 GB DDR3 @ 1333 MHz
Display	LED 14.0" (1366 × 768 pixels) @ 60 Hz
Battery	Six cells
Storage	A 750 GB HDD @ 5400rpm
Video card	A built-in Intel HD Graphics (Ivy Bridge)
	1× HDMI
Communication ports	1× RJ45 (10/100/1000 Mbps)
	4× USB

4 The ENSS: Software Requirements

4.1 The Firewall Stages

As a initial software requirement, the Linux-based OS Raspbian must be installed and configured previously to prepare the initial configuration stage. The full installation process of the OS Raspbian is presented in detail at [22]. The reason to initially install the firewall is to avoid any further attack and this firewall allows us to watch all the Raspberry communication ports and to control all the received/transmitted information. The whole firewall configuration is viewed in Fig. 4.

4.2 The SSH Stages

Once the firewall stage is made, over the same Linux-based OS Raspbian, the SSH protocol is required because SSH let the Raspberry connect with the remote server. On advantage of this configuration is that a remote configuration can be possible instead of an in-situ configuration. As an initial step, it is important to activate SSH protocol because SSH is deactivated by default. The SSH configuration is shown from Figs. 5, 6, 7, 8, 9 and 10. This detailed configuration is presented in [22].

4.3 The VPN Stages

Within this cybersecurity ENSS configuration process, we will start preparing the VPN, PiVPN for the Raspberry computer, PiVPN allows the use of OpenVPN and an easier configuration. In this stage, we summarise the complete VPN configuration from Figs. 10, 11, 12 and 13.

In the following section, we present the test and results stages of our security system over the Raspberry Pi 3B+ computer running an OS Raspbian.

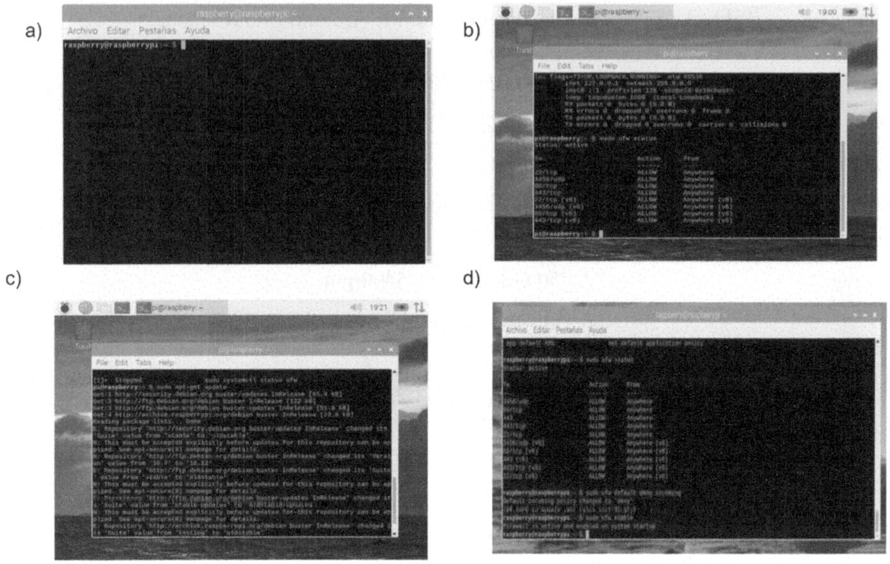

Fig. 5. The Firewall configuration: a) The Raspbian LXT terminal. b) The updating downloading, instruction sudo apt-get update. c) The port activation state for the firewall. d) The firewall service activation.

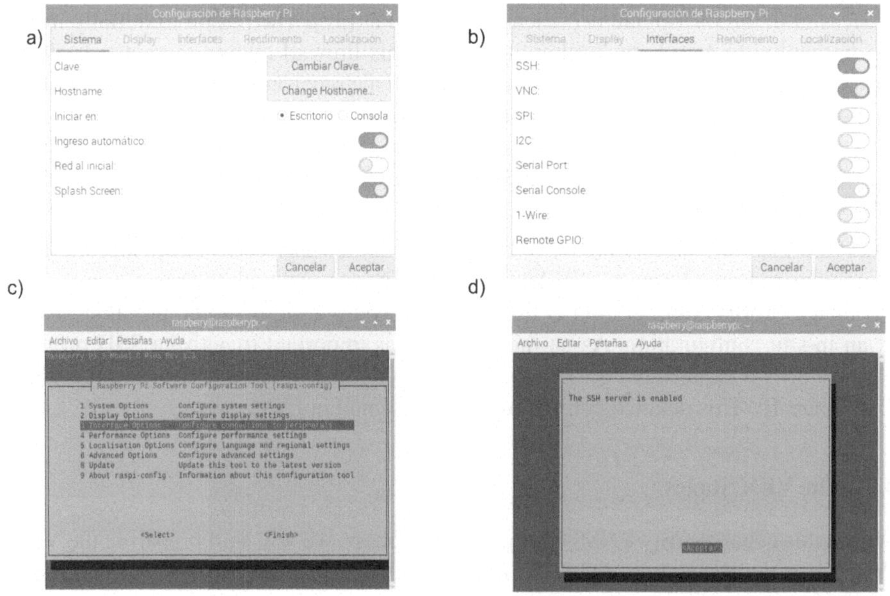

Fig. 6. The SSH configuration: a) The Raspberry Pi 3B+ graphic interface configuration. b) The SSH protocol activation on the Raspberry Pi 3B+ graphic interface configuration. c) The sudo raspi-config command entering result. d) The SSH protocol activation confirmation.

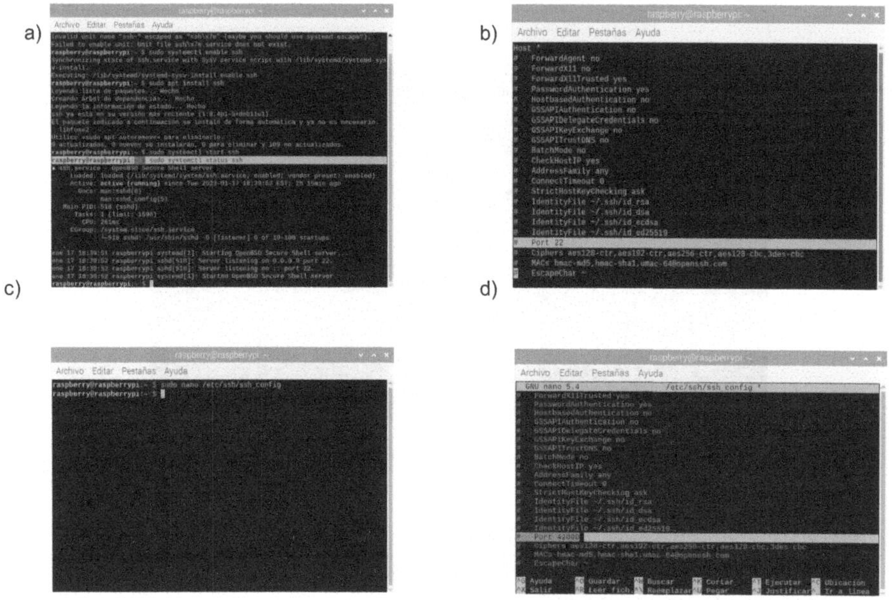

Fig. 7. The verification of SSH: a) The SSH working-state verification. b) The port number location within the SSH configuration. c) The edition instruction of the SSH configuration. d) The port number edition for SSH access, from 22 to 42000.

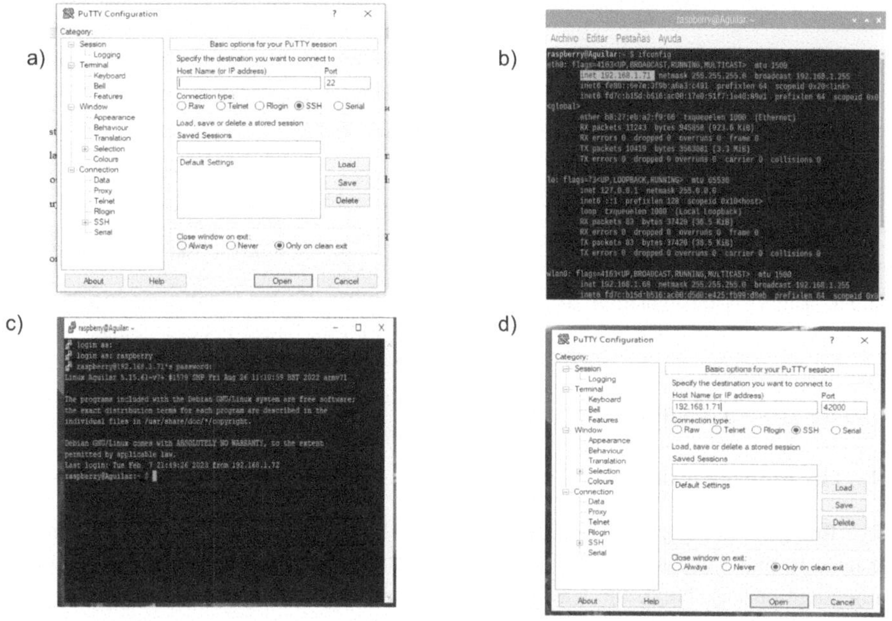

Fig. 8. The SSH connection: a) The putty interface for remote connection to the Raspberry Pi 3B+. b) The IP address of the Raspberry via the *ifconfig* instruction. c) The SSH remote connection to the Raspberry Pi 3B+.

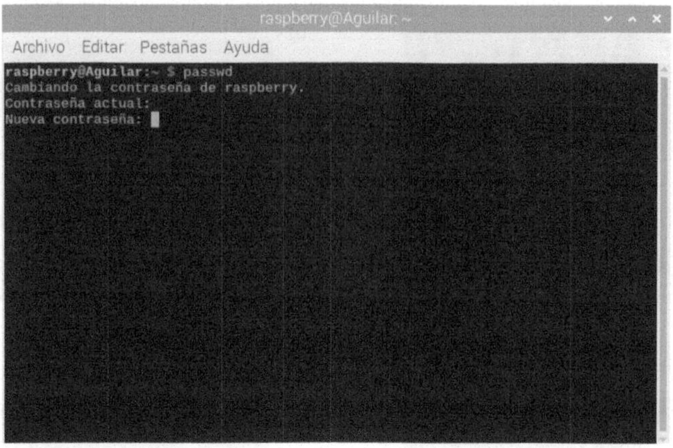

Fig. 9. The Raspberry Pi 3B+ password modification interface for remote access.

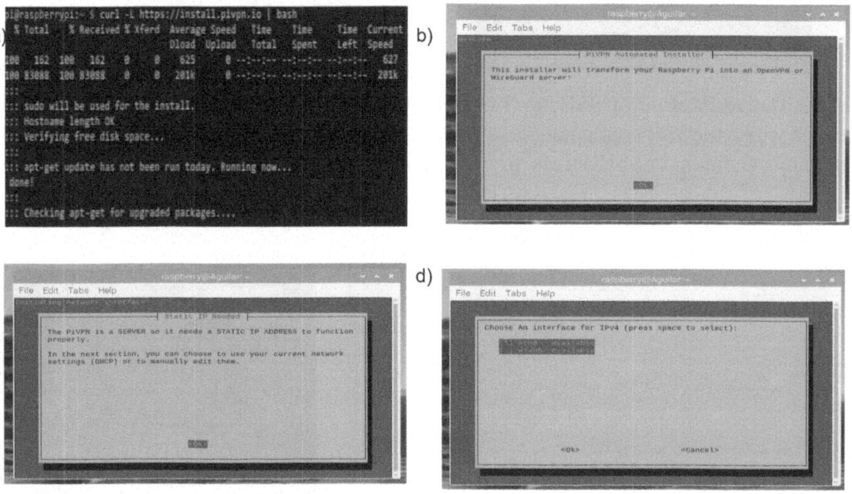

Fig. 10. The VPN configuration: a) The PiVPN test. b) The PiVPN installer message. c) The PiVPN configuration. d) The network selection interface for the OpenVPN addressing.

5 The ENSS Evaluation and Results

5.1 The Firewall Tests

Once the ENSS configuration stage is over, we have to restart the OS Raspbian and we have to make use of PiVPN. In this part, we have to create a user account and an authentication key. Next, the Raspberry creates a file to send it to the remote central computer by the OpenVPN client. This process is viewed from Figs. 14, 15 and 16.

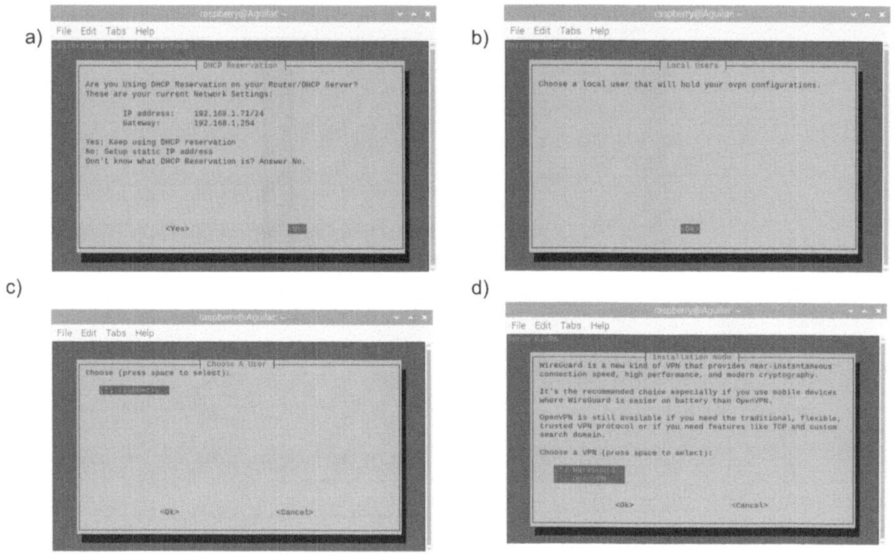

Fig. 11. The OpenVPN configuration: a) The network configuration confirmation of the OpenVPN network. b) The user selection message. c) The choosing configuration for the OpenVPN protocol. d) The selection of the protocol OpenVPN for configuration.

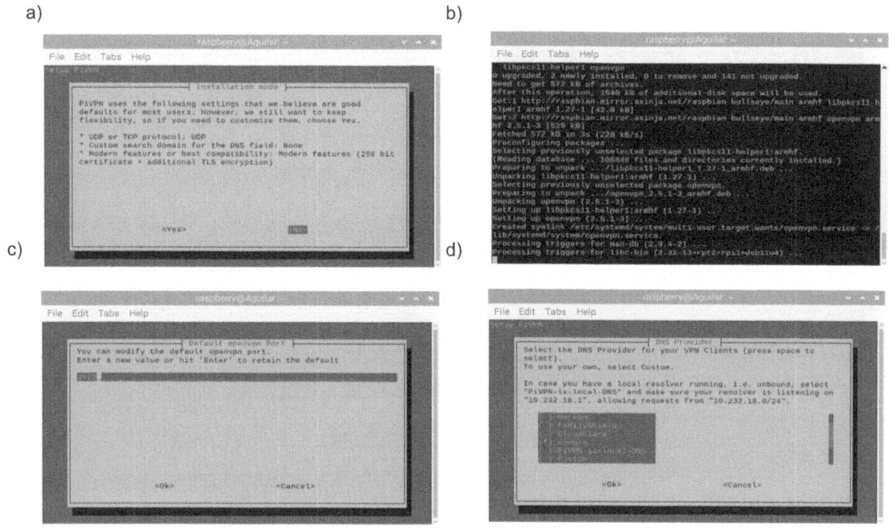

Fig. 12. The VPN configuration: a) The default configuration of the OpenVPN. b) The configuration load of the VPN on the Raspberry Pi 3B+. c) The VPN port modification. d) The DNS selection.

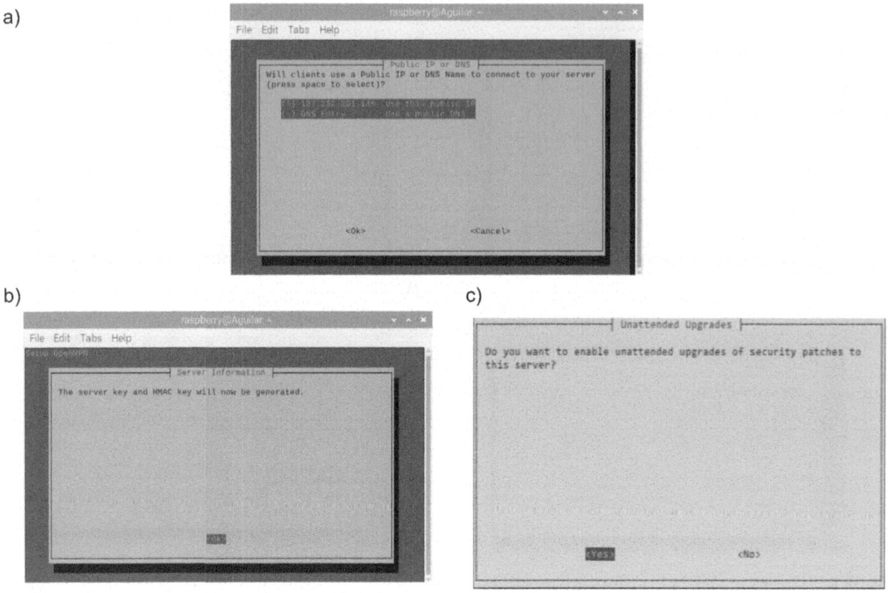

Fig. 13. The DNS configuration: a) The public IP selection for the DNS. b) The authentication confirmation key. c) The choosing of the automatic upgrades on the PiVPN protocol.

Fig. 14. The PiVPN test: a) The VPN user account creation on PiVPN. b) The VPN file explorer on the Raspberry Pi 3B+. c) The VPN file edition on the Raspberry Pi 3B+. d) The network range configuration on VPN.

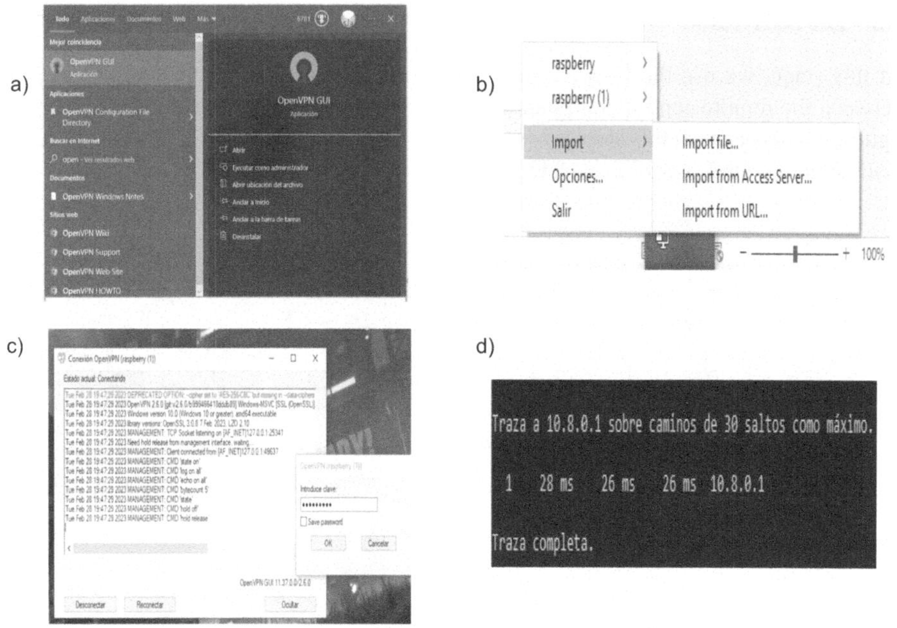

Fig. 15. The OpenVPN running on the remote computer a) The running OpenVPN GUI. b) The importation of the VPN client configuration. c) The access to OpenVPN on the Raspberry Pi 3B+ computer. d) The connectivity test of VPN on the remote computer.

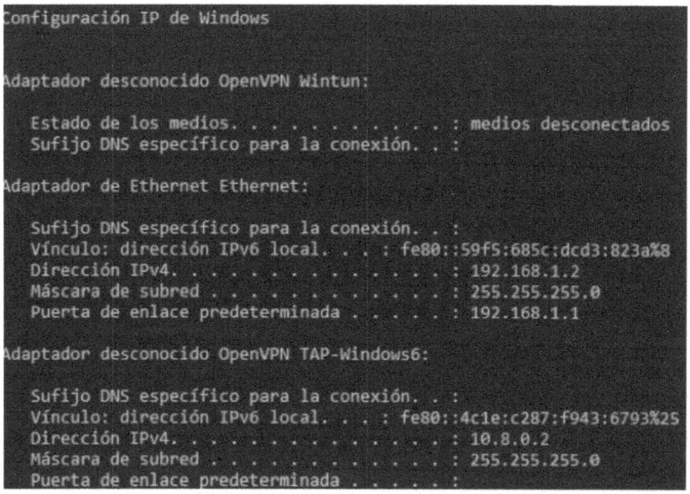

Fig. 16. The implementation test of **VPN** from a remote client computer.

5.2 The SSH Tests

At this stage, we use the File Transfer Protocol (FTP) to let the transference of files between the remote central computer and the Raspberry computer to test the SSH configuration. To perform this step, it is required to download the FTP server. This process is illustrated from Figs. 17 and 18 [22].

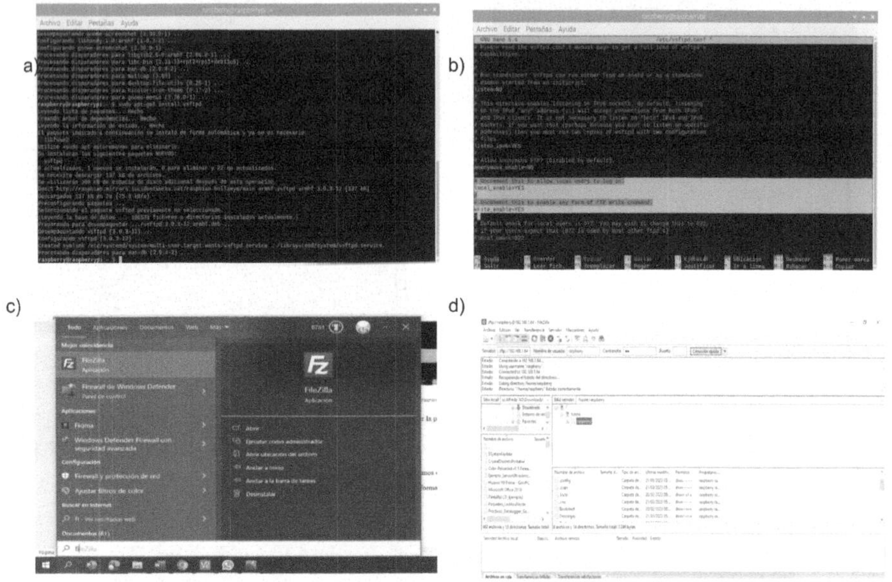

Fig. 17. The SSH test: a) The FTP server installation on the Raspberry Pi 3B+. b) The user enabling of file writing on the Raspberry Pi 3B+. c) The FileZilla interface presentation. d) The FTP connection interface for SSH on the Raspberry Pi 3B+.

5.3 The ENSS Firewall Tests

Finally, to evaluate the ENSS firewall, we have to enter the Raspberry Pi 3B+. This process is shown in Fig. 19. In Fig. 19, the page of the Youtube service is blocked. To make this process, we have to set up the Raspberry Pi 3B+ computer first.

To ensure the proper working of this stage, we save the firewall configuration file, Fig. 19a). In Fig. 19b), we evaluate the firewall by evaluating the firewall functionality in port 2023, then, the firewall assumes the rule and the firewall to try connecting to the VPN server from the client computer (the central remote computer). Hence, the connection fails because of the VPN rules [22].

In Fig. 19c), the error message in red indicates that the VPN cannot makes the connection because of a firewall detail, by a modification of ports, either disabling or enabling the link between the port and the firewall, according to the firewall predetermined rules.

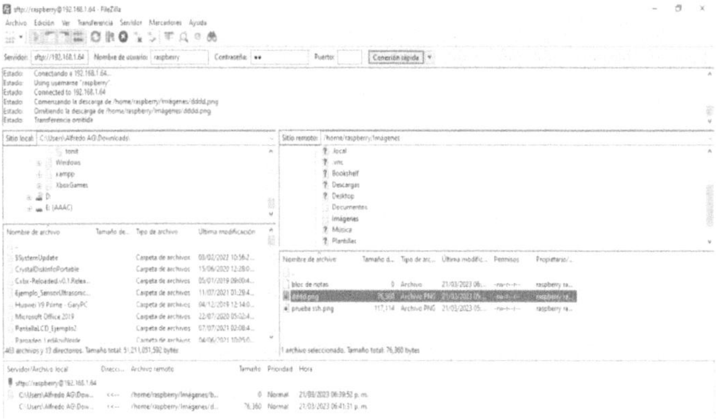

Fig. 18. The information file transfer between the Raspberry Pi 3 model B+ and the remote computer.

Fig. 19. The firewall test: a) The blocking of the Youtube service. b) The firewall verification with OpenVPN on the Raspberry Pi 3B+. c) The firewall is correctly working.

6 Further Research and Conclusions

The implementation of this embedded ENSS over a Raspberry computer will allow us to integrate the ENSS system running over the same WSN central computer which protect not only the WSN itself but also the other remote users: database servers, mobile phones, Cloud-computing computers [22]. However, the security protocols of our in-situ

ENSS device requires permanent maintenance and upgrading. Another further challenge is to integrate the used different OSs into only one OS running in the same Raspberry computer, for instance, in the deployed Raspberry computer over the ENSS is a Raspbian OS [22], while the current WSN uses an Ubuntu-based OS [7]. Therefore, the used security protocols in our embedded ENSS: firewall, SSH, and VPN will be integrated into the same WSN central computer of the WSN. For security functions, our homemade ENSS has this security potential access protection to the environmental WSN.

As ENSS expected functionalities, the purpose of the firewall is to protect the connection between the WSN and a monitoring mobile phone while the SSH protocol blocks the access between the WSN and a remote monitoring central computer. Then, the VPN ensures a private link between the WSN and another cloud-connected monitoring computer to protect the integrity and the reliability of released data from the WSN.

As a security purpose, it is important to consider the links between the WSN and its remote users to keep the integrity and reliability of environmental data because the core of the WSN relies on the Raspberry Pi 3 computer, and then, the ENSS must be integrated into the Raspberry itself. Therefore, our security enhanced WSN will be remotely connected into a GIS as further application in the potential environmental WSN [8, 9]. The aim of interconnecting this security enhanced WSN into a GIS, as the running application software on the remote central computer, is another future research challenge.

Another concerning issue to consider is the battery storage capacity which would be backed up by a solar cell to ensure a more reliable power supply for our WSN. However, another issue is to take into account the adverse meteorological conditions because the Mexican Caribbean zone is frequently exposed to yearly hurricane events, then WSN sensor nodes need to be keeping on save. Other concern is the potential lost during the passing time of the eye of a hurricane [7].

Other potential challenge is that cenotes are highly inaccessible locations to install WSNs to monitor their environmental water parameters and the definition of the chosen deployment environment is crucial for a successful implementation. However, as mentioned in this paper, our future enhanced security environmental WSN will be integrated into a GIS system.

As a final further challenge, this enhanced security WSN would be also more efficiently used in urban areas but because these nodes may require a little of maintenance but for the battery autonomy to keep working any sensor node in contrast whether the same WSN were installed in nature because some cenotes are not accessible and hazardous to access as well [7].

Finally, the scope of this presented ENSS is based on functional embedded systems that can be implemented at a very reasonable cost for applications in outdoors for environmental scenes. Finally, we should mention that this security system detection system is to protect different Cloud-connecting computer devices which are connected with the security enhanced WSN because the environmental data storage is a crucial computational resource to be protected.

References

1. S. K./T. Mexico: A new tourist train in Mexico will destroy indigenous land and livelihoods. Time (2023). [Online]. Available: https://time.com/6245748/maya-train-tulum-yucatan-indigenous-people-land/
2. Gerencia de Planificación Hídrica-Sistema Nacional de Información del Agua, "CONAGUA-sistema Nacional de información del Agua. Gob.mx. [Online]. Available: http://sina.conagua.gob.mx/sina/
3. Metcalfe, C.D., Beddows, P.A., Bouchot, G.G., Metcalfe, T.L., Li, H., Van Lavieren, H.: Contaminants in the coastal karst aquifer system along the Caribbean coast of the Yucatan Peninsula, Mexico. Environ. Pollut. **159**(4), 991–997 (2011)
4. Lizardi-Jiménez, M.A., Hernández-Martínez, R.: Contaminación por Hidrocarburos en la Cuenca Laguna de Bacalar y Biorreactores para su remediación. In: IV Congreso Nacional de Manejo de Cuencas Hidrográficas, pp. 1–4 (2021)
5. Aceves-Zayas, D.G.: Evaluación de la Contaminación por Coliformes Totales y Fecales en Balnearios del sur de Quintana Roo en Relación al Periodo Vacacional de Primavera. Universidad de Quintana Roo, Thesis (2016)
6. Hoogesteijn Reul, A.L., Febles Patrón, J.L., Nava Galindo, V.A.: La contaminación fecal en cenotes de interés turístico y recreacional en el Estado de Yucatán. Ingeniería - Revista Académica de la Facultad de Ingeniería, vol. XIX, no. 4 (2015)
7. Canul, O.M.M., et al.: A deployment of an experimental real-time WSN for monitoring cenote water parameters in urban areas at the city of Cancun. Published GIS LATAM (2023)
8. León-Borges, J.A., Viveros-Jiménez, F., Rodríguez-Mata, A.E., Lizardi-Jiménez, M.A.: Hydrocarbon contamination patterns in the cenotes of the mexican caribbean: the application of principal. Comp. Anal. **105**(5), 758–763 (2020). https://doi.org/10.1007/s00128-020-03026-1
9. León-Borges, J.-A., Lizardi-Jiménez, M.A.: Hydrocarbon pollution in underwater sinkholes of the Mexican Caribbean caused by tourism and asphalt: Historical data series and cluster analysis. Tour. Manag. **63**, 179–186 (2017). https://doi.org/10.1016/j.tourman.2017.06.018
10. Khatri, M., Kumar, A.: Stability inspection of isolated hydro power plant with cuttlefish algorithm. In: 2020 International Conference on Decision Aid Sciences and Application, DASA 2020 (2020)
11. Yetgin, H., Cheung, K.T.K., El-Hajjar, M., Hanzo, L.: A survey of network lifetime maximization techniques in wireless sensor networks. IEEE Commun. Surv. Tutor. (2017)
12. Aldea, E.L.: Raspberry Pi: Fundamentos y Aplicaciones. Ra-Ma, Madrid (2017)
13. Germán, C.R.L., Abarca Jinénez, G.S., Callejas, J.E., Mares Carreño, J., Braulio, M., Zamorategui, A.: Sensores y actuadores: aplicaciones con Arduino. Ciudad de México: Grupo Editorial Patria (2019)
14. Claudio Peña Millahual, Descubriendo Arduino. RedUsers (2020)
15. May-Canul, O.M.: Desarrollo de un prototipo de redes de sensores para monitoreo de cenotes del Estado de Quintana Roo implementado en Raspberry Pi 3, Bachelor degree thesis, QRoo, Cancun, Mexico (2021)
16. Arduino. UNO R3 | Arduino Documentation. docs.arduino.cc (2022). https://docs.arduino.cc/hardware/uno-rev3
17. Arduino® UNO R3. Available: https://docs.arduino.cc/resources/datasheets/A000066-datasheet.pdf
18. Olejnik, L., Kurasinski, A.: Philosophy of Cybersecurity. CRC Press, Boca Raton (2024)
19. Wang, J.: Computer Network Security: Theory and Practice. Springer, Berlin (2009)
20. Kizza, J.M.: Guide to Computer Network Security. Springer Int. Publishing, Cham (2024). Accessed 15 July 2024. [Online]. Available: https://doi.org/10.1007/978-3-031-47549-8

21. Ltd, R.P.: Buy a Raspberry Pi 3 Model B. Raspberry Pi. https://www.raspberrypi.com/products/raspberry-pi-3-model-b/
22. Aguilar-Cristo, A.A.: SSH, Firewall y VPN como sistema de seguridad de red en una placa Raspberry Pi 3 Modelo 3+ para una red de sensores. A bachelor degree dissertation, UQRoo Cancun (2023)

Spatio-Temporal Analysis of Diabetes-Related Hospitalizations: Geographical Areas of Mexico

Carlos Hernandez-Nava[1(✉)], Miguel-Felix Mata-Rivera[1], and Sergio Flores-Hernandez[2]

[1] Unidad Profesional Interdisciplinaria en Ingeniería y Tecnologías Avanzadas del Instituto Politécnico Nacional, 07340 Gustavo A Madero, Mexico City, Mexico
{hernandeznc,mmatar}@ipn.mx

[2] Instituto Nacional de Salud Pública de México, 62100 Cuernavaca, Morelos, Mexico
sergio.flores@insp.mx
https://www.upiita.ipn.mx/

Abstract. The area of geographic information system (GIS) is attracting growing attention because geographic data are now everywhere, in this work with electronic health records. Few studies have explored avoidable diabetes-related hospitalizations in Mexico, and there is no systematic process. This paper provides a spatio-temporal analysis through calculating age adjusted rates by sex and geographical area. This study aims to determine the rates of avoidable hospitalizations as a metric to assess the quality of primary diabetes care prevention, stratifying the country in eight geographical areas. We followed the method used in epidemiology and the approach is mainly based on biostatistics techniques and the GIS process. These results emphasize the importance of working together between GIS experts and epidemiologists. The data presented here reveal that the geographic area with the highest rate of avoidable diabetes-related hospitalizations is the peninsula of Mexico. These findings add substantially to our understanding of how diabetes is cared for and decision makers can generate public health policies and improve health care systems.

Keywords: Spatio-temporal · Data science · Diabetes · Avoidable Hospitalizations

1 Introduction

The area of applied data science is receiving increasing attention because there are more and more data and, in 2024, 328.77 million terabytes are being created every day[1]. In the annual reports "Panorama epidemiológico de las enfermedades no transmisibles en México" of 2020 and 2021 of the Secretaría de Salud de México [1,2], it is concluded that:

[1] https://whatsthebigdata.com/data-generated-every-day/ Date: 07/03/2024.

M. F. Mata-Rivera et al. (Eds.): GIS-LATAM 2024, CCIS 2298, pp. 73–85, 2025.
https://doi.org/10.1007/978-3-031-80017-7_5

> ... the importance of [investigating] these conditions and that in the near future we can have a system... that allows us to group together some of the conditions that make up the metabolic syndrome and even go steps back to the early identification of risks in the population located in Mexican territory.

Although the General Epidemiology Department report, 2021 [2], refers to diseases such as type 2 diabetes mellitus that have a persistently high incidence and are in the early stages, which is alarming. With particular reference to Mexico, in the Ministry of Health, there are currently no procedures in place to integrate the databases, clean the data, and thus have them ready to analyze them, obtain models and support decision-making by health specialists.

A health indicator is a measurement that reflects a given situation. Any health indicator is an estimate (measurement with some degree of imprecision) of a given dimension of health in a specific population [3].

Health indicators serve to describe and monitor the health status of a population. Attributes are characteristics or qualities of health. The dimensions of health are physical, emotional, spiritual, environmental, mental, and social well-being. Indicators are dynamic, under specific temporal and cultural contexts and situations [4]. An attribute that most indicators have is the ability to measure them at different geographical levels (regional, national, and local) and population subgroups (age, sex, ethnicity, among others).

Abedjan et al. [5] refers to the existence of a technical challenge or problem when applying data science techniques in health, which is to handle heterogeneous and multidimensional data, with heterogeneity meaning data from different sources, and multidimensionality being the union of the variables or dimensions provided by each of the sources, for example, data from socioeconomic levels, places of residence, atmospheric conditions, and specific health care habits, and concludes that to design reliable models, it is first necessary to integrate, clean, understand and analyze these data.

Among the most commonly used stratification factors for monitoring health inequalities, are included in the acronym PROGRESS, which in English, Place, Race/ethnicity, Occupation, Gender, Religion, Education, Socioeconomic status, Social capital [6]. Taking into account all conditions sensitive to primary care, the Agency for Healthcare Research and Quality specifies the Prevention Quality Indicators (PQI), in this work are used the following diabetes-related indicators [7]:

PQI 01 Diabetes, short-term complications admission rate,
PQI 03 Diabetes, long-term complications admission rate,
PQI 14 Uncontrolled diabetes admission rate,
PQI 16 Lower extremity amputations among patients with diabetes admission rate, and
PQI 93 Prevention Quality Diabetes Composite

The term crude rate has been used to denominate the rate between cases by study population. It is a general measure that does not take into account the diversity of groups in the population, and in this paper is expressed as the rate per 100,000 inhabitants.

The terms adjusted rate and standardized rate are used here interchangeably, which means the rate obtained by dividing the cases of a specific group by the study population. Differences in age and gender structures between populations are adjusted, allowing direct comparisons to be made. Although age is normally used in this process, other factors (e.g., ethnicity, religion, etc.) can also be used. A single statistic is produced that allows easy comparisons between populations.

Throughout this work, an avoidable hospitalization or a potentially avoidable hospitalization will represent a hospitalization related to ambulatory care sensitive conditions (ACSC), that is, if primary or ambulatory care is timely and effective, it is not necessary to go to the hospital [8]. The avoidable diabetes-related hospitalization rate is the rate of cases that match the ICD code listed in the specification PQI 93 by the study population.

This investigation was carried out to analyze the avoidable rates of hospitalization related to diabetes over time (2010–2022) and space (geographical areas of Mexico). In epidemiological methods, tables and classical graphics are commonly used, even geographical variables are used in studies. Therefore, this work also shows how GIS improves the analysis of epidemiological studies, in this case diabetes-related hospitalizations.

2 Related Work

In this section, related works from the USA, Portugal, and Mexico are presented. They filter diabetes cases that match ICD codes with others used in the literature. To compare results between studies across the world, it is necessary to use the same ICD codes, and for diabetes-related ICD codes listed in the PQI specification by AHRQ is the best option to compare with other studies, regional or national.

Shiraz et al. [9] analyzed the records of 31,934 patients from the Primary Care Clinical Health System in the states of Minnesota, Iowa, and Wisconsin in 2019, in the United States of America. A cross-sectional study is designed for analysis. Their aim is to explore the association between diabetes care in rural and urban areas. And they find that patients who are more deprived and live in a rural area are significantly less likely to receive high-quality diabetes care compared to patients living in less deprived and urban areas, and conclude that public health efforts should focus a little more on rural areas.

Ramalho et al. [10] present the PQI diabetes prevention quality indicators: 1, 3, 14, 16 and the composite indicator 93 in Portugal, where they divide into 5 geographic regions. They also evaluated efficiency at the first level of care using PQI for the years 2016–2017. The regression model they use for the evaluation is Tobit or censored regression model. Among the results they mention that 13 out of 54 groups of health centers manage to become efficient and that in large part people under 45 years of age who are controlled are what reach more efficient diabetes care. Among the conclusions, they say that most primary care health centers are inefficient in diabetes prevention, and by addressing this situation, they could improve the rates of avoidable hospitalizations.

Flores-Hernández et al. [11] present an evaluation of the quality of care of patients with diabetes and present its association with the follow-up of glycemic control. The study was carried out through a cross-sectional analysis of the years 2006 (2,965 patients) and 2012 (4,483 patients); in both cases, the patients are 20 years old or older. The source of the data is the National Health and Nutrition Survey for the respective years.

Multiple regression models (logistic and linear) were created to evaluate changes over the years. The estimated change between was 2.1 more in 2012 than in 2006 (95 CI 1.5-2.7). To evaluate quality, Flores-Hernández et al. used the following criteria: glucose monitoring, doctor visits to treat diabetes, detection of hypertension, detection of dyslipidemia, overweight care, detection of protein in urine, detection of retinopathy, detection of diabetic foot, and whether the patient has pharmaceutical treatment. They concluded that diabetes continues to be a public health emergency in Mexico and that strategies are needed to improve the quality of care of patients with diabetes.

Continuing in the investigation of the challenges in evaluating the quality of diabetes care in Mexico [12], similar to the work of the 2015 publication by Flores-Hernandez et al., estimate quality indicators in primary care and analyze association with glycemic control and use the results of the 2012 and 2018–19 National Nutrition and Health Surveys of people aged 20 years or older, a total of 9,038 people.

To measure quality of care, they take four aspects: diabetes control; surveillance of cardiovascular risk factors; early detection of complications; and follow-up with pharmacological treatment. They use multiple linear regression and a logistic regression model when adding variables of glycemic control and overall quality of care of adults with diabetes. They concluded that population-level studies are needed for better results.

The presented studies focus on analyzing the rates of potentially avoidable hospitalizations related to diabetes, one of them using the same indicators that are used in this study, and the others propose aspects such as diabetes control, early detection of complications, and follow-up of pharmacological treatment. In addition, one of them uses a retrospective observational study with a secondary analysis of databases as is done in this work, and the others make use of the results of surveys and design the cross-sectional study.

3 Data Sources Description

Secondary data sources are those that originally collected data for other purposes. The existing data obtained for this work are considered secondary data.

The source of the data is the open health data website of the Mexican Ministry of Public Health for the years 2010–2022. This work takes the cases of hospital discharges related to diabetes of people 20 years or older, in age groups 20 to 44 years, 45 to 64 years and over 65 years, divided into men and women, and is carried out by geographic areas according to the regionalization defined in the methodology of the National Health and Nutrition Survey 2022 and Planning of the Ensanut Continua[2] 2020-2024.

The open data are in CSV format and are downloaded from the Ministry of Health website [14], specifically the Health Information General Department. In the section hospital discharges there are CSV files from 2010 up to now, and some XLS files with the variable descriptions and catalogs used in the databases. Databases have more than 50 variables and have increased over the years.

The variables used in this work are age, sex, principal condition, and entity, where age is an integer, sex is 1 for men and 2 for women, principal condition for which a person has been hospitalized, contains the ICD code, entity in Mexico this area is called state, and in another level many states create a geographical area.

4 Methodology

The experimental design referred to as secondary data analysis was used. Data were collected from open data sources: DGIS/SS and INEGI from 2010 to 2022. To measure the avoidable rates of hospitalization related to diabetes, the specification of the quality indicator of prevention was used. In fact, similar works are using more and more PQI defined by ARHQ.

The methodology includes: Data collection (Electronic Health Records), Cleaning and Preprocessing (Stratification and Outlier Analysis), Modeling (through biostatistical methods and algorithms), Interpretation (with a biological focus) and Presentation (with statistical evidence). The primary advantages of this methodology are that using data science tools increases the speed of the process in some stages. Data were adjusted or standardized using the direct method for standardization.

Data analysis was performed with the software: STATA v18, R Studio and MS Excel. The missing values are less than 1% and were excluded from the analysis.

This work is a retrospective observational study, it is observational because cases of hospitalizations of patients for some primary condition related to diabetes arose spontaneously, and it is retrospective because the data are obtained from a request after the generation of the data. The years of records are June 2010 to May 2022.

4.1 Methods

The method used follows the foundations of public health methodology, especially epidemiology and biostatistics, but is supported by data science tools, such as database merging, data cleaning tools, and application processing. There are two ways to calculate the crude rate; the first, the naive method or the method

[2] Encuesta Nacional de Salud y Nutrición.

without public health knowledge, is to count the cases of diabetes and divide them by the study population, Eq. 1, which is the population of the geographical area in the period of time of the cases.

$$\text{Crude Rate} = \frac{\text{Diabetes Cases}}{\text{Study Population}} \tag{1}$$

The second is through the specific rates, which are the result of dividing the cases of a specific group by the study population of the same group, Eq. 2, to get the crude rate, just multiply the age group specific rate (Spec Rate) by the age group proportion of the study population in decimal percent (Pop Prop) in Eq. 3.

$$\text{Specific Rate} = \frac{\text{Cases by age}}{\text{Population by age}} \tag{2}$$

$$\text{Crude Rate} = \text{Spec Rate } 20{-}44\text{y} \times \text{Pop Prop } 20{-}44\text{y} \tag{3}$$

In this work to standardize the rates, first, we have to define the population and the diabetes cases stratified by sex and age group; for this step, diabetes cases are the result of the pre-processing and cleaning process. The age-adjusted rate by sex is calculated using the Eq. 4,

$$\begin{aligned} \text{Age Adj Rate} = & (\text{Spec Rate } 20{-}44\text{y} \times \text{Std Pop } 20{-}44\text{y}) \\ & + (\text{Spec Rate } 45{-}64\text{y} \times \text{Std Pop } 45{-}64\text{y}) \\ & + (\text{Spec Rate } 65{+} \times \text{Std Pop } 65{+}) \end{aligned} \tag{4}$$

where, Spec Rate 20–44y is the specific rate for population from 20 to 44 years old, Std Pop 20–44y is the proportion of the standard population from 20 to 44 years old; and the same for the groups from 45 to 64 years old and the group from 65 years old and over. That process is a direct standardization [13], and it is applied when we have an age-structured standard population. And is essential to do because the characteristics of the population are different in each geographical areas, because of its eating habits, housing access and quality of health services, and a comparison of crude rates would misleading.

5 Results

The results presented in this section reveal that the southeast of Mexico has higher rates of avoidable hospitalization related to diabetes than other geographical areas of the country. The geographical area of the peninsula of Mexico and the surrounding areas are the most affected by hospitalizations for diabetes and is related to the geographical areas with the highest rate of obesity in Mexico. According to the results of the 2018 national health and nutrition survey, Tabasco and Quintana Roo had the highest percentages of obesity [?].

Table 1 shows the geographical area of Frontera, which is the area with the lowest adjusted rates over the years, the rates are listed per year, and for women and men, also the crude rate, the lower confidence interval (CI low), the upper confidence interval (CI upp) and the error are shown.

Table 1. Frontera: Crude and Age Adjusted Rates by Sex.

Year	Sex	Crude Rate	Adj Rate	CI low	CI upp	Error
2010	Women	33.52	36.89	35.00	38.79	0.97
2010	Men	24.33	27.31	25.62	29.01	0.86
2011	Women	33.45	36.33	34.48	38.17	0.94
2011	Men	25.26	27.98	26.30	29.65	0.86
2012	Women	36.45	38.72	36.86	40.58	0.95
2012	Men	27.90	30.63	28.91	32.35	0.88
2013	Women	34.93	36.66	34.88	38.43	0.91
2013	Men	26.88	29.10	27.46	30.75	0.84
2014	Women	36.09	37.51	35.74	39.28	0.90
2014	Men	27.54	29.55	27.92	31.18	0.83
2015	Women	48.12	49.34	47.35	51.33	1.01
2015	Men	41.79	44.06	42.12	46.01	0.99
2016	Women	33.04	33.53	31.92	35.14	0.82
2016	Men	26.86	28.10	26.57	29.63	0.78
2017	Women	26.70	26.83	25.41	28.25	0.72
2017	Men	21.18	22.01	20.67	23.34	0.68
2018	Women	34.38	34.30	32.72	35.88	0.81
2018	Men	37.06	37.57	35.87	39.27	0.87
2019	Women	30.88	30.54	29.07	32.01	0.75
2019	Men	31.86	32.43	30.86	34.00	0.80
2020	Women	19.72	19.37	18.22	20.53	0.59
2020	Men	20.59	20.75	19.52	21.99	0.63
2021	Women	19.91	19.39	18.26	20.53	0.58
2021	Men	22.32	22.32	21.06	23.58	0.64
2022	Women	25.20	24.38	23.12	25.64	0.64
2022	Men	27.87	27.61	26.23	28.99	0.71

Table 2 shows the geographical area of the peninsula of Mexico, which is the area with the highest adjusted rates, for women and men. The highest rate was in 2012, 144 women were reached in the hospital, although these hospitalizations could have been avoided because diabetes is an ambulatory care sensitive condition (ACSC).

To observe the whole panorama of avoidable diabetes-related hospitalizations in Mexico, Fig. 1 shows the spatial distribution of adjusted rates in Mexico over the years 2010–2022. In parentheses are the lowest and highest rates per year; it can be seen that in the COVID-19 pandemic the highest rates decreased from 79 in 2019 to 56 in 2020 and 62 in 2021, these are values for women.

Table 2. Peninsula: Crude and Age Adjusted Rates by Sex.

Year	Sex	Crude Rate	Adj Rate	CI low	CI upp	Error
2010	Women	103.78	125.08	120.85	129.31	2.16
2010	Men	76.82	88.98	85.38	92.58	1.84
2011	Women	113.01	133.21	128.96	137.47	2.17
2011	Men	83.07	94.47	90.85	98.09	1.85
2012	Women	125.09	144.72	140.39	149.04	2.21
2012	Men	94.87	106.31	102.55	110.07	1.92
2013	Women	122.93	140.19	136.03	144.36	2.13
2013	Men	90.25	100.27	96.69	103.86	1.83
2014	Women	125.13	140.87	136.78	144.97	2.09
2014	Men	96.52	106.04	102.42	109.66	1.85
2015	Women	116.66	129.90	126.04	133.76	1.97
2015	Men	95.77	104.50	100.96	108.03	1.80
2016	Women	109.81	120.86	117.21	124.51	1.86
2016	Men	88.71	95.96	92.63	99.29	1.70
2017	Women	102.96	111.88	108.44	115.33	1.76
2017	Men	79.64	84.81	81.74	87.88	1.57
2018	Women	95.81	103.36	100.09	106.62	1.66
2018	Men	79.50	84.36	81.34	87.38	1.54
2019	Women	87.57	93.65	90.59	96.70	1.56
2019	Men	75.10	79.22	76.33	82.11	1.47
2020	Women	51.60	54.63	52.33	56.92	1.17
2020	Men	53.47	56.02	53.63	58.41	1.22
2021	Women	60.43	63.51	61.07	65.95	1.24
2021	Men	60.02	62.57	60.07	65.06	1.27
2022	Women	72.66	75.88	73.25	78.51	1.34
2022	Men	66.10	68.41	65.84	70.98	1.31

Regarding men, Fig. 2 shows the spatial distribution of diabetes-related hospitalizations, where it can be seen that the southeast of Mexico has the highest rates.

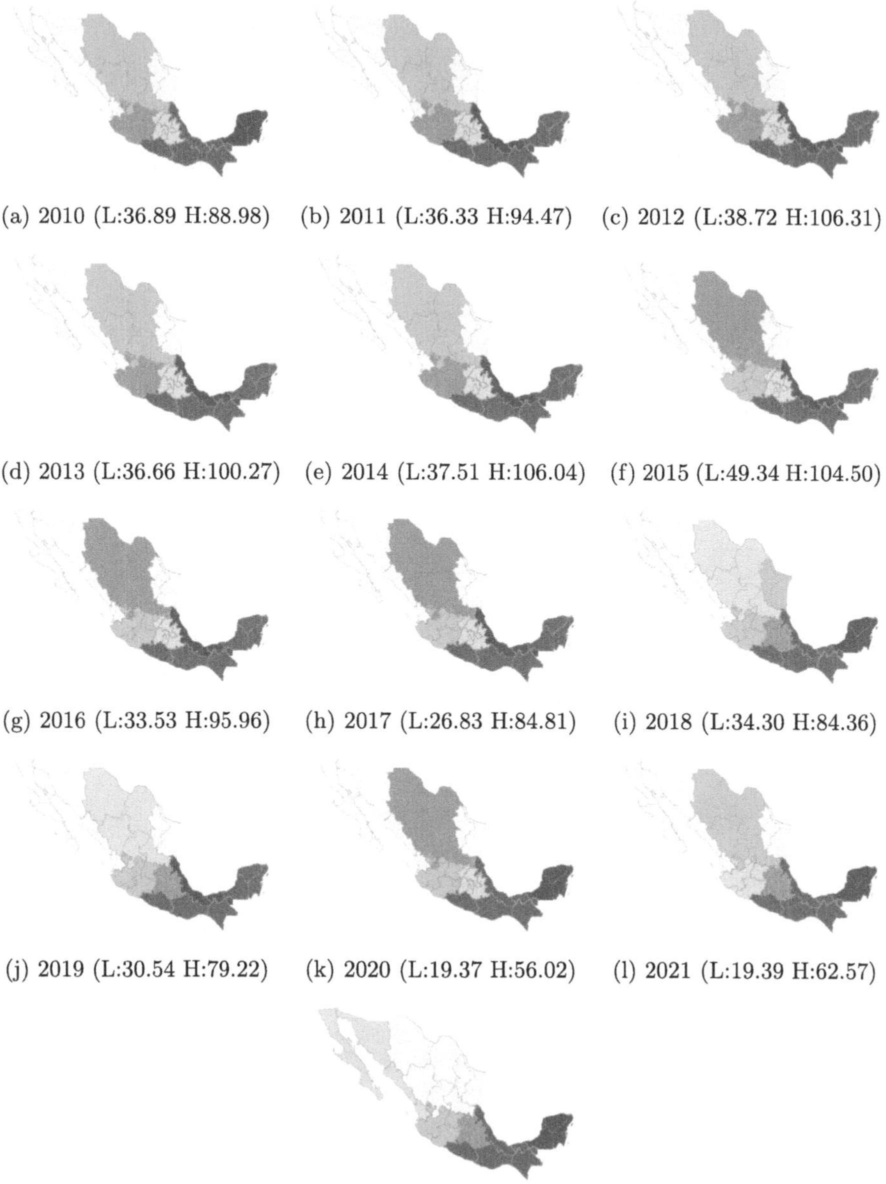

(a) 2010 (L:36.89 H:88.98) (b) 2011 (L:36.33 H:94.47) (c) 2012 (L:38.72 H:106.31)

(d) 2013 (L:36.66 H:100.27) (e) 2014 (L:37.51 H:106.04) (f) 2015 (L:49.34 H:104.50)

(g) 2016 (L:33.53 H:95.96) (h) 2017 (L:26.83 H:84.81) (i) 2018 (L:34.30 H:84.36)

(j) 2019 (L:30.54 H:79.22) (k) 2020 (L:19.37 H:56.02) (l) 2021 (L:19.39 H:62.57)

(m) 2022 (L:24.38 H:68.41)

Fig. 1. Spatio-temporal distribution of Avoidable Diabetes-related Hospitalizations by Geographical Area Of Mexico for Women (L refers to the lowest rate × 100,000 hab. or clearest area and H refers to the highest rate × 100,000 hab. or darkest area).

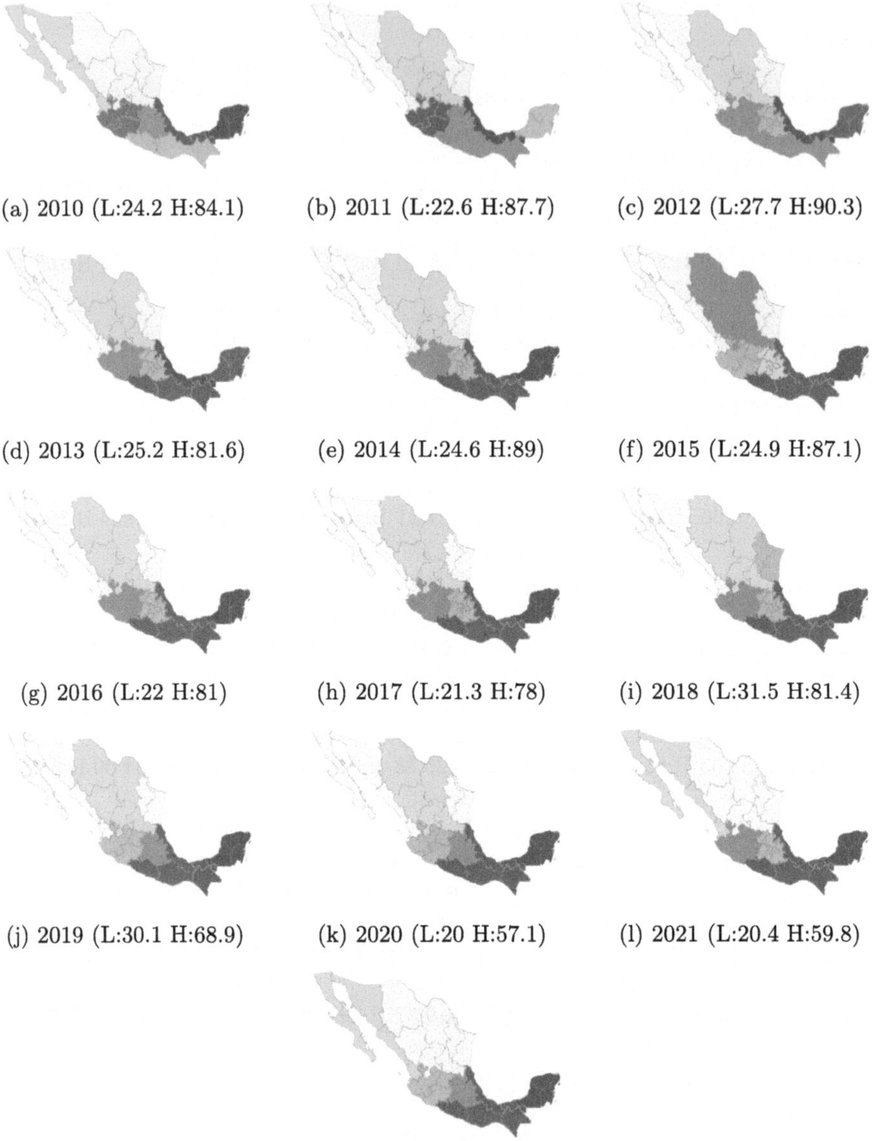

(a) 2010 (L:24.2 H:84.1) (b) 2011 (L:22.6 H:87.7) (c) 2012 (L:27.7 H:90.3)

(d) 2013 (L:25.2 H:81.6) (e) 2014 (L:24.6 H:89) (f) 2015 (L:24.9 H:87.1)

(g) 2016 (L:22 H:81) (h) 2017 (L:21.3 H:78) (i) 2018 (L:31.5 H:81.4)

(j) 2019 (L:30.1 H:68.9) (k) 2020 (L:20 H:57.1) (l) 2021 (L:20.4 H:59.8)

(m) 2022 (L:29.2 H:59.4)

Fig. 2. Spatio-temporal distribution of Avoidable Diabetes-related Hospitalizations by Geographical Area Of Mexico for Men.

6 Conclusions

The results of this study reveal that hospitalization rates related to diabetes could be a metric to measure the quality prevention of diabetes, which means that the primary care level could improve diabetes treatments in early symptoms.

Of eight geographical areas, only one is above the OCDE average of avoidable hospitalizations related to diabetes, this is the peninsula of Mexico. In Fig. 3 the adjusted rates are shown, women of the peninsula of Mexico present the highest rates over the years.

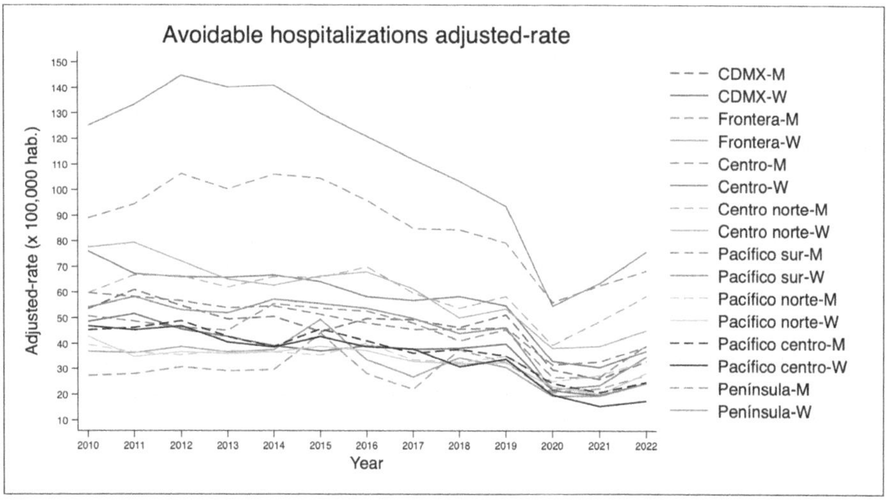

Fig. 3. Avoidable Diabetes-related Hospitalization Rates by Geographical Area.

We have obtained a satisfactory spatio-temporal analysis of avoidable hospitalizations related to diabetes in Mexico stratifying by geographic areas.

The present study has only examined open databases from the public health system of Mexico and does not include the IMSS[3] and ISSSTE[4] databases, two of the main health systems of Mexico, IMSS is the health care system for workers and ISSSTE is the health care system for government workers.

These results provide a significant first step towards a proposal to assess public health care in Mexico at its primary level.

Future research should consider the potential effects of other noncommunicable diseases that are the first cause of death in the world, these diseases could be such as hypertension, cerebrovascular disease, obesity and overweight.

These findings suggest the following recommendations: each geographical area of Mexico must be analyzed per state or small areas, particularly for searching associate factors that could affect or provoke some diseases; another finding

[3] Instituto Mexicano del Seguro Social.
[4] Instituto de Seguridad y Servicios Sociales de los Trabajadores del Estado.

is that the mandatory to collaborate interdisciplinary and multidisciplinary, in accordance with the related areas of knowledge; another contribution is to provide data and information for those who make decisions and formulate public health policies. This work laid out the process for analyzing diabetes-related hospitalizations that could replicate other countries.

The results shown in the tables and figures of this work were calculated with STATA v18, which is the software we recommend, and were validated with R Studio scripts and a spreadsheet with formulas written in MS Excel, where the values were in the confidence interval 95%.

Acknowledgments. This study was funded by the CONAHCYT grant.

Disclosure of Interests. The authors have declared that no competing interests exist.

References

1. Panorama epidemiológico de las enfermedades no transmisibles en México 2020, Dirección General de Epidemiología de México. https://epidemiologia.salud.gob.mx/gobmx/salud/documentos/pano-OMENT/panoepid_ENT2020.pdf. Accessed 10 July 2024
2. Panorama epidemiológico de las enfermedades no transmisibles en México 2021, Dirección General de Epidemiología de México. https://www.gob.mx/cms/uploads/attachment/file/745354/PanoEpi_ENT_Cierre2021.pdf. Accessed 10 July 2024
3. Dicker, R.: Principles of Epidemiology in Public Health Practice. Center for Disease Control and Prevention, CDC (2013)
4. Wolfgang, A., Iris, P.: Handbook of Epidemiology. Springer, Cham (2014)
5. Abedjan, Z., Roller, R., Thoms, J: Data science for healthcare: methodologies and applications. In: Consoli S., Recupero R., Petković M. (eds.). Springer (2019). https://doi.org/10.1007/978-3-030-05249-2
6. Emma L., et al.: Using PROGRESS-plus to identify current approaches to the collection and reporting of equity-relevant data: a scoping review. J. Clin. Epidemiol. **163**, 70–78 (2023). https://doi.org/10.1016/j.jclinepi.2023.09.017. ISSN 0895-4356
7. Agency for Healthcare Research and Quality: U.S. Department of Health and Human Services: Quality Indicator User Guide: Prevention Quality Indicators (PQI) Composite Measures, v2023 (2023). https://qualityindicators.ahrq.gov/measures/pqi_resources
8. Caminal, J., Morales, M., Sánchez, E., Cubells, M., Bustins, M.: Hospitalizaciones prevenibles mediante una atención primaria oportuna y efectiva. Journal Atención Primaria **31**(1), 6–17 (2003)
9. Kurani, S., Lampman, M., Funni, S., et al.: Association between area-level socioeconomic deprivation and diabetes care quality in US primary care practices. JAMA Netw. Open **4**(12), e2138438 (2021). https://doi.org/10.1001/jamanetworkopen.2021.38438
10. Ramalho, A., Souza, J., Castro, P., Lobo, M., Santos, P., Freitas, A.: Portuguese primary healthcare and prevention quality indicators for diabetes mellitus - a data envelopment analysis. Int. J. Health Policy Manag. **11**(9), 1725–1734 (2022). https://doi.org/10.34172/ijhpm.2021.76

11. Flores-Hernández, S., et al.: Quality of diabetes care: the challenges of an increasing epidemic in mexico. results from two national health surveys (2006 and 2012). PLoS One **10**(7), e0133958 (2015). https://doi.org/10.1371/journal.pone.0133958
12. Flores-Hernández, S., Acosta-Ruiz, O., Hernández-Serrato, M., Delgado-Rodríguez, S., Reyes-Morales, H.: Calidad de la atención en diabetes tipo 2, avances y retos de 2012 a 2018-19 para el sistema de salud de México. Salud Pública de México **62**(6), 618–626. Epub 15 de agosto de 2022. https://doi.org/10.21149/11876
13. Nyi Nyi, N.: Easy way to learn standardization: direct and indirect methods. Malaysian J. Med. Sci. **7**(1), 10–15 (2000)
14. Hospital discharges of Mexico. http://www.dgis.salud.gob.mx/contenidos/basesdedatos/da_egresoshosp_gobmx.html. Accessed 25 Oct 2023

School Clustering Through Machine Learning and Geospatial Analysis

Christian A. Flores-Villamil[1(✉)], Huizilopoztli Luna-García[1], Mauricio Ramírez-Villegas[2], Carlos H. Espino-Salinas[1], Alejandro Mauricio-González[1], and José G. Arceo-Olague[1]

[1] Universidad Autonoma de Zacatecas, Zacatecas, Zacatecas, Mexico
chaflovi@uaz.edu.mx

[2] Universidad de Medellin, Medellin, Antioquia, Colombia

Abstract. Schools and school population are prone to safety and health risks due to their proximity to hazardous features, either natural or infrastructural. In Mexico there is an official standard that points out which features to consider when selecting the location for building a school, and how proximal these features can be to the school's location in order to not represent a threat. This work focused on applying both geospatial analysis and unsupervised machine learning techniques to detect the hazardous features per school in Mexico, and group these schools as per the data patterns themselves. For this, a data set containing Mexico's schools and the proximal hazardous features for each school was built by spatially combining multiple official data sets. After that, the K-Modes partitional clustering machine learning algorithm was used with the created dataset. Multiple clustering models were built with this algorithm by testing various K values (number of clusters), and their clustering quality was measured with internal clustering evaluation metrics. The clustering model with the highest quality was the one that grouped Mexico's schools into 11 clusters, each one indicating the most common(s) hazardous feature(s) to the schools of each cluster. The evaluation metrics results for this model were: Silhouette Score (0.72), Calinski-Harabasz Index (32863.96), Davies-Bouldin Index (0.72) indicating strong clustering results, with well-separated and cohesive clusters. The study was carried out by following the Cross Industry Standard Process for Data Mining (CRISP-DM) methodology, consisting in multiple phases and tasks for data mining projects execution.

Keywords: schools · clustering · unsupervised learning · machine learning · geospatial analysis · data mining

1 Introduction

1.1 Background

In Mexico, there is an official standard designed by experts that suggests the ideal conditions for selecting the best place to build a school, according to the

M. F. Mata-Rivera et al. (Eds.): GIS-LATAM 2024, CCIS 2298, pp. 86–104, 2025.
https://doi.org/10.1007/978-3-031-80017-7_6

characteristics of the physical and transformed environment where a given piece of land is located. This document is the Mexican Standard NMX-R-003-SCFI-2011 [1]. Likewise, there is official information on the spatial location of existing schools in the country, as well as attributes related to their identification, economic activity and size as an economic unit. This information is compiled in the data set known as the National Statistical Directory of Economic Units, or DENUE for its acronym in Spanish, and has been compiled and updated based on multiple Economic Censuses [2]. DENUE dataset can be visualized as shown in Fig. 1.

However, there are other official sources through which it is possible to determine some of the hazardous characteristics mentioned in Mexican Standard NMX-R-003-SCFI-2011, and thus determine whether or not a particular site complies with its requirements. These sources include the National Topographic Data Set at a scale of 1:250 000, the National Inventory of Geological Phenomena. Scale 1:250 000, the Geospatial information on municipal management of water and sanitation services, the Geospatial information on municipal management of urban solid waste, and the National Statistical Directory of Economic Units [2].

The hazardous features that were used in this study are present in Table 1:

Table 1. Some hazardous conditions whose proximity to a piece of land makes it unsuitable for school buildings as per the standard [1]

Road	Fuel Depot	Highway	Explosives Depot	Railroad	Mine
Water Treatment	Cemetery	Pipeline	Subsidence Zone	Industrial Zone	Geological Fault
Landslide Zone	Power transmission	Sand Mine	Fuel Station	Flood Zone	Airstrip
Gas Station	Cavern	Cave	Ravine	Dam	Sandy Area
Volcano	Garbage Dump	Swamp	Garbage treatment	Gully	Canyon

The rest of the document is structured in these parts: the related work (literature review), the methodology (research design, data collection, experimental setup, data analysis and results) the discussion (interpretation of the results, implications and limitations of the study) and the conclusions.

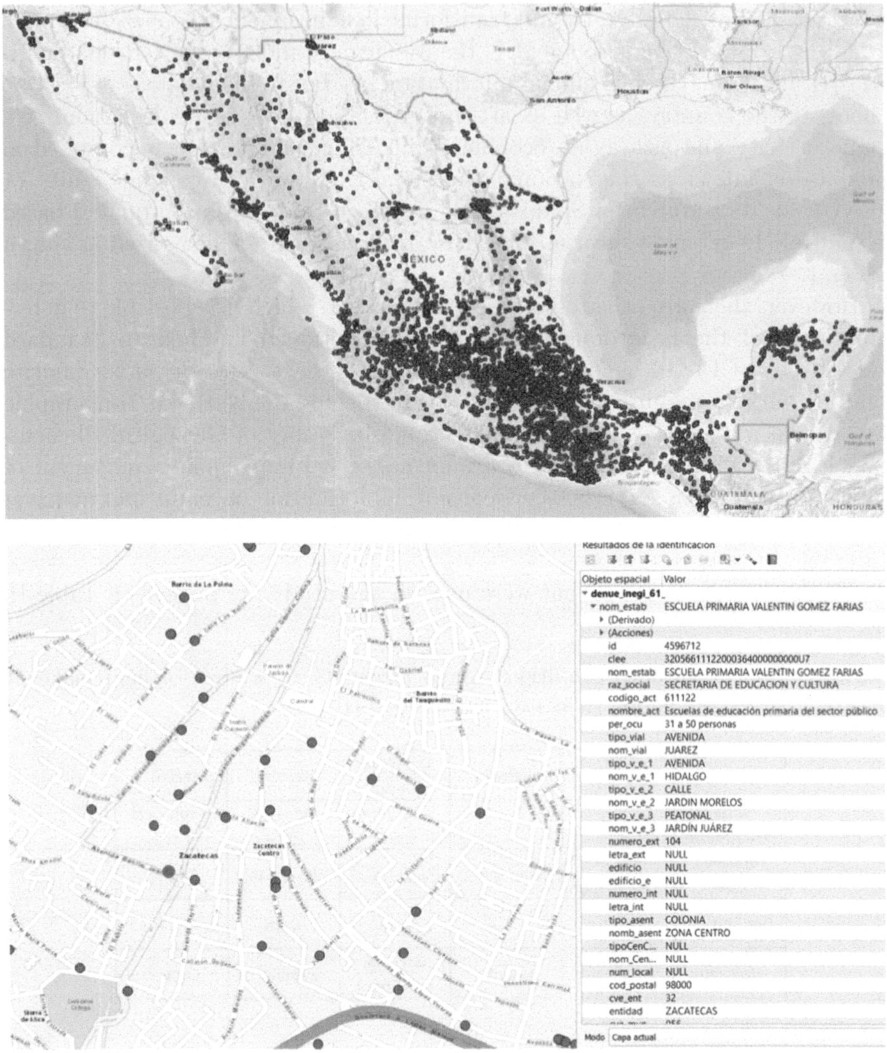

Fig. 1. Visualization of the DENUE Schools Shapefile in a Geographic Information Systems (GIS) software at different scales

1.2 Problem Statement

The environmental setting of schools directly influences the health, safety, accessibility, and motivation of students, which in turn impacts their academic performance and overall well-being. Careful planning and design of the school environment is essential to create an environment conducive to learning and the holistic development of students [3–5].

Aspects such as location in relation to risk zones (such as areas prone to natural disasters, or close to highly hazardous facilities or infrastructure), are crucial and impact the physical safety of students. A well-located and well-designed school can prevent accidents and respond effectively to emergencies [6].

Investigation and consideration of the land characteristics listed in Table 1 are essential to the planning and construction of safe and sustainable schools in Mexico. Ensuring that schools are located on suitable land protects the life, health and well-being of students and the school community as a whole.

1.3 Objective

Generate a machine learning model through the selection and training of an unsupervised learning algorithm, and the use of geospatial analysis techniques, which allows clustering Mexican schools according to their proximity to the hazardous characteristics mentioned by the Mexican Standard NMX-R-003-SCFI-2011. This is not a risk assessment study, as it does not pretend to calculate the probability of a disaster to happen, but it only tries to describe and identify the hazardous features located in proximity to schools.

2 Related Work

2.1 Literature Review

Regarding previous works or studies, there are several types of research depending on the approach used, thus, we can mention the following examples of studies:

1) Studies where compliance with NMX-R-003-SCFI-2011 has been analyzed as such, although not necessarily from a data analysis and processing point of view, but rather from a qualitative point of view by analyzing one or few schools, as well as some or few of the conditions established by the standard. For example:
   - In [7], the educational infrastructure of a sample of 18 preschool schools in the central region of the country was evaluated through the physical survey of data, photographic record and analysis of regulatory compliance, including NMX-R-003-SCFI-2011. However, only certain conditions of the transformed physical environment were evaluated (like proximity to roads, fuel stations, garbage dumps, etc.), without considering those of the natural physical environment. The results show that the percentage of regulatory compliance regarding the location of schools varies among the entities analyzed, as follows: HGO (55.1%), CDMX (46.5%), EDOMEX (34.7%), MOR (31.9%), TLAX (22.2%), QRO (20.2%).
2) Studies that have investigated the impact on the safety and health of the school population due to the proximity of schools to areas prone to natural disasters, or to highly dangerous facilities or infrastructures. These are not studies on machine learning as such. For example:

- In [5] the association between the proximity of 3,669 schools in Michigan, United States to highways and industrial facilities was explored, and a relationship with it and the performance rate on the Michigan Educational Assessment Program tests and the respiratory and neurological risks of the National Air Toxics Assessment was evaluated. Schools closer to such facilities were found to have higher risks of respiratory and neurological illnesses, as well as lower performance rates.
- In [3] the proximity (<75 m) of 1,556 public elementary schools to highways and roads in 10 cities in Canada was determined. By cross-checking information on school location, pollution levels, and census information, it was found that a substantial fraction of students, primarily those attending schools in low-income neighborhoods, may be exposed to elevated levels of air and noise pollution due to proximity to roads. Thus, the location of schools can negatively impact the health and school performance of a large number of students.
- In [6] risk scenarios for atmospheric contamination by benzene (the compound responsible for gasoline odor) from 509 gas stations in three cities in Baja California, Mexico were estimated. By using geospatial analysis and risk mapping, schools near the gas stations (300 m) were located. It was found that, out of a total of 4,654 schools, 421 of them were affected by the contamination of that compound, which meant an exposure of 83,701 students to the pollutant.
- In [4] the relationship between exposure to air pollutants and school performance (average grades) of 1,888 elementary school students in El Paso, Texas, United States was determined. The results showed that the higher the levels of air pollution, the lower the average individual school performance. The authors highlighted the need to establish regulations on the location of schools and adjacent land uses to protect the health of the school population.

3) Studies where the focus has been on clustering public infrastructure facilities such as schools, hospitals, businesses, etc., either in our country or abroad, using unsupervised machine learning techniques.
   - In [8] a clustering model of Mexico's entities was generated based on data from the National Directory of Economic Units of the National Institute of Statistics and Geography (approximately 2 million records, which include all schools in the country, as well as all other types of points of interest), using the K-Medoids algorithm (PAM) and following the CRISP-DM methodology. The result was 4 clusters evaluated with internal validation techniques, and a map showing the geographic distribution of the clusters in the states of the country.
   - In [9] a clustering model of a sample of primary schools in China (845 cases) was generated based on the characteristics of their sports facilities according to data from the General Administration of Sport of China, using the Fuzzy C-Means algorithm. The result was 3 clusters where schools were mainly separated by characteristics such as location, educational levels taught, etc.

- In [10] a clustering model of Indonesian provinces was generated based on data from the Ministry of Education and Culture on the number of libraries per schools of different educational levels (34 records), using the K-Medoids algorithm. The result was 2 clusters, in which provinces with higher and lower number of school libraries were separated.
- In [11] a clustering model of public hospitals in the French health system (388 records) was generated based on characteristics such as number of admissions, mobility index, etc., using the K-Means algorithm. The result was three hospital clusters identified by the algorithm. It was concluded that the flow of patients in the French hospital network is unbalanced between the clusters.

Based on the three types of studies previously described, it is clear that 1) there has not been enough research with regards to the compliance of the existing school infrastructure in Mexico and the NMX-R-003-SCFI-2011, so this study can unveil the current situation at a country-wide level. 2) it has been widely documented that the proximity of hazardous features to schools has an impact in both safety and health of school population. And 3) it is possible to use unsupervised machine learning algorithms to cluster facilities like schools based on their attribution.

3 Methodology

3.1 Research Design

The method used to carry out the analysis and processing of the study data is the one known as CRISP-DM (Cross-Industry Standard Process for Data Mining) [12]. The main phases are summarized in Fig. 2 and described below:

1) Business Understanding: In this phase of the method, tasks are performed to determine the objectives of the study, assess the situation of the problem at hand, define the objectives, and produce a project plan.
2) Data Understanding: This phase of the method consists of carrying out tasks that allow the study data to be known and studied in detail. As for the tasks involved, it could be said that they serve two purposes: on the one hand, to collect, describe and explore the data by means of statistical techniques, and on the other hand, to verify the quality of the data involved.
3) Data Preparation: This phase of the method consists of carrying out tasks to prepare and package the data for subsequent modeling. The tasks involved in this phase include: selection, cleaning, construction, integration and formatting of the data.
4) Modeling: In this phase of the method, algorithms are used to iteratively create models. For this, tasks related to the selection of modeling techniques, the generation of a test design, the generation of models, and the evaluation of models are performed.

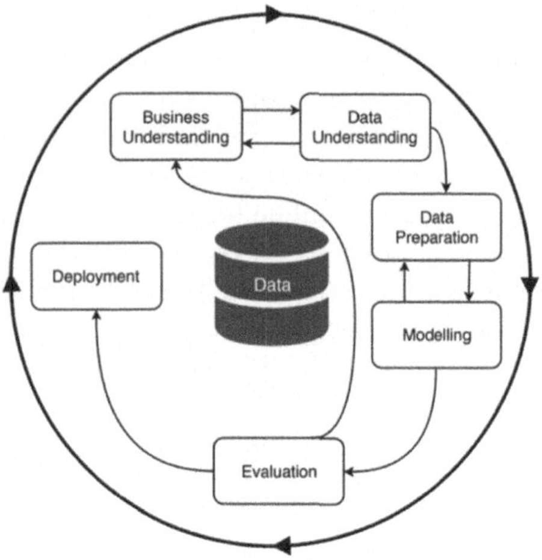

Fig. 2. CRISP-DM Methodology phases [13].

5) Evaluation: In this phase of the method, results are evaluated using performance criteria established at the beginning of the project. To do this, the results are evaluated, a review process is carried out and the next steps are determined.
6) Deployment: In this phase, the implementation of the new knowledge is planned to achieve improvements in an organization, either through the formal application of the model, or the application of modifications in the organization based on the new knowledge. To do this, it is necessary to plan the deployment, plan the control and maintenance, and create a final report [12].

For simplicity sake, in this paper the methodology is not described exactly with the phases and tasks suggested by CRISP-DM, even though such method was indeed employed for the realization of the study.

3.2 Data Collection

As mentioned at the beginning, the objective of this study was to carry out the clustering of schools in Mexico according to the characteristics of the natural and transformed physical environment of their location. These characteristics are not available in the attributes of the original dataset, so it is necessary to compile this information from other sources and merge it with the DENUE source. For this purpose, a search for other geospatial data files in INEGI that represent such characteristics of the physical environment was carried out. The consulted data sources are listed below:

- National Statistical Directory of Economic Units (DENUE) [14]
- National Topographic Data Set at 1:250 000 scale [15].
- National Inventory of Geological Phenomena. Scale 1:250 000 [16]

- Geospatial information on the municipal management of water and sanitation services [17].
- Geospatial information on municipal management of urban solid waste [18].

NMX-R-003-SCFI-2011 Mexican standard contemplates 39 conditions, from physical features (hydrological and geological) to infrastructural ones. However, data was only obtained for 26 of them, which corresponds to 72% of the conditions. However, some conditions involve the use of several data files, such as the one related to highways, roads and railways in which 3 files are used, so the number of files used, and therefore the number of variables, is greater than the total number of conditions covered.

The integration of multiple datasets significantly enhances the accuracy and comprehensiveness of hazard assessment for schools by providing a more complete and nuanced understanding of the various factors that may pose safety and health risks. This, in turn, supports better decision-making and planning for school safety and health.

3.3 Experimental Setup

The experimental setup consisted on:

1) Creating a data set that shows the compliance or non-compliance of each school with respect to the characteristics mentioned in the Mexican Standard.
2) After creating the dataset, a unsupervised machine learning model that clusters these schools and that allows differentiating these institutions from each other according to the characteristics of the Mexican Standard was generated.
3) Finally, the interpretation of the results of the generated model and the proposal of concrete actions based on the hazards detected for each school according to the cluster to which it belongs was carried out.

3.4 Data Analysis

According to the experimental setup steps previously described, the following actions were carried out:

Dataset Creation
For creating the dataset, the Python programming language was used (specifically the Pandas [19] and GeoPandas [20] libraries). A script that processes a shapefile of schools in Mexico from DENUE dataset (the shapefile has a dimension of 148,351 records $\times$ 42 columns) and evaluates its proximity to the various natural and infrastructural features was created.

Initially, it loads the shapefile containing the school facilities, converts its coordinate reference system to EPSG:4326, filters relevant columns, and removes duplicate entries. It then defines a function that takes the schools dataset and the condition layer, converts the coordinate reference system of the conditions layers to EPSG:4326, calculates the nearest distance between features in these layers (Table 2), and flags schools within a specified distance threshold (Table 3). The proximity flags have values of 1 or 0, indicating whether each school is within the specified distance of each natural or infrastructural feature. The distance threshold is specified by the official standard, and if not specified, a default 500 m/250 m (the latter for cemeteries, roads and railroads only) distance was applied (the 500 m default distance was chosen because it is the most commonly used one in the standard). The frequency of hazardous conditions close to schools is shown in Fig. 3. The data set is reduced from 148,351 records to 111,174 records due to deduplication and exclusion of schools not considered by the Standard (e.g., sports, language or arts schools). Only preschools, elementary schools, middle schools, high schools, and higher education schools are maintained.

The script sets up a dictionary of multiple conditions layers, each with its path, optional filter criteria, and distance threshold, and iteratively processes each layer by calling the function. After processing, it removes duplicate school entries and columns related to distances, and saves the final dataset to a CSV file.

Table 2. Schools in the data set and their distance from the natural and infrastructural hazardous features (in meters). Dataset dimensions: 111174 rows × 30 distance columns (descriptive columns not counted)

#	id	nom_estab	nombre_act	tipo_asent	entidad	geometry	distance inundacion	distance barranca	...	distance vialidad	distance via ferrea
1	157454	JARDIN DE NIÑOS DR MARIA MONTESSORI	Escuelas de educación preescolar del sector pú...	LOCALIDAD	BAJA CALIFORNIA SUR	POINT (-114.89723 27.68990)	57154.4	482532.92	...	542.54	424296.42
2	157455	PRIMARIA NARCISO MENDOZA	Escuelas de educación primaria del sector público	LOCALIDAD	BAJA CALIFORNIA SUR	POINT (-114.89679 27.68976)	57111.5	482560.93	...	562.46	424283.71
...	...	...	...	...	...	...	...	...	...	...	...
111173	4370376	JARDIN DE NIÑOS FERNANDO OROZCO Y BE	Escuelas de educación preescolar del sector pú...	COLONIA	VERACRUZ DE IGNACIO DE LA LLAVE	POINT (-96.91554 18.86699)	55402.87	11642.61	...	420.23	0.87
111174	4510524	COLEGIO DE BACHILLERES DEL ESTADO DE YUCATAN N...	Escuelas de educación media superior del secto...	COLONIA	YUCATÁN	POINT (-89.40457 20.99813)	32589.07	551638.31	...	33.98	0.18

Clustering Model Generation

For generating the clustering model, the Python programming language was used again. This time, another script using the scikit-learn [21], Numpy and kmodes [22] libraries was created. This script loads the binary dataset (CSV file) which contains the school information along with the proximity flags to the various hazardous features (Table 3).

Descriptive columns are dropped to focus only on the binary proximity flags for clustering. It tests a range of cluster numbers (from 2 to 15) using the K-Modes algorithm, which is suitable for clustering categorical data.

Table 3. Schools in the data set and their flags indicating compliance with distance threshold defined in the standard. Dataset dimensions: 111174 rows × 30 flag columns (descriptive columns not counted)

#	id	nom_estab	nombre_act	tipo_asent	entidad	geometry	flag inundacion	flag barranca	...	flag vialidad	flag via ferrea
1	157454	JARDIN DE NIÑOS DR MARIA MONTESSORI	Escuelas de educación preescolar del sector pú...	LOCALIDAD	BAJA CALIFORNIA SUR	POINT (-114.89723 27.68990)	0	0	...	0	0
2	157455	PRIMARIA NARCISO MENDOZA	Escuelas de educación primaria del sector público	LOCALIDAD	BAJA CALIFORNIA SUR	POINT (-114.89679 27.68976)	0	0	...	0	0
...	...	...	...	...	...	...	...	...	...	...	...
111173	4370376	JARDIN DE NIÑOS FERNANDO OROZCO Y BE	Escuelas de educación preescolar del sector pú...	COLONIA	VERACRUZ DE IGNACIO DE LA LLAVE	POINT (-96.91554 18.86699)	0	0	...	0	1
111174	4510524	COLEGIO DE BACHILLERES DEL ESTADO DE YUCATAN N...	Escuelas de educación media superior del secto...	COLONIA	YUCATÁN	POINT (-89.40457 20.99813)	0	0	...	1	1

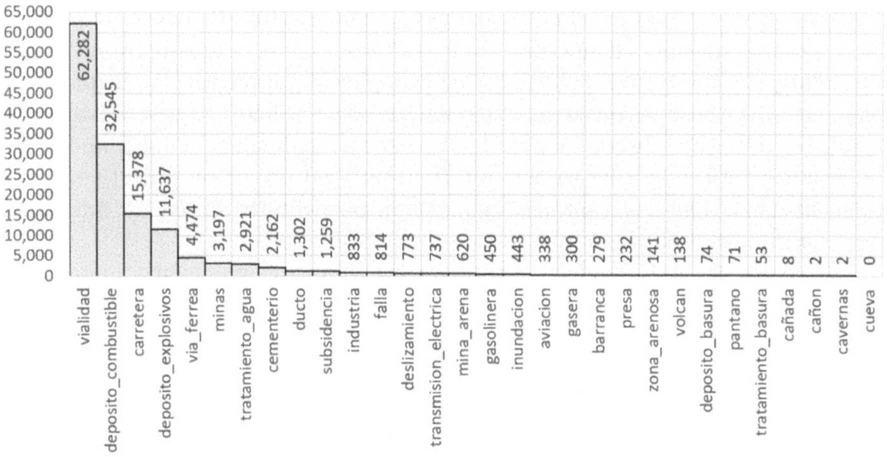

Fig. 3. Frequency of hazardous conditions close to schools

K-Modes is an unsupervised machine learning algorithm categorized as a partitional clustering algorithm. Partitional clustering is a method of data analysis that focuses on dividing a dataset into several groups [23]. This process seeks to create groups of data that maximize the similarity between objects within the same group, while minimizing the similarity between objects assigned to different groups [24]. Partitioning is performed such that each group contains at least one data point and each data point belongs to at least one group [23]. In this process, each data object is iteratively assigned to a group based on its similarity to other objects in the same group, with the goal of optimizing specific functions until convergence is reached [25].

K-Modes begins by initializing the cluster centroids. Unlike K-Means which uses means, K-Modes initializes using modes (the most frequent category in each attribute). The initial centroids can be chosen randomly or using specific strategies like the Huang method [26].

Each data point (school) is assigned to the cluster whose centroid it is closest to. The distance between a data point and a centroid is calculated using a simple matching dissimilarity measure, which counts the number of mismatches in categorical attributes. For binary data, this is equivalent to the Hamming distance:

$$Disimilarity(x, y) = \sum_{i=1}^{m} x_i = I(x_i \neq y_i) \tag{1}$$

where I is an indicator function that is 1 if $x_i \neq y_i$ and 0 otherwise.

For each number of clusters, it calculates clustering metrics including Silhouette Score, Calinski-Harabasz Index, and Davies-Bou Index to evaluate the quality of the clusters. The optimal number of clusters is determined based on the best combination of metrics results [27]. K-Modes clustering is applied to the data using the optimal number of clusters identified.

Using unsupervised machine learning techniques like K-Modes clustering offers several specific advantages over traditional risk assessment methods, particularly in the context of analyzing complex datasets with multiple variables, such as those involved in assessing risks for schools. These advantages include: enabling the discovery of hidden patterns, managing complex and high-dimensional data, adapting to new information, and providing objective, data-driven insights. These advantages make them particularly suited for analyzing large, multifaceted datasets in risk assessment scenarios.

The choice of the K-Modes clustering algorithm can significantly impact the overall quality and reliability of the clustering results, especially when dealing with categorical data, as is common in many real-world scenarios. The reason is that it provides a method well-suited for categorical data, offers interpretability, efficiency, and scalability. However, the quality of the results is still highly dependent on factors such as the choice of K, the initialization method, and the alignment of the algorithm with the problem's characteristics. Properly addressing these factors ensures that K-Modes clustering delivers meaningful and actionable insights.

The K-Modes clustering model is saved for future use. The dataset with the original descriptive columns and the cluster labels is saved as a new CSV file. This CSV file indicates the cluster assignment for each school. This file combines the original descriptive data with the clustering results, making it easy to analyze which schools belong to which cluster.

Clustering Model Interpretation

For interpreting the clustering model, the Excel program was used. The CSV file produced by the second script was loaded in Excel. A new attribute containing the count of proximity flags per school was created.

Finally, a Pivot table that summarizes the clustering results of schools based on their proximity to the various hazards identified by the previous Python scripts was created. It categorizes schools into a number of distinct clusters (according to the best k value), where each cluster represents a different hazard profile for the schools.

The table (Table 4) provides the following information for each cluster: Average hazards per school, Number of schools, Percentage of schools, Minimum number of hazards, Maximum number of hazards, Description. The total row at the bottom aggregates these values for all schools. This pivot table helps in understanding the distribution and characteristics of hazard exposure among different groups of schools, facilitating better hazard management and resource allocation.

3.5 Results

In order to determine the best k value, performance metrics for each k were calculated. Since ground truth labels are not available for this dataset, internal metrics that evaluate the clustering quality were used instead of external metrics [27]. Metrics can be interpreted this way:

Silhouette Score: Higher values indicate better-defined clusters. A higher silhouette score suggests that the clusters are well-separated and distinct.

Calinski-Harabasz Index: Higher values indicate better-defined clusters. This index measures the ratio of the sum of between-cluster dispersion and within-cluster dispersion.

Davies-Bouldin Index: Lower values indicate better clustering. This index measures the average similarity ratio of each cluster with its most similar cluster, hence lower values are preferred [21].

According to the evaluation metrics, out of the tested values, $k = 11$ is the best one since it has a high Silhouette Score (0.72) and Calinski-Harabasz Index (32863.96), while having a low Davies-Bouldin Index (0.72). For these reasons the model produced with $k = 11$ is the one used for the final analysis. Comparison of metrics results can be found in Fig. 4.

The results obtained from the modeling were represented as labels in the data set, indicating the cluster number to which each record belongs. Likewise, in parallel, it was possible to perform the sum of hazard for each school. Figure 5 shows the distribution of schools by the number of nearby hazardous features, without taking into account the clustering results. Table 4 summarizes the results of the K-Modes clustering and describes what kind of scenario each cluster describes. Figure 6 shows how the spatial data set actually looks with the K-Modes clustering labels.

4 Discussion

4.1 Analysis of Results

Based on the 11 clusters defined by the K-Modes algorithm and summarized in Table 4, some actions could be carried out in order to decrease the risk for the schools according to the cluster they belong:

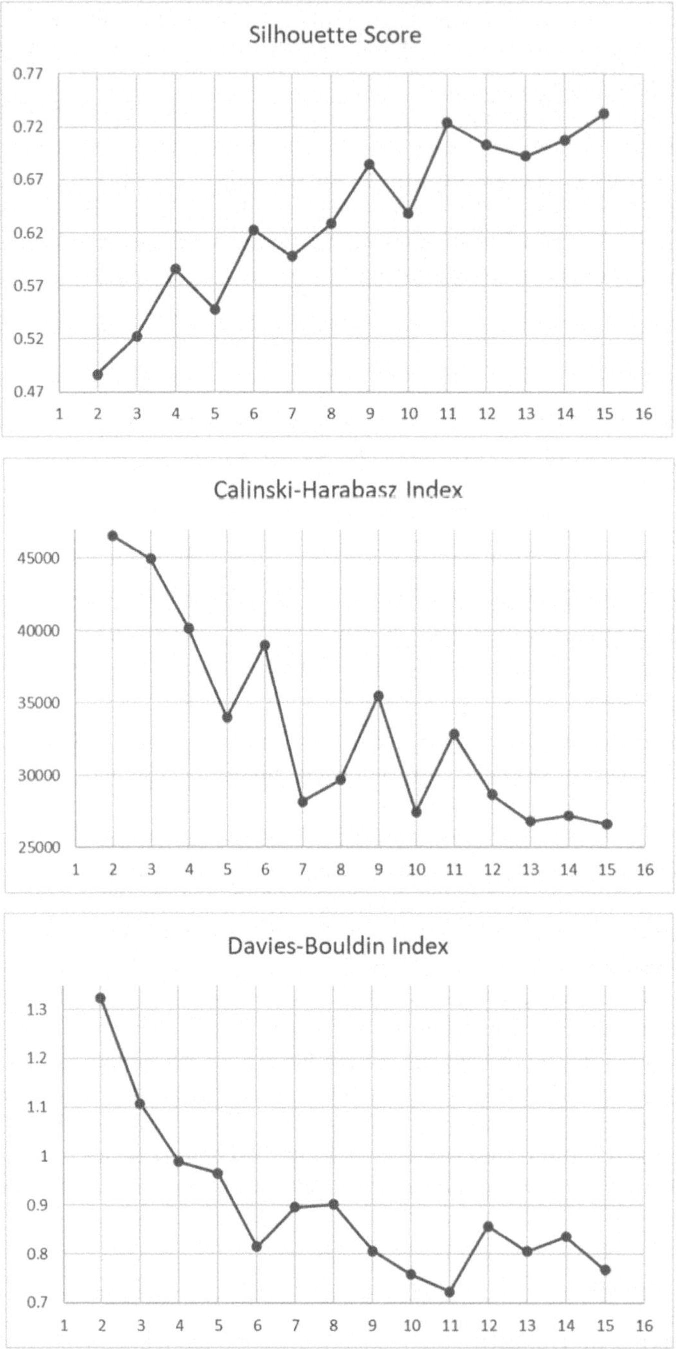

Fig. 4. Internal evaluation metrics results. The graphs show that K = 11 is the best option as it has high Silhouette and Calinski-Harabasz Index Scores, while having a low Davies-Bouldin Index Score

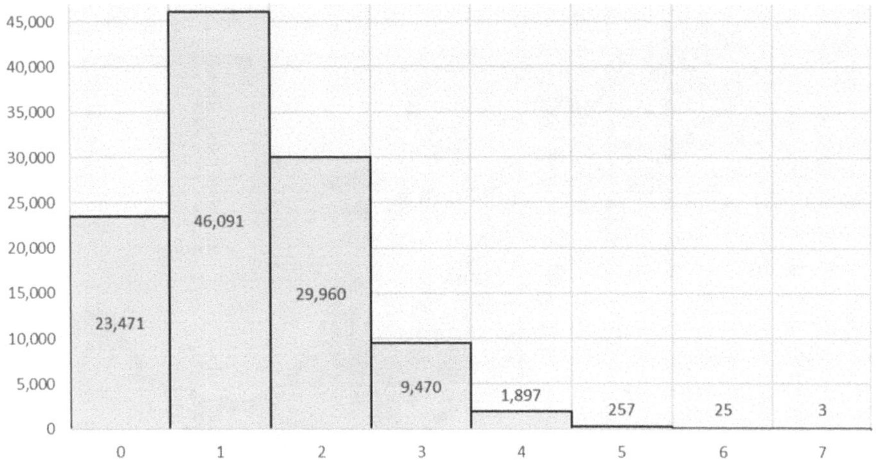

Fig. 5. School count per close hazardous conditions frequency

Table 4. Summary of the K-Modes Clustering results

K Modes Cluster	School Count per cluster	School Percentage per cluster	Average near hazard per cluster	Min. Near hazard Count per cluster	Max Near hazard Count per cluster	Description
2	34165	31%	1.2	1	5	Schools near a road
8	27599	25%	0.1	0	3	Schools with no nearby hazards
9	11238	10%	2.2	2	7	Schools close to a road and a fuel depot
7	10133	9%	1.2	1	5	Schools near a fuel depot
1	8448	8%	2.4	2	7	Schools close to a road and a highway
0	7147	6%	1.9	1	5	Schools near a road and an explosives depot
10	5260	5%	1.2	1	5	Schools near a highway
6	4298	4%	2.9	2	6	Schools near a road, a fuel depot and an explosives depot
5	1383	1%	2.1	1	6	Schools near a road and a cemetery
3	1186	1%	1.6	1	5	Schools near a water treatment plant
4	317	0%	1.7	1	5	Schools near a fuel depot and a landslide area
Total	111174	100%	1.2	0	7	

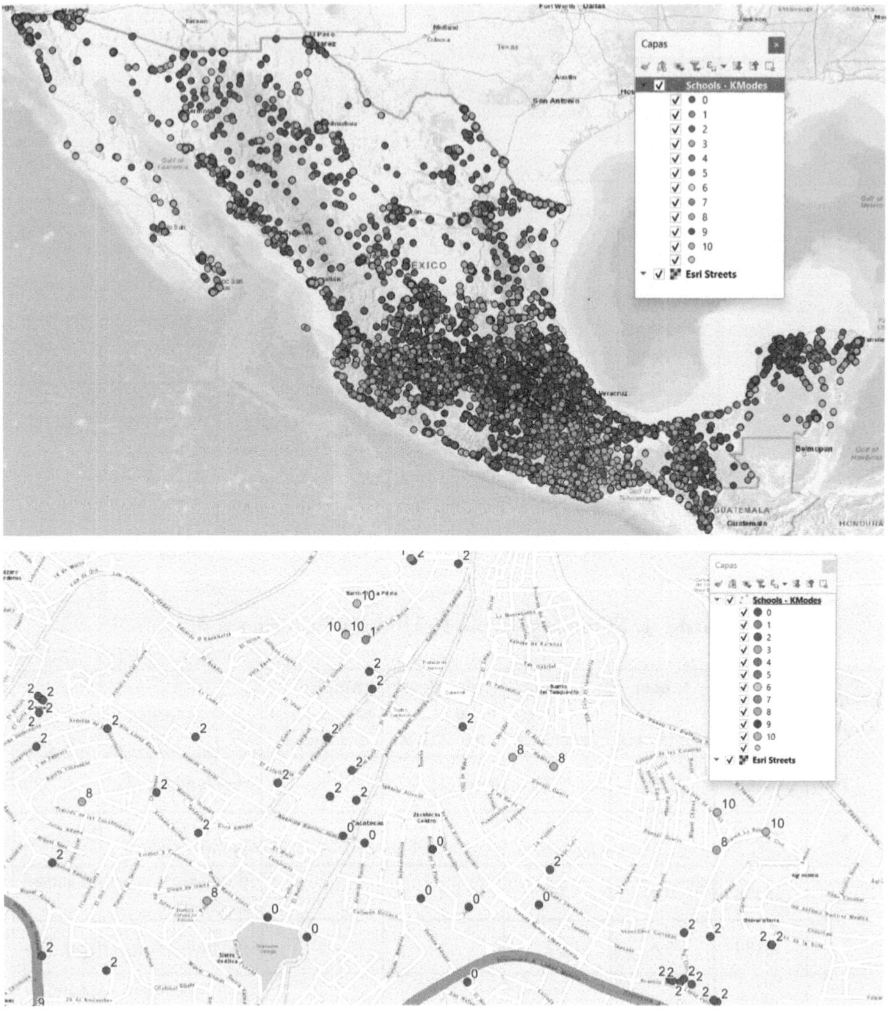

Fig. 6. Visualization of the DENUE Schools Shapefile in a Geographic Information Systems (GIS) software at different scales, with K-Modes clustering labels

Schools near a Road (Cluster 2): This cluster groups 34,165 schools, which represents 31% of the total. To prevent accidents, fences or barriers between the school and the road can be installed. Safe pedestrian crossings with traffic lights and crossing guards during school hours can be created. Speed bumps can be implemented and speed limits near the school zone can be reduced. Students can be educated on road safety and the importance of using designated crossings.

Schools with No Nearby Hazards (Cluster 8): This cluster groups 27,599 schools, which represents 25% of the total. These schools do not have any nearby hazards, which places them in relatively safe environments. It is crucial to maintain conditions that ensure the absence of hazards. This involves continuous monitoring of the environment to ensure that no new hazards emerge, and the implementation of policies and practices that reinforce existing safety, preventing the introduction of new hazards.

Schools Close to a Road and a Fuel Depot (Cluster 9): This cluster groups 11,238 schools, which represents 10% of the total. Evacuation plans that account for the specific hazards of a road and a fuel depot can be created and practiced. Air quality can be monitored and have protocols for poor air quality days. Also students and staff can be educated on the dangers of the fuel depot and road safety measures.

Schools near a Fuel Depot (Cluster 7): This cluster groups 10,133 schools, which represents 9% of the total. For these schools a response plan for fuel leaks, fires, or explosions can be developed. Regular drills for scenarios involving fuel hazards can be conducted. Also there can be coordination with local fire departments and emergency services for rapid response strategies.

Schools Close to a Road and a Highway (Cluster 1): This cluster groups 8,448 schools, which represents 8% of the total. Stricter traffic control measures, including pedestrian bridges can be implemented. Noise barriers and soundproofing in classrooms to mitigate highway noise can be used. Air quality with plants, air purifiers, and ventilation systems can be monitored and improved.

Schools Near a Road and an Explosives Depot (Cluster 0): This cluster groups 7,147 schools, which represents 6% of the total. Blast-resistant windows can be installed and building structures reinforced. Drills for both evacuation and shelter-in-place scenarios can be regularly practiced. Potential risks and safety procedures can be communicated to the school community.

Schools Near a Highway (Cluster 10): This cluster groups 5,260 schools, which represent 5% of the total. Robust safety barriers and pedestrian overpasses or underpasses can be put in place. Noise reduction and air quality improvement measures can be implemented as described for schools close to roads and highways.

Schools Near a Road, a Fuel Depot, and an Explosives Depot (Cluster 6): This cluster groups 4,298 schools, which represents 4% of the total. A thorough risk assessment considering all three hazards can be conducted. An integrated safety plan that addresses evacuation, air quality, noise, and blast protection can be developed. Emergency drills can be regularly practiced, and the school community can be educated on all potential hazards.

Schools Near a Road and a Cemetery (Cluster 5): This cluster groups 1,383 schools, which represents 1% of the total. Minimal risks from the cemetery can be ensured, but general safety practices for road hazards can be maintained. Respectful boundaries can be maintained and also to ensure students understand the importance of the cemetery.

Schools Near a Water Treatment Plant (Cluster 3): This cluster groups 1,186 schools, which represents 1% of the total. Water quality can be regularly tested to ensure there are no contaminants. Plans for scenarios involving chemical spills or leaks from the treatment plant can be developed. A communication line with the water treatment plant for timely updates on any incidents can be implemented.

Schools Near a Fuel Depot and a Landslide Area (Cluster 4): This cluster groups 317 schools, which represents almost 0% of the total. Regular assessments to monitor landslide risks can be conducted. Evacuation drills for both fuel-related incidents and landslides can be practiced. Contingency plans for temporary relocation if landslide risks become imminent can be considered.

4.2 Implications and Limitations

The research has the potential of being highly convenient and useful, as it allowed to identify and address a wide range of natural and anthropogenic hazards for scholar infrastructure. The application of advanced geospatial analysis and machine learning techniques allowed to suggest informed, accurate and effective actions according to each cluster's characteristics, contributing to safer and more sustainable urban and educational development.

Conducting this study can have social relevance, as its results not only can support in the protection of the life and well-being of the school population, but can also contribute to safer urban development, evidence-based public policy making, and the promotion of equity and social justice. In addition, it can drive the use of advanced technologies in solving critical problems, demonstrating that scientific research can have a direct and positive impact on society.

A limitation for this study was the lack of data for all the hazardous conditions described by the official standard (specially natural features). As mentioned, data was found for 72% of the conditions. However, as shown in Fig. 3, most of the close features to schools are infrastructural ones, so its probable that the missing natural conditions are not very common as are the ones included in the study.

Another limitation is regarding the distance thresholds defined by the official standard. In most of the cases, a specific distance from the school location to the hazardous feature is not clearly mentioned, and so a default distance threshold had to be used instead, which can overestimate or underestimate the real impact the hazardous feature could have in the reality. However, the analysis is useful to get an understanding of the possible risks each school in the country could have and take actions accordingly.

Internal clustering evaluation metrics like the Silhouette Score and the Davies-Bouldin Index are useful tools for assessing the quality of clustering when ground truth labels are not available. However, they come with certain limitations that can affect the reliability and interpretability of the results. These limitations include the fact that they are relative, sensitive to the number of clusters and distance measures, and may favor certain cluster structures over others. Additionally, they do not capture the real-world relevance or domain-specific significance of clusters. As such, they should be used cautiously and ideally in conjunction with other methods, such as external validation or domain expert input, to ensure the clustering results are both mathematically sound and practically meaningful.

5 Conclusion

The realization of the present work allowed us to employ both machine learning and geospatial analysis techniques to successfully generate models that detect and group schools that may be located in potentially dangerous areas due to the surrounding natural and infrastructural conditions. In fact, as was verified in the results evaluation phase, it was possible to carry out the clustering of the schools according to their proximity to such conditions. Also, according to the results of the model evaluation, the metrics showed that the clustering had a good quality, so the clustering patterns found are acceptable. It is important that the population of each school is aware of the hazardous factors nearby so that measures can be implemented to ensure the safety and health of everyone.

References

1. Secretaría de Economía. Norma Mexicana NMX-R-003-SCFI-2011. ESCUELAS-SELECCION DEL TERRENO PARA CONSTRUCCION-REQUISITOS. https://www.gob.mx/cms/uploads/attachment/file/104884/NMX-R-003_Escuelas_Seleccion_del_terreno.pdf
2. Instituto Nacional de Estadística y Geografía. Directorio Estadístico Nacional de Unidades Económicas (DENUE) (2022)
3. Amram, O., Abernethy, R., Brauer, M., Davies, H., Allen, R.W.: Proximity of public elementary schools to major roads in Canadian urban areas. Int. J. Health Geogr. **10** (2011)
4. Grineski, S.E., Clark, S.E., Collins, T.W.: School-based exposure to hazardous air pollutants and grade point average: a multi-level study. Environ. Res. **147**, 164–171 (2016)
5. Kweon, B.-S., Mohai, P., Lee, S., Sametshaw, A.M.: Proximity of public schools to major highways and industrial facilities, and students' school performance and health hazards. Environ. Plan B Urban Anal. City Sci. **45**(2), 312–329 (2018)
6. García-Zarate, M.A., Arellano, E., Villada-Canela, M., Barajas-Carrillo, V.W.: Risk scenarios, based on the IDLH of benzene, in the population near gas stations of three cities in Baja California, Mexico. J. Earth Environ. Sci. **4**(1), 1–7 (2016)
7. Pacheco Martínez, N.J.: Evaluación del impacto de la infraestructura física educativa en la educación. RIDE Revista Iberoamericana para la Investigación y el Desarrollo Educativo (2021)
8. Espinosa-Zúñiga, J.J.: Aplicación de metodología CRISP-DM para segmentación geográfica de una base de datos pública. Ingeniería Investigación y Tecnología, vol. XXI, no. 1 (2020)
9. Xia, J., Wang, J., Chen, H., Zhuang, J., Cao, Z., Chen, P.: An unsupervised machine learning approach to evaluate sports facilities condition in primary school. PLoS One (2022)
10. Rahim, R., Santoso, J.T., Jumini, S., Bhawika, G.W., Susilo, D.: Unsupervised data mining technique for clustering library in Indonesia. Libr. Philos. Pract. (2021)

11. Chrusciel, J., et al.: Making sense of the French public hospital system: a network-based approach to hospital clustering using unsupervised learning methods. BMC Health Serv. Res. **XXI**(1244) (2021)
12. IBM. Conceptos básicos de ayuda de CRISP-DM. https://www.ibm.com/docs/es/spss-modeler/saas?topic=dm-crisp-help-overview
13. Martínez-Plumed, F., et al.: CRISP-DM Twenty Years Later: From Data Mining Processes to Data Science Trajectories (2019)
14. Instituto Nacional de Geografía e Informática. Directorio Estadístico Nacional de Unidades Económicas (DENUE). https://www.inegi.org.mx/app/descarga/?ti=6
15. Instituto Nacional de Geografía e Informática. Conjunto Nacional de Datos Topográficos a escala 1:250 000. https://www.inegi.org.mx/app/biblioteca/ficha.html?upc=794551091968
16. Instituto Nacional de Geografía e Informática. Inventario nacional de fenómenos geológicos. Escala 1:250 000. https://www.inegi.org.mx/app/biblioteca/ficha.html?upc=889463842767
17. Instituto Nacional de Geografía e Informática. Información geoespacial sobre la gestión municipal de los servicios de agua y saneamiento. https://www.inegi.org.mx/app/biblioteca/ficha.html?upc=889463858560
18. Instituto Nacional de Geografía e Informática. Información geoespacial sobre la gestión municipal de los residuos sólidos urbanos. https://www.inegi.org.mx/app/biblioteca/ficha.html?upc=889463858577
19. The Pandas development team, "Pandas."
20. Jordahl, K., et al.: geopandas/geopandas: v0.8.1 (Version v0.8.1)
21. Pedregosa, F., et al.: Scikit-learn: machine learning in Python. J. Mach. Learn. Res. **12**, 2825–2830 (2011)
22. de Vos, N.J.: kmodes categorical clustering library (2015). https://github.com/nicodv/kmodes
23. Balusamy, B., Abirami, N., Kadry, S., Gandomi, A.H.: Big Data: Concepts, Technology and Architecture, Wiley (2021)
24. de Vries, N.J., Olech, L.P., Moscato, P.: Introducing clustering with a focus in marketing and consumer analysis. In: Business and Consumer Analytics: New Ideas. Springer (2019)
25. Ni, H., Dong, X., Zheng, J., Yu, G.: An Introduction To Machine Learning In Quantitative Finance. World Scientific Publishing Company (2021)
26. Huang, Z.: Extensions to the k-Means Algorithm for Clustering Large Data Sets with Categorical Values (1998)
27. Sarkar, D., Bali, R., Sharma, T.: Practical Machine Learning with Python. Apress (2018)

Spatial Regression Models on Sexual Violence Against Women in Mexico City

Francisco Carrillo-Brenes[1(✉)], Luis M. Vilches-Blázquez[2], and Sandra Dinora Orantes-Jiménez[1]

[1] Centro de Investigación en Computación, Instituto Politécnico Nacional, 07700 Mexico City, Mexico
fcarrillob2022@cic.ipn.mx
[2] Ontology Engineering Group, Universidad Politécnica de Madrid, 28031 Madrid, Spain

Abstract. Sexual violence persists as a significant global public matter, manifesting in gender-specific ways. It is a pervasive phenomenon, with high prevalence rates reported across the globe, affecting individuals in a multitude of ways—physically, psychologically, and socially. This study focuses on female victims of sexual violence and employs a combination of spatial autocorrelation (Global and Local Moran's) and four distinct regression models (Geographically Weighted Regression) to analyze the prevalence of sexual violence against women in Mexico City. The regression models employed a range of demographic and socio-economic variables, in addition to police records, to identify any spatial clustering and to examine the factors influencing the geographical distribution of the cases. The selected model was compared with the Ordinary Least Squares and Generalized Method of Moments models. The findings revealed significant concentrations of sexual violence in specific urban areas, underscoring the role of poverty levels, victims' age group, and average years of schooling. Furthermore, spatial variations in these factors were identified, emphasizing varying vulnerabilities across different local areas.

Keywords: Sexual violence · Regression Model · Geographically Weighted Regression · Moran's Index · Geospatial analysis

1 Introduction

According to the World Health Organization (WHO), sexual violence persists as a significant global public concern, with significant physical, psychological, and social ramifications [2]. As estimated by the WHO on a global scale, this issue exhibits gender-specific aspects, with 6% of women aged 15–49 years reporting a history of non-partner sexual violence. In high-income regions of Northern America and Australia, the estimated prevalence is even higher, reaching 15% and 19%, respectively. Significant prevalence rates are also reported in Latin America and the Caribbean, with 11% of women experiencing non-partner sexual violence. In Mexico, the estimated lifetime prevalence of intimate partner violence (IPV) among women aged 15 years and older is 24%. However, data on non-partner violence in Mexico during 2018 is inconclusive [1].

M. F. Mata-Rivera et al. (Eds.): GIS-LATAM 2024, CCIS 2298, pp. 105–121, 2025.
https://doi.org/10.1007/978-3-031-80017-7_7

In order to elucidate and comprehend the phenomenon of sexual violence against women, some works have employed regression models as a mean of investigating this research problem. Notably, some studies have utilized traditional regression models, such as Ordinary Least Squares (OLS) or logistic regression. Kearns et al. [3] employed the OLS model to identify the relationship between sexual violence and gender inequality. Garza and Franklin [4] analyzed the police response to sexual violence. Ajayi et al. [5] and Aboagye et al. [6] used logistic regression to identify the relationship between alcohol use, inadequate family financial support, and exposure to sexual violence. They discovered a relationship between sexual violence and multiple high-risk fertility.

Another regression model that is frequently utilized is Geographically Weighted Regression (GWR). This model was employed to examine the spatial variability in the association between male partner alcohol misuse, income and educational level, with intimate partner violence against women in Ghana [7]. Similarly, Fontes et al. [8] employed GWR to model intimate partner sexual violence considering variables such as educational level, alcohol use and economically active women. Moreover, Horsefield et al. [9] investigated the correlation between sexual violence and alcohol misuse perpetrated by men. The aforementioned studies compared their GWR models with OLS, but the employed OLS model did not take into account the spatial attributes of the data.

Additionally, some studies have integrated techniques such as Local Moran's Index with regression models. For example, a logistic regression model was applied to the hotspots identified through the use of Moran's Index in [10]. Andresen [11] employed a multinomial logistic regression model to analyze the clusters identified through the Local Moran method. Notwithstanding the employment of an array of autocorrelation and regression models in a multitude of related works, to the best of our knowledge, no contribution has employed Moran's Indexes to identify spatial clusters of female sexual violence and, subsequently, to explore how variables applied to a spatial regression model affect these clusters. This offers a more nuanced understanding of spatial patterns that extends beyond the examination of a singular type of cluster (hotspots).

The contribution of this research is the utilization of sophisticated spatial analysis techniques, including Geographically Weighted Regression (GWR) and Moran's I. These techniques are used in accordance with the methodologies outlined in [12, 13], with the aim of examining the geographical distribution of sexual violence against women in Mexico City. The objective of our analysis is to elucidate the manner in which socioeconomic variables influence the spatial distribution of reported sexual violence cases. This work not only identifies spatial clusters of sexual violence but also highlights the socioeconomic variables present in those clusters through GWR models, thereby providing insights into the extent to which different factors contribute to the observed patterns in the data.

This paper is structured as follows: Sect. 2 outlines the geographical context, data sources, and analytical techniques employed in the study. Section 3 presents the results, and Sect. 4 discusses the findings and offers some conclusions.

2 Materials and Methods

2.1 Study Area

The area of study is Mexico City, the capital and most populous city of Mexico. This city is one of the most significant in North America. This study focuses on the 2,431 urban micro-statistical areas, also known as *Áreas Geoestadísticas Básicas* (AGEB), defined by the National Institute of Statistics and Geography (INEGI) in Mexico. These areas represent a highly detailed level of geographic division within the city, allowing for a granular analysis of spatial patterns and correlations. Each of these units can be conceptualized as a neighborhood or sector, collectively encompassing the entirety of Mexico City.

2.2 Data Sources

Dependent Variable
Given the constructed regression models, the dependent variable was defined as the number of female victims of sexual violence. The dataset comprises 3,639 registered victims from January 2019 to December 2023. This variable was derived from the dataset of victims of various crimes[1], and it includes detailed information on the gender and age of the victims. For the purposes of this study, only the records pertaining to female victims were selected.

Independent Variables
In addition to the dependent variable, several independent variables related to the female population were considered, given that the dependent variable belongs exclusively to female victims. These variables correlate with socio-demographic and economic factors, which are postulated to impact the prevalence of sexual violence, as evidenced by related work [6–9]. The following independent variables were considered:

1. Victims by Age Group. The dataset employs a categorization of victims into three age groups: 0–18 years, 19–64 years, and 65 years and older. This categorization facilitates an understanding of the distribution of sexual violence across different life stages.
2. Population. The total female population in each micro-statistical area.
3. Illiteracy Rate. The number of female individuals who are unable to read or write.
4. Population with Incomplete Education. The number of females who have not completed their basic education.
5. Population at Schools. The population currently enrolled in educational institutions between the ages of 18 and 24.
6. Average Years of Schooling. The average number of years of schooling completed by the female population.
7. Economically Active Population. The number of females of working age who are engaged in employment or who are actively seeking employment.

[1] https://datos.cdmx.gob.mx/dataset/victimas-en-carpetas-de-investigacion-fgj.

8. Economically Inactive Population. The number of females who are not part of the labor force.
9. Population with Employment. The number of females in the population who are currently employed in some capacity.
10. Population without Employment. The number of females in the population who are currently unemployed.
11. Homes with Dirt Floors. The number of residential units with dirt floors, which is indicative of a lower socio-economic status.
12. Poverty Percentage. The range of poverty percentages per micro-statistical areas.

These variables were selected based on their potential relevance to the incidence of sexual violence. The variables related to the numbers of the female population were collected from the INEGI[2], and those associated with socio-economic aspects and poverty percentages[3] were gathered from the CONEVAL (*Consejo Nacional de Evaluación de la Política de Desarrollo Social*, in Spanish) [14].

2.3 Study Design

Our approach involves determining whether the data pertaining to the victims exhibited spatial autocorrelation. This is accomplished through the calculation of Moran's I statistic [15]. In the event of the detection of spatial autocorrelation, the identification of spatial clusters is conducted through the utilization of Local Indicators of Spatial Association (LISA) [16].

Once spatial autocorrelation has been identified, three different metrics are employed to correlate diverse variables. In light of the findings, four Geographically Weighted Regression (GWR) models [17] are developed for the purpose of examining the relationship between sexual violence and a range of population and socio-economic variables. Subsequently, the most suitable model is then compared to other regression models using the Kolmogorov-Smirnov test [18] to ascertain the p-value of the general model. Following the application of the regression models, the impact of specific variables within the Moran's I clusters is analyzed, thereby offering a more nuanced understanding of the socio-economic factors at play in these areas.

2.3.1 Global and Local Moran

In order to obtain the spatial autocorrelation between the different areas of Mexico City, the Global Moran's Index [15] was first employed and then the Anselin Local Moran's Index [16]. The Global Moran Index is an extension of the Pearson coefficient with spatial weights that measure the spatial correlation between spatial units. This index is represented in Eq. 1 [15]:

$$I = \frac{n}{\sum_{i=1}^{n}\sum_{j=1}^{n} w_{ij}} \frac{\sum_{i=1}^{n}\sum_{j=1}^{n} w_{ij}(y_i - \overline{y})(y_j - \overline{y})}{\sum_{i=1}^{n}\sum_{j=1}^{n} w_{ij}} \tag{1}$$

[2] https://www.inegi.org.mx/app/scitel/Default?ev=10.

[3] https://www.coneval.org.mx/medicion/paginas/pobreza_localidad_urbana.aspx.

where y_i denotes n observations with mean $\overline{y}$ that are spatially connected via weights w_{ij}.

The Local Moran's index is a statistical tool that quantifies the degree of spatial autocorrelation between locations. It provides a formal representation of the identification of clusters between local areas, as illustrated by Eq. 2.

$$I_i = \left(\frac{x_i - \overline{X}}{s^2}\right)\sum_{j-1}^{n} w_{ij}\left(x_j - \overline{X}\right) \tag{2}$$

where I_i is the Local Moran's index for the location I, x_i is the value of an attribute at location i, $\overline{X}$ is the mean of the corresponding attribute,s^2 is the variance of the attribute, w_{ij} are the spatial weights between locations I, and j and n is the total number of locations in the dataset.

Both indices were employed to ascertain whether victims of sexual violence exhibited spatial autocorrelation at the general level. The Global Moran's I offers an overall measure of spatial autocorrelation across the entire study area, whereas the Local Moran's I facilitates the identification of specific areas (clusters) exhibiting high or low spatial autocorrelation.

2.3.2 Metrics

In order to obtain the degree of correlation between the variables that may be employed in the regression models and the number of cases of sexual violence, three distinct metrics were utilized. Two of these metrics, Bivariate Moran's I and Pearson's correlation, were utilized to assess the relationship between variables and the number of victims of sexual violence. Furthermore, the Bivariate Moran's Index is associated with a P-value and a Z-score, which quantify the strength and significance of the relationship between the dependent and the independent variables. The third metric, the Variance Inflation Factor (VIF), was employed to assess the presence of collinearity among the variables, thereby facilitating the determination of which variables should be included or excluded in the models.

Bivariate Moran's Index

The bivariate Moran's Index represents an extension of Moran's Index, facilitating the calculation of spatial autocorrelation between two variables. This index is particularly useful for exploring spatial relations within a specific region. The calculation of this index is performed using Eq. 3 [19], which is presented below:

$$I = \frac{n\sum_{i=1}^{n}\sum_{j=1}^{n} w_{ij}(x_i - \overline{x})\left(y_j - \overline{y}\right)}{\left(\sum_{i=1}^{n}\sum_{j=1}^{n} w_{ij}\right)\sum_{i=1}^{n}(x_i - \overline{x})} \tag{3}$$

where n is the number of observations, x_i and y_i are the values of the variables X and Y, $\overline{x}$ and $\overline{y}$ are the means of the variables, and w_{ij} is the spatial weights between the locations.

Pearson Correlation

The Pearson's correlation coefficient is a measure of the linear relationship between two variables [20]. It is calculated using the Eq. 4:

$$r = \frac{\sum_{i=1}^{n}(x_i - \overline{x})(y_i - \overline{y})}{\sqrt{\sum_{i=1}^{n}(x_i - \overline{x})^2 \sum_{i=1}^{n}(y_i - \overline{y})^2}} \tag{4}$$

where r is the Pearson coefficient, x_i and y_i are the values of the variables, and $\overline{x}$ and $\overline{y}$ are the means of the variables. This coefficient ranges from -1 to 1, where 1 indicates a perfect positive relationship and -1 a perfect negative relationship between the variables. In this study it was used to see the relationship between the dependent and the independent variables.

Variance Inflation Factor (VIF)

The Variance Inflation Factor (VIF) [21] is a statistical measure that quantifies the degree of multicollinearity among the independent variables in a regression model. It is calculated using Eq. 5:

$$VIF_i = \frac{1}{1 - R_i^2} \tag{5}$$

where R_i^2 is the coefficient of determination of the regression of variables I on all other independent variables. A VIF value exceeding 10 is indicative of high multicollinearity, which can render the regression model unstable and the regression coefficient estimates unreliable.

2.3.3 Regression Models

In this study, three regression models were employed, each incorporating a spatial aspect. These were Geographically Weighted Regression (GWR), Ordinary Least Squares (OLS), and Generalized Method of Moments (GM Lag), all utilizing the same spatial weight matrix.

Geographically Weighted Regression (GWR) [17] allows for the modeling of spatially varying relationships by providing localized parameter estimates for each location. The model is expressed by Eq. 6:

$$y_i = \beta_0(u_i, v_i) + \sum_{k-1}^{p} \beta_k(u_i, v_i)x_{ik} + \epsilon_i \tag{6}$$

where (u_i, v_i) are the coordinates of location i, $\beta_0(u_i, v_i)$ is the intercept, $\beta_k(u_i, v_i)$ are the coefficients and ϵ_i is the error term.

Ordinary Least Squares (OLS) is a traditional regression model that estimates the relationship between a dependent variable and one or more independent variables [22]. Despite being a global model, OLS can be extended to account for spatial aspects using a spatial weight matrix, as expressed by Eq. 7:

$$y = X\beta + \epsilon \tag{7}$$

where y is the dependent variable, X is the matrix of independent variables,β is the vector of coefficients, and ϵ is the error term.

The Generalized Method of Moments (GM Lag) [23] addresses potential endogeneity employing instrumental variables and incorporating spatial lag terms, as expressed by Eq. 8:

$$y = \rho Wy + X\beta + \epsilon \tag{8}$$

where y is the dependent variable, Wy is the spatially lagged dependent variable, X is the matrix of independent variables, β is the vector of coefficients, ρ is the spatial autoregressive coefficient, and ϵ is the error term.

The three models were compared, and the model with the best fit was selected based on its performance metrics, including R2 and Mean Absolute Error (MAE). Additionally, the p-value obtained by the Kolmogorov test, a statistical test used to determine whether a sample of data follows a specific distribution, was considered. This approach is particularly useful when the theoretical distribution is not fully specified, as it allows for the comparison of the empirical distribution of the data with any specified theoretical distribution [18].

Once the optimal model was determined, the analysis of the significance of various variables within the spatial clusters identified using Local Moran's Index proceeded. This approach allowed us to understand how different demographic, socioeconomic, and spatial factors contribute to the incidence of sexual violence in Mexico City.

3 Results

The initial step involved the identification of clusters of victims of sexual violence in Mexico City using spatial autocorrelation techniques. First, a Global Moran's Index to assess the overall spatial correlation of female victims of sexual violence across all areas was conducted. The results of the Global Moran's Index are summarized in Table 1, which provides insights into the spatial distribution and clustering tendencies of these incidents.

Table 1. Spatial correlation of female victims of sexual violence using Global Moran's

Global Moran's Index	P-value	Z-score
0.2511	0.001	20.40

The spatial correlation analysis, as indicated by the Global Moran's Index (Table 1), revealed a notable spatial autocorrelation among areas with respect to sexual violence victims in Mexico City, resulting in a value of 0.2511. This finding is substantiated by the p-value of 0.001 and a z-score of 20.40, which confirm the presence of spatial autocorrelation within the study area. Subsequently, Local Moran's Index was employed to identify distinct clusters (hotspots and coldspots), and outliers (doughnuts and diamonds), as illustrated in Fig. 1.

Figure 1 demonstrates that a notable number of cases (hotspots) of reported sexual violence incidents in Mexico City are concentrated in the central areas of the city. This

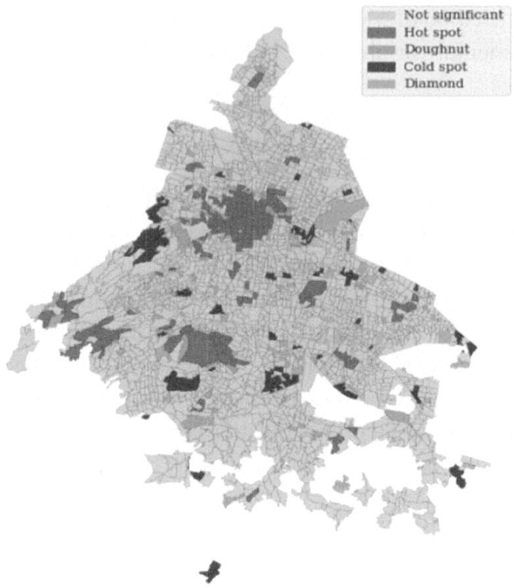

Fig. 1. Clusters identified using Anselin's Local Moran's Index

spatial clustering analysis offers valuable insights into the geographical distribution and tendencies of sexual violence, identifying areas of heightened concern within the city. The identification of these clusters is crucial for understanding the spatial distribution of sexual violence and for pinpointing areas with significantly higher or lower incidences. The identified clusters were then used to analyze the significance of the variables of the model within each cluster, thereby providing insights into how these factors impact sexual violence in different areas of Mexico City.

Following the acquisition of the spatial correlation analysis, the Pearson correlation, bivariate Moran's I, and VIF (see Table 2) were calculated for the variables under consideration. These values were taken into account when selecting the variables for the regression models.

As illustrated in Table 2, certain variables exhibiting a high Pearson correlation also display a high VIF value. Such examples include population, both those who are economically active and those who are inactive, as well as the population with and without employment. The elevated VIF values may render regression models unstable and susceptible to inaccuracies. Considering these findings, four distinct GWR models were devised, each employing a distinct set of criteria and variables.

- Model 1. This model was implemented using all the variables irrespective of their VIF value and the correlations calculated.
- Model 2. It was implemented using variables with a VIF value of less than 10.
- Model 3. The model was obtained using variables with a VIF under 5, irrespective of the correlation value, given that both Pearson and Bivariate correlations are low for the variables representing average years of schooling and poverty percentages.

Table 2. Metrics calculated for the variables under consideration

Variables	Pearson Correlation	Bivariate Moran's Index			VIF
		Index	P-value	Z-score	
Victims (0–18 years old)	0.484	0.118	0.001	9.646	1.079
Victims (19–64 years old)	0.935	0.236	0.001	19.834	1.222
Victims (≥ 65 years old)	0.115	0.022	0.052	1.728	1.019
Population	0.394	0.135	0.001	10.991	508.572
Illiteracy Rate	0.270	0.092	0.001	7.330	7.752
Population with incomplete education	0.261	0.092	0.001	7.414	5.614
Population at Schools	0.363	0.120	0.001	9.946	9.828
Average years of Schooling	0.010	0.022	0.028	1.881	2.351
Economically Active Population	0.413	0.159	0.001	12.904	3722731.602
Economically Inactive Population	0.354	0.104	0.001	8.457	109.414
Population with Employment	0.414	0.159	0.001	12.931	3595089.660
Population without Employment	0.311	0.115	0.001	9.205	1627.793
Homes with Dirt Floor	0.134	0.011	0.177	0.879	1.571
Poverty Percentage	−0.018	−0.022	0.033	−1.810	2.214

- Model 4. This model was implemented using variables with the highest VIF, which exceed 10, and thus represent variables with a higher correlation.

The results of this implementation are shown in Table 3, which presents the GWR models along with their corresponding variables. Additionally, this table shows the p-value resulting from the Kolmogorov test, the statistic of this test, R2, and the MAE of the model.

Model 3 was selected as the optimal model based on its superior performance, as evidenced by its R2 value of 0.959, which is the highest among all models. This indicates that Model 3 is the most effective in explaining the variance in the dependent variable, suggesting a superior fit. Furthermore, the MAE value of the model is 0.014,

Table 3. GWR models

Variables	GWR Model (1)	GWR Model (2)	GWR Model (3)	GWR Model (4)
Victims (0–18 years old)	0.229	0.232	0.231	
Victims (19–64 years old)	0.951	0.958	0.961	
Victims (≥ 65 years old)	0.159		0.160	0.209
Population	−0.026			
Illiteracy Rate	0.001	−0.008		
Population with incomplete education	0.001	0.005		
Population at Schools	0.005	0.022		
Average years of Schooling		0.018	0.013	
Economically Active Population	20.932			92.804
Economically Inactive Population	−0.010			−0.146
Population with Employment	−20.486			−90.251
Population without Employment	−0.384			−1.809
Homes with Dirt Floor	−0.384	−0.025	−0.010	
Poverty Percentage		0.013	0.005	
P-value	0.0	0.0	0.0	$8.34*10^{-27}$
Statistic	0.392	0.387	0.418	0.11
R2	0.958	0.955	0.959	0.188
MAE	0.014	0.015	0.014	0.082

which is among the lowest compared to the other models, indicating a higher degree of prediction accuracy and a lower incidence of errors in the model's predictions. The p-value for Model 3 is 0.0, indicating that the results are statistically significant and that the model's predictors are reliable. The statistic value for Model 3 is 0.418, which, although not the lowest, is within an acceptable range for model performance. The selected model includes variables with a VIF value of less than 5, which ensures that multicollinearity is kept in check and maintains the stability and reliability of the model's coefficients. Notwithstanding the low Pearson and bivariate correlations, key variables such as the average years of schooling and poverty percentages have been included in the model, thereby ensuring that important demographic and socio-economic factors are not excluded from the analysis.

With Model 3 selected, a comparative analysis was conducted of the performance of this model against OLS and GM Lag, both of which employ a spatial weight matrix. Although these models do not return coefficients at a regional level, as GWR does, they serve as a valuable reference point for evaluating the overall efficacy of spatial regression techniques. The comparison highlights the advantages of utilizing GWR for capturing local variations and spatial heterogeneity. The findings of this comparison are presented in Table 4.

Table 4. Regression models comparative

Variables	GWR Model (3)	OLS	GM Lag
Victims (0–18 years old)	0.231	0.284	0.282
Victims (19–64 years old)	0.961	0.868	0.861
Victims ($\geq$ 65 years old)	0.160	0.064	0.064
Average years of Schooling	0.013	0.011	0.010
Homes with Dirt Floor	−0.010	−0.001	−0.001
Poverty Percentage	0.005	0.001	0.001
P-value	0.0	0.0	0.0
Statistic	0.418	0.423	0.420
R2	0.959	0.957	0.958
MAE	0.014	0.112	0.111

The results presented in Table 4 demonstrate that the GWR model exhibits superior performance in terms of R2, the statistical measure, and MAE. Although the p-value is similar across all three models according to the Kolmogorov test, the coefficient values demonstrate that the GWR model has superior performance in fitting the spatial variations. In particular, the GWR model provides more precise estimates for the coefficients of key variables, such as victims in different age ranges. These variables exhibit higher and more accurate coefficients in the GWR model compared to the OLS and GM Lag models.

Moreover, the R2 value for the GWR model is marginally higher (0.959) than for the OLS (0.957) and GM Lag (0.958) models, indicating that the GWR model accounts for a slightly greater proportion of the variance in the data. Furthermore, the mean absolute error (MAE) for the GWR model is significantly lower (0.014) in comparison to the OLS (0.112) and GM Lag (0.111) models, indicating that the GWR model provides more precise predictions.

The statistical values are nearly identical across the models, with the GWR model exhibiting a value of 0.418, while the OLS and GM Lag models demonstrated values of 0.423 and 0.420, respectively. This consistency across models indicates that all models perform well, but the GWR model shows slight superiority in terms of overall fit and predictive accuracy.

Fig. 2. The impact of the average years of schooling on (a) hotspots, (b) coldspots, (c) doughnuts, and (d) diamonds

Subsequently, the results of Local Moran's I are utilized to examine the behavior of specific variables from the GWR model within the identified clusters. Figure 2 depicts the impact of the average years of schooling on the prevalence of hotspots (a), coldspots (b), doughnuts (c), and diamonds (d). Moreover, the percentage of poverty was identified as a variable that exerted an influence on the models. Despite the relatively minor effect, it was statistically significant and exhibited low collinearity. Figure 3 illustrates the impact of this variable on hotspots (a), coldspots (b), doughnuts (c), and diamonds (d).

Fig. 3. The impact of the poverty percentages on (a) hotspots, (b) coldspots, (c) doughnuts, and (d) diamonds.

4 Discussion

The application of spatial autocorrelation methods, such as the Global and Local Moran's Indices, is of particular significance in the analysis of the geographic distribution of sexual violence in urban areas. The Global Moran's Index facilitated the identification of non-random spatial patterns in Mexico City, indicating that incidents of sexual violence are not randomly distributed but tend to cluster in specific areas. This indicates the presence of underlying factors that influence the concentration of these incidents in specific zones. Conversely, the implementation of the Local Moran's Index on data pertaining to victims of sexual violence facilitated the discernment of distinct clusters wherein the prevalence of sexual violence is more or less concentrated, with a particular emphasis on the GWR coefficients associated with the four clusters identified through the Local Moran's Index.

The results of our analysis indicate that the concentration of hotspots is predominantly located in the central areas of Mexico City. This suggests that these regions are particularly vulnerable and may require targeted interventions. In contrast, the distribution of cold spots is not confined to a particular region; rather, they are dispersed throughout the city. With regard to outliers, the doughnut clusters are dispersed, yet some of the micro-statistical areas are in close proximity to hotspots, which aligns with the cluster definition of a low surrounded by high values. A similar distribution is observed for diamonds, which are also dispersed throughout the city. Some of the areas in question are situated in close proximity to cold spots, which aligns with the definition of a diamond.

The employment of a range of metrics, including the Bivariate Moran's Index, Pearson correlation, and VIF, was instrumental in evaluating the interrelationships between the variables and the prevalence of sexual violence. The Bivariate Moran's Index facilitated the elucidation of the spatial autocorrelation between the variables and sexual violence, whereas the Pearson correlation enabled the determination of the strength of the relationships. The VIF was of paramount importance in the assessment of multicollinearity, thereby ensuring the robustness and reliability of our regression models.

Furthermore, the VIF proved to be an invaluable tool in the application of GWR, as it addressed the issue of multicollinearity among independent variables and identified the most pertinent variables for model implementation, while simultaneously reducing its variability. The value led us to conclude that the third model, which incorporates variables such as average years of schooling and poverty percentages, represents the most optimal model. These variables were found to have a significant impact on sexual violence incidents, despite exhibiting low Pearson and Bivariate correlations. They proved to be crucial in capturing the socioeconomic factors affecting sexual violence.

The third model demonstrated that the age of victims is a particularly salient factor when fitting the model to the data. To illustrate, the variable representing victims aged 19–64 exhibited a positive impact, indicating that regions with a higher prevalence of sexual violence victims in this age group tend to have a higher overall incidence of reported sexual violence.

A comparison of this model with the other two regression models, OLS and GM Lag, reveals that GWR exhibits superior performance in terms of R2, MAE, and the statistic resulting from the Kolmogorov test. Although both the OLS model and GM Lag employ a geographic weights matrix that considers area changes, the result is a single value for the entire study area. In contrast, GWR reveals how this relationship varies significantly across different regions of the city, thus allowing the visualization of the disparate impacts of the variables used in the study. However, GWR also has inherent limitations, including increased computational complexity and the potential for multicollinearity. These issues have been addressed in this study through the use of VIF.

The observation of these differences at the local level in the various clusters identified by Local Moran's I statistic indicates that the age of victims has a positive impact on the model in the different clustered areas. The average years of schooling, as illustrated in Fig. 2, also exerts a positive influence in all the areas identified as hotspots to a certain degree, indicating that elevated levels of education are associated with elevated incidences of reported sexual violence. This may suggest that in these particular regions, individuals with higher levels of education are either more likely to report incidents of sexual violence or that there is a greater awareness and recognition of what constitutes sexual violence, leading to higher reporting rates. This behavior is analogous in cold spots, with a few areas exhibiting a negative impact, which could indicate that in these regions, increased education is associated with lower rates of sexual violence. A comparison of the other clusters reveals a similar behavior to that observed in the hotspots, with a comparable degree of variation. This is an expected outcome, given that the model GWR considers the spatial neighbors, with the majority of these areas situated in close proximity to the hotspots. In a manner similar to diamonds with coldspots, the impact of the variable is comparable to that observed in the coldspots, despite the presence of high values surrounded by low values.

In comparison to the results presented in [9], the variable in question exhibited a negative coefficient, indicating that individuals with lower educational levels are more likely to engage in sexual violence. This is contrary to our findings. The discrepancy can be attributed to the distinct dependent variable and the presence of other social and structural variables in the region that are not comparable to the socio-cultural context of Mexico City.

With respect to the poverty percentage variable, a positive correlation exists between higher poverty rates and reported sexual violence in hotspots. However, not all hotspots exhibit high poverty rates, suggesting that even modest increases in poverty may be associated with elevated rates of sexual violence. This suggests that even at lower levels, poverty represents a significant risk factor for sexual violence in these regions.

In contrast, the poverty percentage variable has a negative coefficient in most of the coldspot areas, indicating that higher levels of poverty are associated with lower incidences of reported sexual violence. This could indicate that in these regions, the link between poverty and sexual violence may be less pronounced, or that other factors are attenuating the impact of poverty on sexual violence rates. In some areas of the coldspots, the poverty percentage variable has a positive coefficient, indicating that higher poverty levels are associated with higher incidences of reported sexual violence. This is similar to the relationship observed in the hot spots. This variability indicates that the relationship between poverty and sexual violence may vary considerably across regions, potentially due to differences in local conditions, social service availability, and community dynamics.

This study presents significant findings regarding the application of GWR and its correlation with Local Moran's clusters. It is important to note, however, that sexual violence is often underreported. It is frequently caused by factors such as social stigma, fear of retaliation, and a lack of trust in the legal system [1]. This could lead to some misunderstanding of the circumstances, but it is evident that some variables are indeed related and can, to some extent, explain the reporting patterns observed in specific zones, which have been classified as hotspots or coldspots.

5 Conclusions and Future Work

This work has provided a comprehensive spatial analysis of sexual violence against women in Mexico City, underscoring the pivotal role of spatial considerations in comprehending and confronting this pervasive issue. Four distinct GWR models were developed and subsequently analyzed. The most fitting model was selected for comparison with other regression models that utilize spatial weights or coordinates. In this case, we have employed both the OLS and GM Lag regression models. The GWR model illustrated the pivotal role of variables such as age, education, and poverty in elucidating the spatial distribution of sexual violence. It is imperative that future research and policy efforts address the limitations of underreporting in order to fully understand and combat sexual violence.

As future work, we intend to consider additional variables, such as surveys about security in Mexico City and other population variables related to characteristics such as beliefs or skin color. Moreover, we plan to extend our analysis to encompass other regression models. Furthermore, the regression models applied to each cluster will be considered, allowing for the examination of separate models at varying levels. Additionally, temporal patterns will be explored to gain a more comprehensive understanding of the dynamics of sexual violence in urban settings. The potential for integrating qualitative data to obtain deeper insights into the lived experiences of survivors and the socio-cultural contexts influencing reporting and victimization rates will also be analyzed.

References

1. World Health Organization. Violence against women prevalence estimates, 2018: global, regional and national prevalence estimates for intimate partner violence against women and global and regional prevalence estimates for non-partner sexual violence against women. World Health Organization (2021). https://iris.who.int/handle/10665/341337
2. Chaudhury, S., Bakhla, A.K., Murthy, P.S., Jagtap, B.: Psychological aspects of rape and its consequences. Psychol. Behav. Sci. Int. J. **2**, 555–586 (2017). https://doi.org/10.19080/PBSIJ.2017.02.555586
3. Kearns, M.C., D'Inverno, A.S., Reidy, D.E.: The association between gender inequality and sexual violence in the US. Am. J. Prev. Med. **58**(1), 12–20 (2020). https://doi.org/10.1016/j.amepre.2019.08.035
4. Garza, A.D., Franklin, C.A.: The effect of rape myth endorsement on police response to sexual assault survivors. Violence Against Women **27**(3–4), 552–573 (2021). https://doi.org/10.1177/1077801220911460
5. Ajayi, A.I., Mudefi, E., Owolabi, E.O.: Prevalence and correlates of sexual violence among adolescent girls and young women: findings from a cross-sectional study in a South African university. BMC Women's Health **21**, 299 (2021). https://doi.org/10.1186/s12905-021-01445-8

6. Aboagye, R.G., Donkoh, I.E., Okyere, J., et al.: Association between sexual violence and multiple high-risk fertility behaviours among women of reproductive age in sub-Saharan Africa. BMC Public Health **24**, 432 (2024). https://doi.org/10.1186/s12889-023-17444-3
7. Amegbor, P.M., Yankey, O., Rosenberg, M.W., Sabel, C.E.: Examining spatial variability in the association between male partner alcohol misuse and intimate partner violence against women in Ghana: a GWR analysis. J. Interpers. ViolenceInterpers. Violence **36**(23–24), NP12855 (2021). https://doi.org/10.1177/0886260519900299
8. Fontes, K.B., Alarcão, A.C.J., Nihei, O.K., Pelloso, S.M., Andrade, L., de Barros Carvalho, M.D.: Regional disparities in the intimate partner sexual violence rate against women in Paraná State, Brazil, 2009–2014: an ecological study. BMJ Open **8**(2), e018437 (2018). https://doi.org/10.1136/bmjopen-2017-018437
9. Horsefield, O.J., Lightowlers, C., Green, M.A.: The spatial effect of alcohol availability on violence: a geographically weighted regression analysis. Appl. Geogr.Geogr. **150**, 102824 (2023). https://doi.org/10.1016/j.apgeog.2022.102824
10. Angaw, D.A., Melesse, A.W., Geremew, B.M., Tesema, G.A.: Spatial distribution and determinants of intimate partner violence among reproductive-age women in Ethiopia: spatial and multilevel analysis. BMC women's health **21**, 1–13 (2021). https://doi.org/10.1186/s12905-021-01218-3
11. Andresen, M.A.: Predicting local crime clusters using (multinomial) logistic regression. Cityscape **17**(3), 249–262 (2015)
12. Reyal, H.P., Dissanayake, N., Gunarathna, H., Soysa, D., Fernando, M.S., Senarathna, L.: Association between individual-level socioeconomic factors and intimate partner violence victimisation in women: a systematic review protocol. BMJ Open **14**(3), e080117 (2024). https://doi.org/10.1136/bmjopen-2023-080117
13. Herbert, A., et al.: Exploring the causal role of intimate partner violence and abuse on depressive symptoms in young adults: a population-based cohort study. BMC Med. **20**, 1–13 (2022). https://doi.org/10.1186/s12916-021-02182-3
14. CONEVAL. La Pobreza Urbana en México: Un Enfoque Geoespacial. https://www.coneval.org.mx/Medicion/Documents/Pobreza_urbana/Documentos_metodologicos/Nota_tecnica.pdf. Last Accessed 21 June 2024
15. Getis, A.: Spatial autocorrelation. In: Fischer, M., Getis, A. (eds.) Handbook of Applied Spatial Analysis. Springer, Berlin, Heidelberg (2010). https://doi.org/10.1007/978-3-642-03647-7_14
16. Anselin, L.: Local indicators of spatial association—LISA. Geogr. Anal.. Anal. **27**(2), 93–115 (1995). https://doi.org/10.1111/j.1538-4632.1995.tb00338.x
17. Fotheringham, A.S., Brunsdon, C., Charlton, M.E.: Geographically weighted regression. The Sage Handbook of Spatial Analysis **1**, 243–254 (2009)
18. Smirnov, N.: Table for estimating the goodness of fit of empirical distributions. Ann. Math. Stat. **19**(2), 279–281 (1948)
19. Lee, S.I.: Developing a bivariate spatial association measure: an integration of Pearson's r and Moran's I. J. Geograph. Syst. **3**, 369–385 (2001). https://doi.org/10.1007/s101090100064
20. Pearson, K.: VII. Note on regression and inheritance in the case of two parents. Proc. R. Soc. Lond.Lond. **58**(347–352), 240–242 (1895). https://doi.org/10.1098/rspl.1895.0041
21. O'brien, R.M.: A caution regarding rules of thumb for variance inflation factors. Qual. Quan. **41**, 673–690 (2007). https://doi.org/10.1007/s11135-006-9018-6
22. Draper, N.R., Smith, H.: Applied Regression Analysis, vol. 326. John Wiley & Sons (1998)
23. Hansen, L.P.: Large sample properties of generalized method of moments estimators. Econom. J. Econom. Soc. **50**, 1029–1054 (1982)

Geographic Gamification Strategies in Mathematics Education: Enhancing Linear Algebra Learning at the Technological University of Cancún

Irvin Arlin Chan Ac(✉), Kermin Dayan Peña Santoyo, Sergio Roberto Preza Medina, Sandra Hernández Chacón, and Yamit López Cetina

Universidad Tecnológica de Cancún, Carretera Cancún-Aeropuerto Km. 115, S.M. 299, Mz. 5, Lt. 1, C.P. 77500 Cancún, Quintana Roo, Mexico
iachan@utcancun.edu.mx

Abstract. Innovative education in the Mexican context does not necessarily require sophisticated or inaccessible hardware and software. Educators must understand global educational innovation trends without being confined to them. Ramírez-Montoya et al. [1] identified creativity, entrepreneurship, and implementation as key conceptual axes in Mexican Higher Education Institutions, emphasizing the importance of policy support for sustainable educational innovations. Active educational methodologies, particularly gamification, have gained prominence for enhancing digital skills and motivating learning through game design elements in non-game contexts [2]. Before implementing new educational practices and tools, educators must assess their effectiveness in teaching-learning processes, with advanced technologies, such as artificial intelligence (AI), playing a crucial role. Machine learning, particularly clustering techniques, helps personalizing education by identifying learning preferences and segmenting student groups [3, 4]. This study proposes using gamification in Linear Algebra learning and a logistic regression model to evaluate the effectiveness of educational innovations in the learning processes. Students in the Technological University of Cancún's TSU in Maintenance program experienced gamified linear algebra learning, integrating academic data into the artificial intelligence algorithm to determine innovation effectiveness and educational needs, ultimately personalizing education. The research question explored the impact of gamification tools on student performance in linear algebra.

Keywords: Gamification · Educational Innovation · Artificial Intelligence Algorithms · Personalized Learning · Logistic Regression · Smart Education

1 Introduction

Educational innovation in the Mexican context does not necessarily require the application of sophisticated or inaccessible hardware or software for certain communities. However, this paradigm must be understood by every educator who chooses to pursue

M. F. Mata-Rivera et al. (Eds.): GIS-LATAM 2024, CCIS 2298, pp. 122–137, 2025.
https://doi.org/10.1007/978-3-031-80017-7_8

innovation in their daily practice. It is crucial to comprehend global trends in educational innovation without being limited by them. Ramírez-Montoya et al. [1] have indicated that educational innovation within the context of Mexican Higher Education Institutions (HEIs) is associated with three conceptual pillars: creativity, entrepreneurship, and intervention or implementation. Moreover, they emphasize the need for educational policies that support educational innovation and its research to ensure sustainability long enough for implementations to gain social relevance. These authors encourage educators and educational researchers to "continue gathering, researching, and designing strategies to obtain more quantitative and qualitative information" on educational innovation.

Among active educational methodologies, gamification stands out for its seamless integration with the digital skills that students may develop. It is a technique designed to motivate and enhance learning using game design elements in non-game contexts [2]. The term emerged in 2002 when Pelling, a British game developer, applied gaming concepts to user interfaces in applications to make electronic transactions more enjoyable and faster. Recent trends position gamification as an innovation that converges, from an educational research perspective, between studies on teacher perspectives and the development of transversal competences.

However, before implementing new educational practices and tools, educators must consider the effectiveness these innovations will generate in teaching-learning processes. This consideration is crucial in research on educational innovation, where the use of advanced technologies is becoming a pressing need to address research problems. The use of artificial intelligence (AI) for critical decision-making in organizations has increased and evolved. Through AI algorithms, a mathematical model can be "trained" to associate organizational goals with supplied data sets, for instance, to predict whether a new employee will remain in a company based on data such as age, gender, income, work history, etc.

Machine learning, particularly clustering, has been the subject of study by various authors. Gironés et al. [3] have explored the application of clustering techniques in the personalization of education and how these techniques can be adapted to students' learning preferences. Clustering algorithms allow the segmentation of student groups with similar learning characteristics, facilitating the adaptation of pedagogical strategies [4]. This approach can be considered a tool for identifying behavioral patterns and learning preferences, contributing to personalized education. It is important to note that machine learning can be managed using various tools, such as neural networks. Works like [5] provide an overview of neural networks and their application in classification and prediction problems, highlighting their ability to model complex relationships. Another study, [6], focuses on the implementation of an Intelligent Tutoring System aimed at learning algebra, exploring how these networks can be adapted to enhance mathematics education.

Thus, this research proposed to develop an AI model that could determine the effectiveness of an educational innovation (gamification) in the learning process of a group of students with defined characteristics. This would allow for data-driven curricular and educational intervention decisions based on the academic achievement that students are expected to attain, while also integrating data that would be difficult to analyze, such as learning styles, attitudes toward mathematics, and background knowledge.

During the development of the following project, students from the University Higher Technician (TSU) in Maintenance program at the Division of Engineering and Technology at the Technological University of Cancún (UTC) experienced educational innovation through the gamification of Linear Algebra learning in the first trimester of the educational program. This approach combined technology, educational games, and positive reinforcement strategies. However, the implementation generated input and output data on academic performance in the subject, which were integrated into the AI algorithm along with the academic background data to determine the innovation's effectiveness and establish patterns of educational needs. In the long term, this will enable personalized education and the optimal use of each student's intrinsic abilities. The research question, meticulously analyzed by advanced technologies, was: What is the impact of gamification tools on student academic performance in learning Linear Algebra?.

2 Development

2.1 Background

Education has undergone a significant transformation with the incorporation of advanced technologies and innovative methodologies. Gamification has emerged as a promising technique to enhance student engagement and performance. Gamification involves the use of game design elements in non-game contexts to motivate and increase student participation in the learning process [2].

Research in educational innovation highlights the importance of integrating active methodologies that promote digital skills and meaningful learning. Previous studies have demonstrated that gamification can enhance intrinsic motivation and academic performance [5]. However, the effectiveness of this methodology in specific contexts, such as linear algebra learning, requires rigorous evaluation through both quantitative and qualitative approaches.

2.2 Problem Statement

The objective of this research is to determine whether gamification has a positive effect on the learning of linear algebra in a group of students enrolled in the University Higher Technician (TSU) in Maintenance program at the Division of Engineering and Technology at the Technological University of Cancún (UTC). The research question is: What is the impact of gamification tools on student academic performance in learning the Linear Algebra course?

To address this question, a logistic regression model was developed to predict the improvement in student performance using various academic and demographic variables. This approach allows for the identification of the factors that most significantly influence the effectiveness of gamification, and evaluates whether this methodology contributes meaningfully to the learning of linear algebra.

2.3 Research Design

The study aimed to evaluate the impact of gamification teaching strategies applied at a Linear Algebra course at a University Higher Technician program in Maintenance, measured as achievement levels, but integrating indirectly related data like admission exam results, learning styles tests, and attitude toward mathematics tests; supported by an IA model. For that purpose, a semi-experimental quantitative approach was used, due to the impossibility of fully randomizing experimental units (groups of students); although the application of standardized data collection tools, as well as the support of machine learning algorithms, allowed the establishment of significant quantitative inferences about the effectiveness of gamification strategies.

2.4 Sample and Study Group

During the spring trimester of the 2023–2024 academic year, a group of 48 students was selected for the study. All of the students were signed in the first trimester of the program. 28 students belonged to a control group, which received traditional education strategies in the subject Linear Algebra, whereas 20 students were in the experimental group, which received gamification teaching strategies in the same subject.

2.5 Data Collection Tools

The study was carried out during 13 weeks with 3–4 lessons per week, summing a total of 6 h per week on the subject of Linear Algebra. Therefore, the research was limited to 78 course hours. Measurement instruments used in this research were:

Linear Algebra achievement test: 20 questions multiple choice achievement test, which allowed evaluation of both 4 different units of the course program as follows: Unit 1, Numerical systems: 4 questions; Unit 2, Algebra: 5 questions; Unit 3, Equations and inequations: 5 questions and Unit 4, Linear Algebra: 6 questions. This test was applied to both groups (experimental and control) at the beginning (pre-test) and at the end (post-test) of the course.

Attitude toward Mathematics Inventory (ATMI): to evaluate factors involved in students' expectations from the subject [5]. It's divided into 4 subcategories: Enjoying mathematics, Motivation to do mathematics, Self-confidence about mathematics, and Perceived value of mathematics. The 4 subcategories were analyzed independently during this research. This test was applied to both groups in a physical format at the end of the course.

Kolb's learning styles test: to assess 9 items that allow determining University students' learning styles. Each item contributed to 4 different learning styles (Diverger, Converger, Assimilative, Accommodator) [6]. This test was mandatorily presented by every student at the beginning of autumn trimester 2023–2024.

Academic performance skills and knowledge predictive test, area Mathematical thinking (EXANI-II): used in Mexican higher education admission processes, specifically measuring students' basic skills developed throughout background formation [7]. This test was presented by every student during the admission process before the autumn trimester 2023–2024.

2.6 Implementation Process

In the experimental group, gamification strategies were implemented during the Linear Algebra course. A set of 4 main teaching-learning digital tools was selected and/or developed according to each Unit's learning objectives. For Unit 1 "Numerical systems", a Kahoot instrument challenged student's teams to identify different considerations on pure and complex imaginary numbers; in Unit 2 "Algebra" another Kahoot activity was implemented, to help students developing basic algebraic operations. In Unit 3 "Equations and inequations", the University of Colorado's PhEt simulation tools allowed instructing challenges for students to obtain relationships among variables. Lastly, in Unit 4 "Linear Algebra", a guided set of exercises with the help of the technological education platform Educaplay served for students to make sure about their advance at understanding operations with matrixes. Throughout the course, students obtained prizes and awards that contributed to their unit grades with the help of the platform KeepTheScore, where they could monitor their advances in the form of "monedas" (coins) (Figs. 1, 2, 3, 4 and 5).

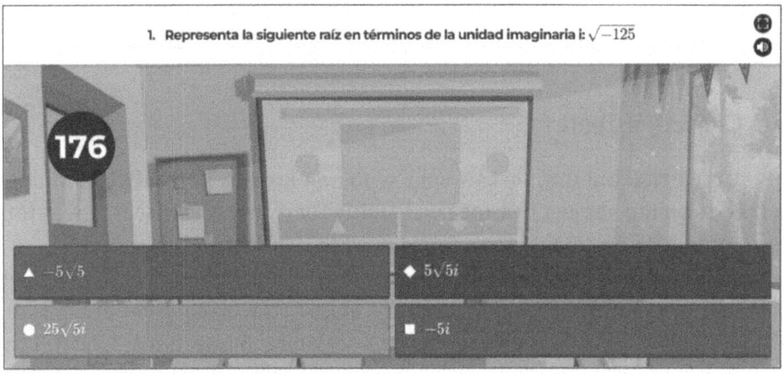

Fig. 1. Kahoot resource used at Unit 1 "Numerical systems".

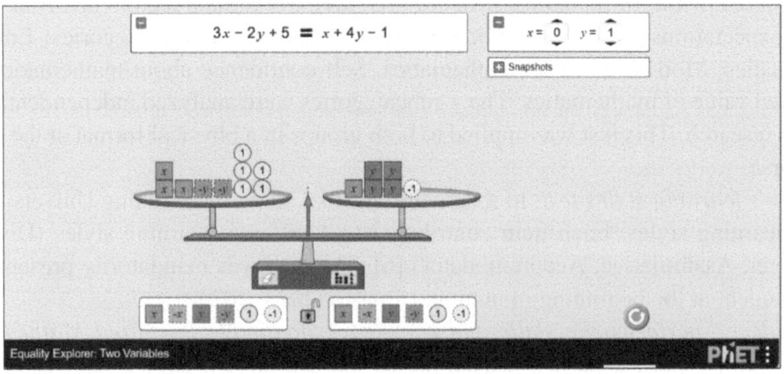

Fig. 2. PhEt simulator used in Unit 3 "Equations and inequations".

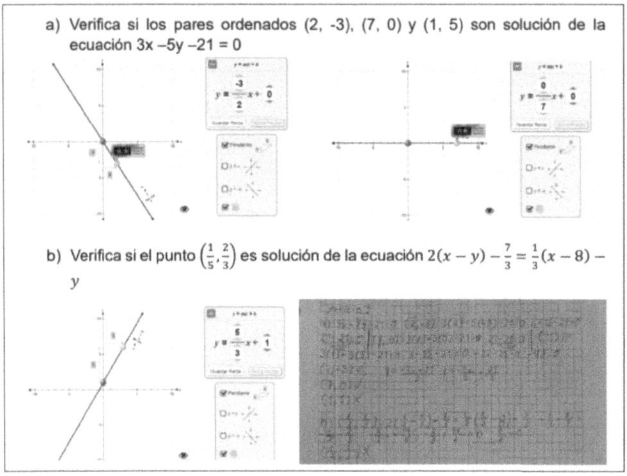

Fig. 3. PhEt simulator used for autonomous challenges at Unit 3 "Equations and inequations".

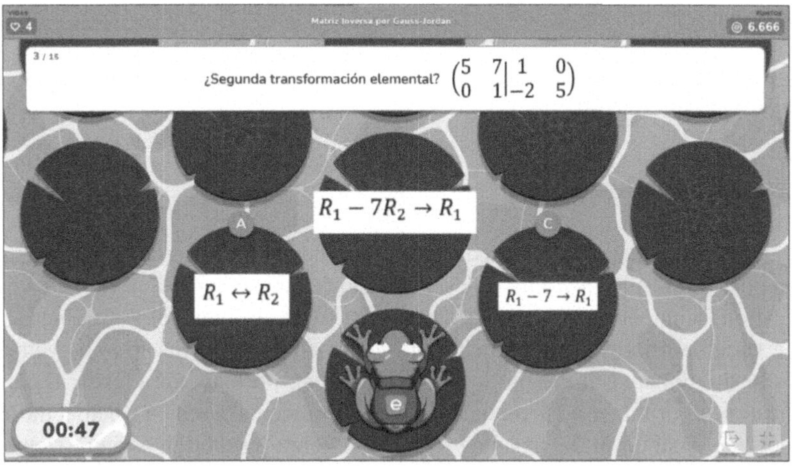

Fig. 4. Educaplay game designed to introduce advances in Unit 4 "Linear Algebra".

2.7 Data Analysis and Predictive Machine Learning Model Preparation

Data obtained at the achievement pre-test and post-test, attitude toward mathematics, as well as background information from students (Mathematical thinking at EXANI-II test and Kolb's learning styles test), were ordered and treated in a variable matrix adding a final column for Gamification strategies applied (yes or no). Using this database, a logistics regression model was trained through machine learning algorithms to state the level of effectiveness of applying gamification strategies considering related variables like learning styles, attitude/motivation, and background formation. The construction procedure and testing of that model are shown in the following section.

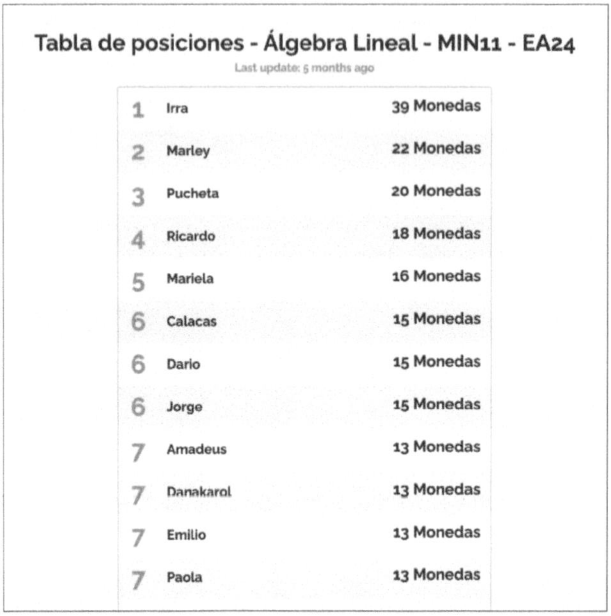

Tabla de posiciones - Álgebra Lineal - MIN11 - EA24

Last update: 5 months ago

1	Irra	39 Monedas
2	Marley	22 Monedas
3	Pucheta	20 Monedas
4	Ricardo	18 Monedas
5	Mariela	16 Monedas
6	Calacas	15 Monedas
6	Dario	15 Monedas
6	Jorge	15 Monedas
7	Amadeus	13 Monedas
7	Danakarol	13 Monedas
7	Emilio	13 Monedas
7	Paola	13 Monedas

Fig. 5. KeepTheScore platform used for students to monitor their advances throughout the course in form of "monedas" (coins).

3 Results and Discussion

The research was conducted using a dataset of 48 students, with variables including pre-test and post-test results, learning styles, admission exam scores (EXANI), and whether gamification techniques were applied. The logistic regression model was trained to predict the variable Improvement, which indicates whether there was an improvement in the post-test compared to the pre-test. The following presents the logistic regression classification algorithm used to predict and classify students based on whether the application of gamification in the teaching of linear algebra resulted in an improvement in their performance. This improvement is understood as the positive difference between the post-test and pre-test results, administered at the end and the beginning of the Linear Algebra course, respectively. This pre-post representational level analysis offers an appropriate comparison of knowledge, as illustrated in early algebra problem analysis studies [8].

To assess the impact of teaching linear algebra through gamification strategies, a logistic regression algorithm was used, which requires a rigorous process of data preparation and division [22]. This step is crucial to ensure the validity and reliability of the obtained results. The following section provides a detailed description of the implemented procedure (Fg. 6).

The DataFrame containing the variables obtained from the tests applied to the students was uploaded to an algorithm on the Google Colab platform which is a platform to run Python programs and data analysis (Fig. 7):

+ Código + Texto

```
#Importar las librerías
import pandas as pd
import numpy as np
import seaborn as sns
import matplotlib.pyplot as plt
from sklearn.model_selection import train_test_split, cross_val_score
from sklearn.linear_model import LogisticRegression
from sklearn.preprocessing import StandardScaler
from sklearn.metrics import classification_report, accuracy_score, roc_auc_score
import joblib
from sklearn.model_selection import train_test_split
```

Fig. 6. Inclusion of Libraries for the Logistic Regression Classification Model

```
#mostramos los primeros 5 registros de nuestro dataframe
pd.set_option('display.max_columns', None)
estudiantes_df.head(5)
```

	Grupo	Matrícula	Nombre	Pre-Test	PromSub1	PromSub2	PromSub3	PromSub4	Estilo de aprendizaje	EXANI Pensamiento Matemático	Gamificación	Post-Test
0	MI11	23333097	ARIAS HERNANDEZ MANUEL BENJAMIN	25.0	3.2	2.50	2.2	3.6	ACOMODADOR	1000.0	No	70.0
1	MI11	23333110	CABRERA RODRIGUEZ JENNIFER	25.0	3.0	3.50	4.0	4.2	ASIMILADOR	980.0	No	35.0
2	MI11	23333127	CHABLE GOMEZ ERIK ARTURO	20.0	3.2	3.50	2.8	4.2	DIVERGENTE	940.0	No	50.0
3	MI11	23333131	CHUMBA SILVA ALEXIS DE JESUS	10.0	4.0	3.00	3.0	5.0	ACOMODADOR	920.0	No	80.0
4	MI11	23333107	DE LA CRUZ DE LA CRUZ IGNACIO	5.0	3.4	3.25	3.4	3.4	DIVERGENTE	1040.0	No	30.0

Fig. 7. DataFrame with the Variables Resulting from the Tests Administered to the Students.

The data was prepared by including a new variable called "improvement," to determine if gamification positively contributed to the student's learning (Figs. 8 and 9).

```
#Paso 1: Preparar los datos
# Crear la columna 'Mejora' con lo cual se analiza la diferencia positiva entre el post-test y el pre-test para determinar
# que la gamificación ayudó de manera positiva al aprendizaje del estudiante

estudiantes_df['Mejora'] = estudiantes_df['Post-Test'] - estudiantes_df['Pre-Test']
estudiantes_df['Mejora'] = estudiantes_df['Mejora'].apply(lambda x: 1 if x > 0 else 0)

# Codificación de variables categóricas
estudiantes_df['Gamificación'] = estudiantes_df['Gamificación'].apply(lambda x: 1 if x == 'Sí' else 0)
estudiantes_df['Estilo de aprendizaje'] = estudiantes_df['Estilo de aprendizaje'].astype('category').cat.codes
```

Fig. 8. Creation of the "improvement" Variable to Assess the Impact of Gamification on the Positive Difference Between Post-Test and Pre-Test.

Feature Selection and Target Variable

Initially, relevant features, also known as independent variables [23], were selected, which are considered to influence the improvement in student performance. The chosen features or variables include:

	Grupo	Matrícula	Nombre	Pre-Test	PromSub1	PromSub2	PromSub3	PromSub4	Estilo de aprendizaje	EXANI Pensamiento Matemático	Gamificación	Post-Test	Mejora
0	MI11	23333097	ARIAS HERNANDEZ MANUEL BENJAMIN	25.0	3.2	2.50	2.2	3.6	0	1000.0	0	70.0	1
1	MI11	23333110	CABRERA RODRIGUEZ JENNIFER	25.0	3.0	3.50	4.0	4.2	1	980.0	0	35.0	1
2	MI11	23333127	CHABLE GOMEZ ERIK ARTURO	20.0	3.2	3.50	2.8	4.2	3	940.0	0	50.0	1
3	MI11	23333131	CHUMBA SILVA ALEXIS DE JESUS	10.0	4.0	3.00	3.0	5.0	0	920.0	0	80.0	1
4	MI11	23333107	DE LA CRUZ DE LA CRUZ IGNACIO	5.0	3.4	3.25	3.4	3.4	3	1040.0	0	30.0	1

Fig. 9. Resulting DataFrame with the Incorporation of the "improvement" Variable and Categorization.

Pre-Test: Initial score before the educational intervention.
PromSub1 to PromSub4: Averages in four related subjects analyzed through the Attitude toward mathematics inventory (ATMI).
Learning Style: Category classifying the student's preferred type of learning.
EXANI Mathematical Thinking: Score on a standardized test of mathematical thinking.
Gamification: Indicator of the gamification strategies application (yes/no).
The dependent variable, termed 'Improvement,' represents the enhancement in student performance following the application of gamification strategies. In logistic regression, the dependent variable [24] is represented as categorical or dichotomous (and one or more independent or explanatory variables) to obtain an estimate.

Data Splitting

To train and evaluate the model, the data were divided into two sets: one for training and one for testing, as required in a supervised learning algorithm [25]. For training, a pre-labeled and classified dataset is necessary. This division was carried out using the 'train_test_split' function from the 'sklearn' library, which is widely recognized in the field of machine learning (Fig. 10).

```
[ ] #Paso 2. División de los datos en los arreglos de entrenamiento y, prueba
    #x; variable independiente x y y variable dependiente.
    from sklearn.model_selection import train_test_split

    features = ['Pre-Test', 'PromSub1', 'PromSub2', 'PromSub3', 'PromSub4', 'Estilo de aprendizaje', 'EXANI Pensamiento Matemático', 'Gamificación']
    X = estudiantes_df[features]
    y = estudiantes_df['Mejora']

    X_train, X_test, y_train, y_test = train_test_split(X, y, test_size=0.2, random_state=42)
```

Fig. 10. Creation of Training and Testing Arrays for the Logistic Regression Algorithm.

Implementation of the Logistic Regression Model

To train the model, we used the sklearn library, known for its efficiency and simplicity in the field of machine learning. Specifically, we employed the 'LogisticRegression' class to construct our model (Fig. 11).

```
[ ] #Paso 3. Entrenamiento del modelo usando Regresión Logística
    from sklearn.linear_model import LogisticRegression

    model = LogisticRegression(max_iter=1000)  # Aumentar las iteraciones si es necesario
    model.fit(X_train, y_train)

        LogisticRegression
    LogisticRegression(max_iter=1000)
```

Fig. 11. Training of the Logistic Regression Model.

Details of the Process

Model Instantiation: We created an instance of the logistic regression model using LogisticRegression(). The parameter max_iter = 1000 was set to ensure the convergence of the optimization algorithm. Increasing the maximum number of iterations may be necessary if the model does not converge with the default value, providing flexibility in model adjustment.

Model Training: We used the fit method to train the model with the training data (X_train and y_train). This method adjusts the model's coefficients to minimize the loss function, thus finding the best representation of the relationship between the independent features and the dependent variable.

Additional Considerations

Convergence: Setting max_iter = 1000 ensures that the model's iterative process has enough steps to achieve convergence. This is crucial for obtaining accurate coefficients that maximize the likelihood function.

Regularization: Although not specified in the provided code, logistic regression in sklearn by default applies L2 regularization to prevent overfitting. This regularization is important for improving the model's generalization to new data.

Training the logistic regression model is a critical step in our research as it allows us to capture the underlying relationships between the selected features and the improvement in student performance.

Evaluation Process

We used a variety of standard evaluation metrics from machine learning literature to assess the performance of our model. These metrics include accuracy, precision, recall, and the confusion matrix, providing a comprehensive view of the model's performance (Fig. 12).

Evaluation Metrics

1. **Accuracy:** Accuracy is defined as the proportion of correct predictions among the total number of cases evaluated. It is a global metric that provides an initial indication of the model's performance:

   Accuracy is calculated as: accuracy = accuracy_score(y_test, y_pred)

```
[ ] #Paso 4. Evaluación del modelo

    from sklearn.metrics import accuracy_score, precision_score, recall_score, confusion_matrix
    import matplotlib.pyplot as plt
    import seaborn as sns

    # Predicciones
    y_pred = model.predict(X_test)

    # Métricas de evaluación
    accuracy = accuracy_score(y_test, y_pred)
    precision = precision_score(y_test, y_pred)
    recall = recall_score(y_test, y_pred)-
    conf_matrix = confusion_matrix(y_test, y_pred)

    # Mostrar la matriz de confusión
    plt.figure(figsize=(8, 6))
    sns.heatmap(conf_matrix, annot=True, fmt='d', cmap='Blues',
        xticklabels=['Predicted Negative', 'Predicted Positive'], yticklabels=['Actual Negative', 'Actual Positive'])
    plt.xlabel('Predicted')
    plt.ylabel('Actual')
    plt.title('Confusion Matrix')
    plt.show()

    # Mostrar métricas
    print(f'Accuracy: {accuracy:.2f}')
    print(f'Precision: {precision:.2f}')
    print(f'Recall: {recall:.2f}')
```

Fig. 12. Evaluation of the Logistic Regression Model with Accuracy, Precision, Recall, and Confusion Matrix Calculation.

2. **Precision:** Precision measures the proportion of true positives among all cases that were predicted as positive. This metric is crucial in contexts where the cost of false positives is high:

   Precision is calculated as: precision = precision_score(y_test, y_pred)
3. **Recall:** Also known as sensitivity, measures the proportion of true positives correctly identified among all positive cases. It is particularly important in scenarios where false negatives have a high cost:

   Recall is calculated as: recall = recall_score(y_test, y_pred)
4. **Confusion Matrix:** The confusion matrix is a tool that provides a detailed view of the model's performance by showing the frequencies of correct and incorrect predictions for each class (Fig. 13):

Model Effectiveness

The evaluation of the logistic regression model showed an overall accuracy of 70%, with a precision of 88% and a recall of 78%. These results indicate that the model is effective in predicting improvements in student performance. The high precision suggests that when the model predicts an improvement, it is highly likely to be correct, while the 78% recall indicates that the model correctly identifies most cases of improvement.

Generation of the ROC Curve

To generate the ROC curve, predicted probabilities for each instance in the test set are first calculated. These probabilities are then used to determine the true positive rates (TPR) and false positive rates (FPR) at various thresholds, enabling the construction of the ROC curve. The area under the curve (AUC) is 0.78, as indicated in the legend. The AUC is an aggregated metric that summarizes the performance of the ROC curve in a single value. An AUC of 0.78 indicates that the model has a reasonable ability to

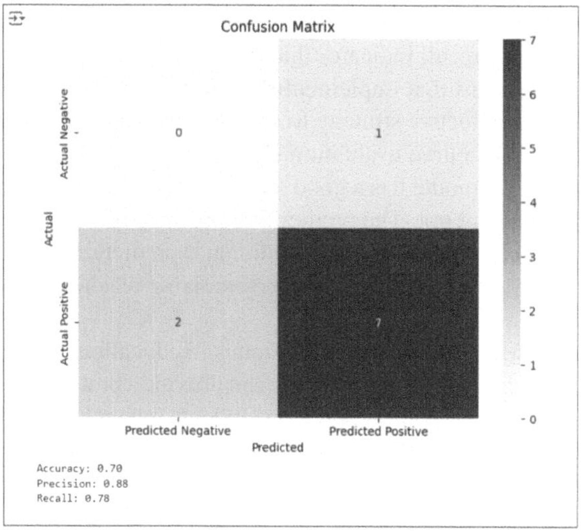

Fig. 13. Resultant Confusion Matrix.

distinguish between positive and negative classes. The horizontal shape of the ROC curve at TPR = 0.78 might indicate an issue with how FPR and TPR values are computed, or it could suggest a specific behavior of the model that requires further investigation (Fig. 14).

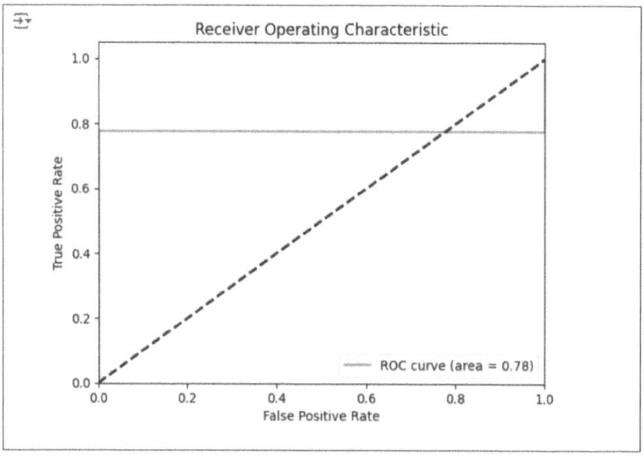

Fig. 14. ROC Curve Graph for Evaluating the Logistic Regression Model.

Discussion

The results suggest that gamification has a positive impact on learning linear algebra, as demonstrated by the logistic regression model. The model's high precision and sensitivity indicate that it is effective in predicting improvements in student performance. The high precision suggests that when the model predicts an improvement, it is highly likely to be correct, while the 78% recall indicates that the model correctly identifies most cases of improvement. This means that implementing gamification in the teaching process of linear algebra can be an effective strategy to enhance students' academic performance.

Furthermore, the ROC curve evaluation showed a significant area under the curve (AUC), indicating that the model has a good ability to distinguish between students who improved and those who did not. The prediction for a specific student case also demonstrated that the model can be used to make individual predictions about the probability of improvement, which could be useful for personalizing teaching strategies according to each student's needs.

In summary, the use of gamification techniques in education, supported by artificial intelligence models such as logistic regression, can provide a powerful tool for improving learning and personalizing education based on students' characteristics and needs. This study provides a solid foundation for future research and practical applications in the field of educational innovation.

This study also aims to extend the innovative educational framework regarding the use of Geographic Information Systems (GIS) with maps that visualize the results obtained from students and their high school backgrounds. This approach will serve as an academic observatory to analyze student profiles, their learning styles, and their performance in mathematical thinking assessments, and to undertake future collaborative work with higher education institutions to improve mathematics teaching. The data collected will contribute to a big data database, allowing the development of robust classification algorithms applicable to new students entering higher education at the Technological University of Cancún. Anticipating the impact of gamification on learning mathematics or other innovative teaching methods will facilitate personalized educational strategies and improve overall educational outcomes. This represents a second phase of the present work, for which a geographical representation prototype was developed to visualize the high school institutions from which students come.

The underlying technology for data exploitation and geographic representation through interactive maps is implemented using Python, APIs, and data analysis components, as illustrated in the following images (Figs. 15 and 16).

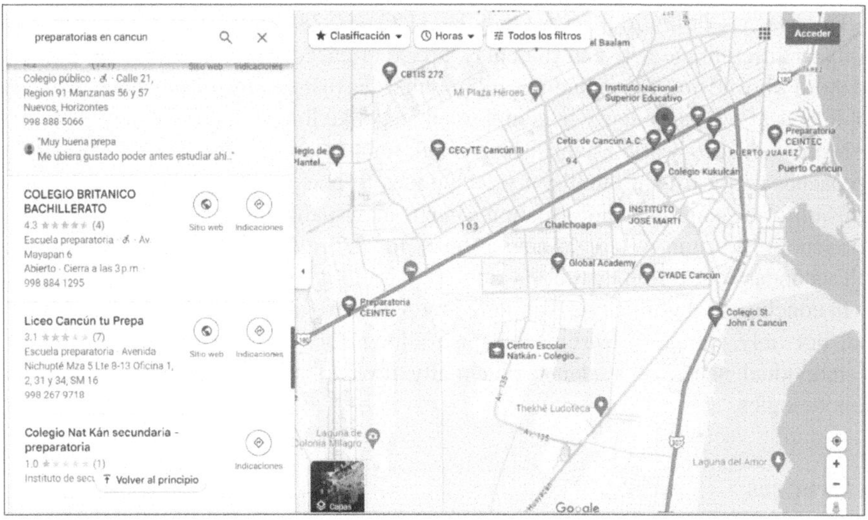

Fig. 15. Screen prototype for geolocation of upper secondary institutions from which the students originate.

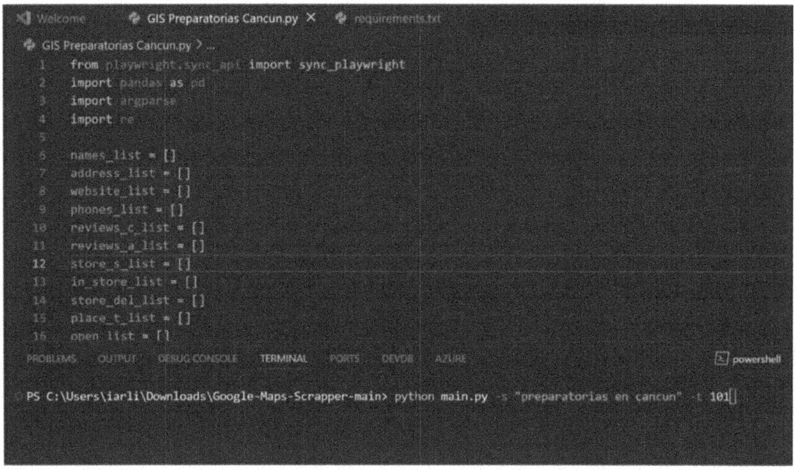

Fig. 16. Algorithm developed in Python for data representation in geographic information maps.

4 Conclusions

This study has demonstrated that the integration of gamification in teaching linear algebra has a positive impact on students' performance. By applying a logistic regression model, it was identified that gamification not only enhances students' motivation but also significantly contributes to their academic achievement. The results, which show an overall accuracy of 70%, with a predictive precision of 88% and a recall of 78%, highlight the model's effectiveness in predicting improvement in learning.

The analysis of the ROC curve and the AUC of 0.78 further reinforce the model's ability to differentiate between students who experienced a performance improvement and those who did not. These findings support the idea that gamification can be a powerful tool in education, particularly in complex subjects like linear algebra.

Moreover, this work establishes a solid foundation for the use of data-driven approaches and artificial intelligence techniques to personalize education. The future inclusion of a geographic information system to visualize students' results based on their school of origin will open new avenues for improving teaching in collaboration with secondary education institutions.

In conclusion, gamification, supported by predictive models such as logistic regression, not only enhances learning but also allows for the adaptation of teaching to the individual needs of students, potentially revolutionizing traditional educational methodologies.

References

1. Ramírez-Montoya, M.S., De Agüero-Servin, M., Pompa-Mansilla, M., Hernández-Romo, A.K., Hernández-Alvarado, M.A., Sánchez-Mendiola, M.: La investigación de la innovación en la educación superior en México y el mundo: 2015–2020. de Innovación Educativa en Educación Superior: una mirada 360, México, Imagia Comunicación, pp. 43–80 (2021)
2. Deterding, S.: Gamification: designing for motivation. Interactions **19**, 14–17 (2012)
3. J.C.-R., J.M.-A. J., C.-Q.R.: Gironés-Roig, Minería de datos: Modelos y Algoritmos (2017)
4. R.P.A., Mandale, A.A.: Improved Undergraduate Software Capstone Project Development with Adoption of Industry Practices. J. Eng. Educ. Transf. **34**(4), 74–89 (2021)
5. S. Y. L., Chapman, E.: Development of a short form of the attitudes toward mathematics inventory. Educ. Stud. Math. **82** (1), 146–164 (2013)
6. Kolb, D.: Experiential Learning: Experience as the Source of Learning and Development. Prentice-Hall, Englewood Cliffs, New Jersey (1984)
7. CENEVAL: Examen Nacional de Ingreso a la Educación Superior (EXANI-II). CENEVAL, [Online], [En línea]. Available: https://ceneval.edu.mx/examenes-ingreso-exani_ii/. [Último acceso: 1 08 2024]
8. Turkmen, G.P., Soybas, D.: The effect of gamification methodology on students' achievements and attitudes towards mathematics. Bartın Univ. J. Faculty Educ. **8**(1), 258–298 (2019)
9. Sánchez-Mendiola, M., Escamilla-De Los Santos, J., Moreno-Arellano, C.I.: La naturaleza de las innovaciones educativas, de Innovación educativa en educación superior: una mirada 360, México, pp. 21–43. Imagia Comunicación (2021)
10. Russo, S., Lavicza, Z.: An overview of gamification and gamified educational platforms for mathematics teaching, de Eleventh Congress of the European Society for Research in Mathematics, Utrecht, Netherlands (2019)
11. Rozhenko, O.D., Darzhaniya, A.D., Bondar, V.V., Mirzoian, M.V.: Gamification of Education as an Addition to Traditional Educational Technologies at the University. CEUR Workshop Proceedings, pp. 457–464 (2021)
12. Parra-Sánchez, J.S., Torres-Pardo, I.D., Martínez-De Meriño, C.Y.: Personalización de recursos para la enseñanza de matemáticas universitarias usando inteligencia artificial. Revista Interamericana de Investigación, Educación y Pedagogía **16**(1), (2023)
13. Palmero, L.R.: La teoría del aprendizaje significativo: una revisión aplicable a. Revista Electrónica de Investigación e Innovación Educativa y Socioeducativa **50**, (2011)

14. Ortíz-Colón, A.M., Jordán, J., Agredal, M.: Gamificación en educación: una panorámica sobre el estado de la cuestión. Educação e Pesquisa **44**, e173773 (2018)
15. Mendoza-Velasco, D.J., Cejas-Martínez, M.F., Alban-Yanez, C., Marisol-Ortega, Y.: The Open Algorithm Based on Numbers (ABN) as an Educational Innovation for Teaching and Learning in Ecuador. Int. Electron. J. Math. Educ. **15**(3), (2020)
16. Lee, J.Y., Pyon, C.U., Woo, J.: Digital twin for math education: a study on the utilization of games and gamification for university mathematics education. Electronics **12**, 3207 (2023)
17. M. S. Jiménez, Observatorio Tec (2023). [En línea]. Available: https://observatorio.tec.mx/edu-news/andragogia-adaptando-el-aprendizaje-para-los-adultos/#:~:text=La%20andragog%C3%ADa%20se%20refiere%20al,esta%20etapa%20de%20la%20vida.
18. Espín-Mendoza, I.V.: Gamificación como estrategia educativa del proceso de enseñanza aprendizaje de matemáticas en estudiantes de bachillerato, Ambato. Pontificia Universidad Católica del Ecuador, Ecuador (2021)
19. Carrillo Mariana et al, redalyc (2009). [En línea]. Available: https://www.redalyc.org/pdf/4677/467746249004.pdf
20. Alcoba-González, J.: La clasificación de los métodos de enseñanza en la educación superior. Contextos Educativos **15**, 93–106 (2012)
21. U. X. R. d. C. F.-M. A. M. U. X. R. d. C. F.-M. Ana Medrano: Un análisis de la producción de representaciones al solucionar problemas de álgebra temprana en estudiantes de primaria. Educación Matemática **34**(3), 10–41 (2022)
22. Usuga, I.: Preparación de Datos Para Aprendizaje Automático. Universidad Torcuato Di Tella, Buenos Aires (2023)
23. R. S. M. F. Valentín Pando Fernández, Regresión logística multinomial, Dialnet, vol. 2004, no 18, pp. 323–327 (2004)
24. G. G. P. D. G. B. R. G. M. R. García Péreza, Modelo de regresión logística para estimar la dependencia según la escala de Lawton y Brody, Elsevier, vol. 36, no 7, pp. 365–371 (2010)
25. J. I., Carlos Barrionuevo, I.S.: Reconocimiento de emociones a través de expresiones faciales con el empleo de aprendizaje supervisado aplicando regresión logística. Repositorio Institucional de la UNLP, pp. 491–500 (2020)
26. Velásquez Henao, J.D.: Neuroscheme: un lenguaje para el modelamiento de redes. Neuronales Artif. **72**(47), 75–83 (2005)
27. Montoya Pérez, Dy.M.S.S.: Implementación de redes neuronales artificiales en un sistema tutorial inteligente orientado al aprendizaje del algebra. Revista Virtu@lmente **6**(1), 73–87 (2018)
28. J., K.J., S.H.: Hamari, Does gamification work? — A literature review of empirical studies on gamification. In: Proceedings of the Annual Hawaii International Conference on System Sciences (2014)
29. Wool-folk, Dialnet (1996). [En línea]. Available: https://dialnet.unirioja.es/descarga/articulo/5897814.pdf

Spatial Analysis of Student Feedback on Learning Management Systems in Mathematics: Leveraging GIS for Enhanced Insights

Eduardo Eloy Loza Pacheco[1](✉), Mayra Olguin Rosas[1], Dulce Loza-Pacheco[1], Mayra Lorena Díaz Sosa[1], Georgina Eslava Garcia[1], Miguel Torres Ruiz[2], and Christian Carlos Delgado Elizondo[1]

[1] Universidad Nacional Autónoma de México, Acatlán Edomex, 08544 MEX, Mexico
{eduardo.loza,mlds,geslava}@acatlan.unam.mx

[2] Centro de Investigacion en Computo, Alcaldía Gustavo A. Madero, C.P. 07700 CDMX, Mexico
mtorres@ipn.mx

Abstract. The use of Learning Management Systems is Important in Hybrid courses especially in Mathematics. In addition to that since the COVID LMS are a important mechanism to enforce the learning at home for students. However, the feedback from students is important to adapt the learning objects so students can learn and study in a more effective way. On the Other hand, Geographic Information Systems helps to represent a reason spatial information to give more accurate information about where objects are located. Natural Process Language has different applications for example to understand written and speak language. It is use in web search engines, translate, intelligent assistants. The present work with GIS and NLP is used to measure the level of effectiveness a LMS called TEDI have in students of Mathematics by analyzing their locations, responses in order to build the LMS system more effective to students.

Keywords: Artificial Intelligence · Natural Process Language · Smart education · Learning Management Systems

1 Introduction

Collecting, understanding, processing, and generating insights about text data is called natural language process. (NLP) [1]. Additionally, NLP refers to a branch of computer science that empowers the ability to understand texts and spoken words [3]. NLP is implemented in hardware and software to understand audio or text data. NLP is a known field of Artificial Intelligence (AI) with a wide variety of applications such as web search engines, translation applications, intelligent assistants, etc. Text data is an example of unstructured data where this kind of data can be found in different sources such as web pages, social media portals, the Internet of things, interconnection with other computers,

M. F. Mata-Rivera et al. (Eds.): GIS-LATAM 2024, CCIS 2298, pp. 138–147, 2025.
https://doi.org/10.1007/978-3-031-80017-7_9

industrial data (automobiles), telecommunications, press, data from sensors, RFID, NFC, photos, videogames, etc. This kind of data needs to be preprocessed before a computer can use it. The text data needs to be processed in lower case, removal of punctuations and stop words, spelling corrections, etc.

On the other hand, Learning Management Systems (LMS), help students to empower their knowledge. Examples of these technologies are well-known such as Moodle, Blackboard, and Google Classroom. Professors use LMS to implement Hybrid courses, presential, and online courses. At the end of the semester, students give feedback on the use of a platform called TEDI [2]. Finally students live sometimes very far from school that affects the way students are ready for their classes and learn.

2 Related Work

The widespread of new technologies allows NLP to be applied in various fields, such as healthcare, commerce, etc. NLP can revolutionize education. For example, NLP technologies, provide information about the relevant points of a text. NLP transforms text to audio and reads to teachers and students, through videos, and tutorial textbooks. These elements can help people with some disability. Additionally, NLP can help to offer intelligent Tutoring and recommend students some topics in the future [3]. For example, in Fig. 1 we can see some scenarios where NLP Technologies can be helpful in education.

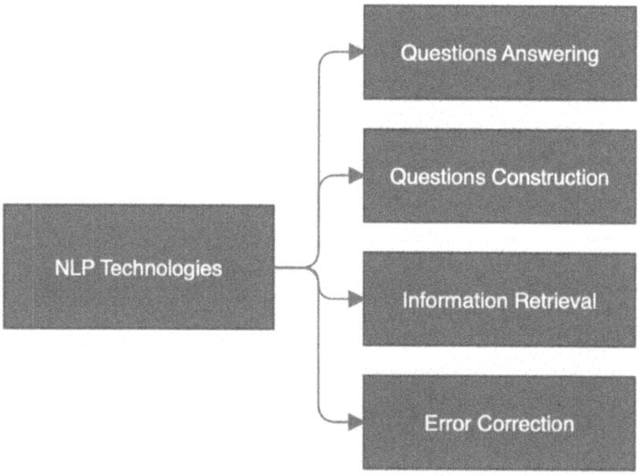

Fig. 1. Scenarios where NLP Technologies can be applied. Taken from [3]

In [4] discuss the importance of NLP in students of K-12, and how different digital environments can help for teaching young students. The work mentions eleven technologies used for education. For example, it mentions NLP4ALL which is an NLP tool that analyzes tweets from political parties to help students to understand the political proposal from different parties. Convo is a conversational programming agent. Con-voBlocks to help students learn programming and build a bot that facilitates the learning of AI. Finally [4] shows the most frequent NLP tasks that can be found in NLP learning tools that are: text classification, speech recognition, dialogue, speech synthesis, question answering, text processing, etc.

In [5] shows a study of the impact of COVID-19 in education, using sentiment analysis about more than 13 thousand tweets. The article uses Deep Neural networks to train the model. The article shows how negatively the COVID-19 epidemic affected students and teachers. Additionally, [6] shows how NLP can be integrated into the Software engineering process for example for creating requirements in a more effective way and used to help students in the software engineering courses.

In [7] mentions how NLP methods can be implemented in education. Especially to process students' feedback and annotate their views about certain subjects. It also mentions the high number of articles addressing education, Artificial Intelligence, and NLP. Mentions important technologies for Python, R, and Java with libraries such as NLTK for Python, OpenNLP for R and Java, etc.

Research about NLP and geospatial data is an interesting topic that can help in many areas like urban planning, transportation, environmental management etc. as it is shown in [9], NLP can be important to a wide variety of spatial data infrastructures. For example in [10] they propose a BB-GPT: A frame work for machine learning to learn geographic information data. Finally in [11], they mention to use NLP to enchance the capability of traditional GIS.

3 The Educative Platform Used

TEDI is an educational platform that uses Moodle (see Fig. 2). This educative platform is designed to give students, teachers, and managers an integrated system with the following characteristics: robust, accessible. The aim is to create a personalized learning environment for teachers to create everything. The system has more than 3721 users from different courses. The system is available for curricular courses from the Bachelor of Applied Mathematics and Computers Science. The system also helps students with hard topics such as Numerical Methods, Calculus, and Algebra and increases the efficiency of students [2].

4 Spatial Analysis

The courses of Numeric Analysis and Calculus are predominantly men, seventy per-cent men, and the rest women. To date, we have no compiled information about, non-binary, and other genders (Fig. 3).

There is an important issue that it is necessary to address adequately. The impact of the location of the students. Students have preferred locations where they access the TEDI platform. This information is important because gives us information about the location on the campus where students use the platform and where more network traffic the institution has. It is important to add more access points, routers, and switches in other words provide network provisioning [6]. On the other hand, students who are outside the campus network can have significant delays because of the internet service provider. So, the integration of spatial localization is important to reason about different aspects the student can answer about the effectiveness of the platform. And give new features that a machine-learning model can use. MapKit technology can help to map the location of the internet connections [8].

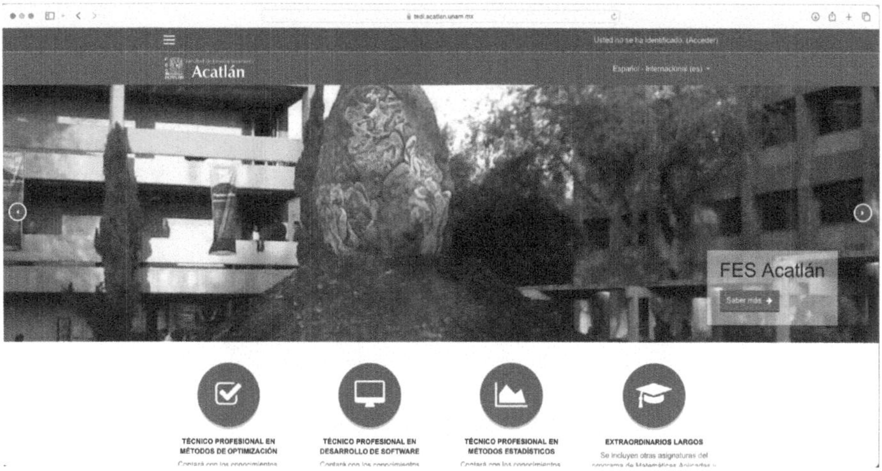

Fig. 2. TEDI Education Platform.

Fig. 3. Students from FES Acatlán

5 Spatial Location of Students

Students are geographically dispersed in the metropolitan zone of Mexico, Mexico City and State of Mexico. For example, students from generation 2016 of the Bachelor of Applied Mathematics and Computer Science live very disperse from the university at FES Acatlán. in Table 1 some locations where students live are shown. In the table we can see information about street, colony, postal code, municipality.

As we see student live very far from FES Acatlán, for example we can find location as far nearly 30 km from Tlahuac to Naucalpan (where University is). This journey to

Fig. 4. FES Acatlán Campus using Mapkit.

students is very difficult because many of the students use public transportation and they require to take more than one bus or subway (Fig. 5).

This is one of the reasons TEDDI platforms is one of the best options to students to take a hybrid course. Because students often need to study at home, and other in the public transportation.

6 Methodology

TEDI is an educational platform that uses Moodle (see Fig. 2). This educative platform is designed to give students, teachers, and managers an integrated system with the following characteristics: robust, and accessible. The aim is to create a personalized learning environment for teachers to create everything. The system has more than 3721 users from different courses. The system is available for curricular courses from the Bachelor of

Table 1. Locations where students live.

Street	Col	Del	PC
Juan Colorado 117	Benito Juarez	Nezahualcoyotl	57000
20 De Noviembre N11	San Rafael Chamapa	Naucalpan De Juarez	53660
Calle Santa Cruz No. 443	Los Olivos	Tlahuac	13210
Juan Escutia Mz 14 Lt 8	San Miguel	Chimalhuacan	56335
Nicolas Bravo 19	Martires De Rio Blanco	Naucalpan De Juarez	53780
Heroes 62	Guerrero	Cuauhtemoc	06300
Benito Juarez 7	San Mateo Nopala Zona Norte	Naucalpan De Juarez	53224
4 And. Xamiltepec Mz C Lote 4	Mesa De Los Hornos	Tlalpan	14420
Cda. Francisco Banuet Num. 100	Constitucion De La Republica	Gustavo A. Madero	07469
Juan De Dios Peza 65	Mexico Primera Seccion	Nezahualcoyotl	57620
2Da De Cochabamaba	Las Americas	Naucalpan De Juarez	53040
Participacion Mz 6 Lt 29	Ejercito Del Trabajo Ii	Ecatepec De Morelos	55238
Ave. El Polvorin S/N	Santa Maria Huecatitla	Cuautitlan	54831
Prol Felipe Angeles Mz 43 Lt 9	Torres De Potrero	Alvaro Obregon	01840
Prolongacion Constitucion 551	San Pablo Chimalpa	Cuajimalpa De Morelos	05050
Carlos Marx Mz 20 Lt 13	Allapetlalli	Iztapalapa	09960
Callejon Palacio Segunda Cerrada 5	La Asuncion	Iztapalapa	09000
Acahuales Numero 35A	Ampliacion San Marcos Norte	Xochimilco	16038
Camino A Belen 85 Int H 113	Cove	Alvaro Obregon	01120
Bosques De Europa No. 316	Bosques De Aragon	Nezahualcoyotl	57170
Cerrada Norte 85 60	Sindicato Mexicano De Electricistas	Azcapotzalco	02060

Applied Mathematics and Computer Science. The system also helps students with hard topics such as Numerical Methods, Calculus, and Algebra and increases the efficiency of students [2] (Fig. 6).

Fig. 5. Distance from Tlahuac to Naucalpan municipality.

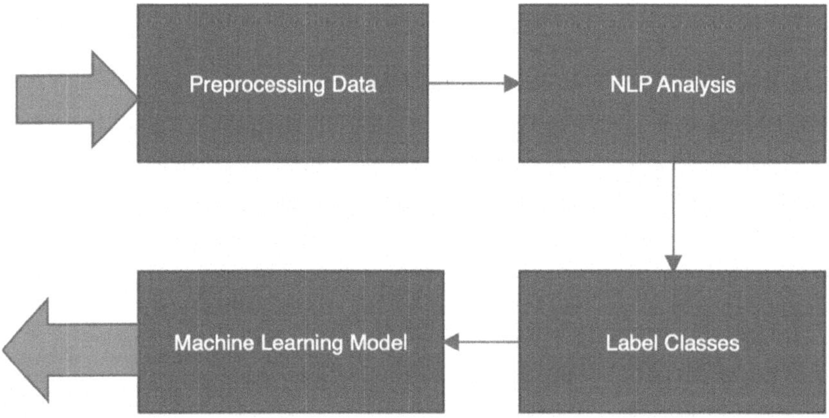

Fig. 6. Framework proposed for the construction of proposed frameworks to analyze students' responses.

6.1 Preprocessing

In the Stage of preprocessing, we applied a survey for the courses of Calculus I and Numeric Methods, in the spring of 2023. The survey is composed of 53 questions, 25 questions yes or no questions and the rest are open questions where students could write a short answer. The following table shows an example of these questions in Spanish and their translation to English. An example is shown in Table 2. In the questions we show a series of question regarding to the locations of their home and whether the location is relevant to their performance at school.

6.2 NLP Analysis

In NLP Analysis, it is necessary to process the information, divide the text into tokens, delete stop words, articles, prepositions, and reduce the words using synonyms, and

Table 2. Example of some answers of students from Stage 1: Preprocessing

Question	English	Spanish	Answer
0	Gender	Genero	Femenino
1	Did you enjoy using the platform	Fue de tu agrado utilizar la plataforma	Yes
2	What improvements would you make to the course?	¿Qué mejoras harías?	no poner vídeos en la plataforma que no sean hechos por el docente
3	Does the teacher explains clearly?	¿El docente explica con claridad?	le gusta su materia y lo transmite
4	Do you live far from school?	¿Vives lejos de la escuela?	Si
5	The location of your school complicates your school performance?	¿La lejania de tu casa complica la efectividad que tienes en la escuela?	Si, muchas veces llego cansado. O con pocas ganas

antonyms. Finally, lemmatize to find the root word (See Sect. 5). To analyze the importance of the text we are analyzing it is important to know the frequency of repetition. The frequency allows us to recognize the general sentiment during Calculus and Numeric methods. In the Analysis phase, we need to use the positive examples of the class to find a pattern of words that are used to describe a successful way of teaching, and build learning objects. Also the analysis whether the location affects their learning process.

6.3 Label Classes

For every open question, we identify two classes if the feedback was adequate or not. So the labels are 0 or 1. In total were built 25 datasets for every question. Table 3 shows the question: Does the Teacher explain Clearly? The datasets have these structures to obtain a machine-learning model.

Table 3. Question for Calculus and Numeric Methods Does the location of where you live affecte the effectiveness of you learning

Answer	Yes/No
Si	1
Ninguno, gracias	0
Ninguno, gracias	0
No	0
No responde	0
No respondio	0
Sin cometarios	0
Si muchas veces no alcanzo a llegar a tiempo a las clases	1
Muchas veces	1
Tengo que poner las clases mas tarde	1
Si	1
A veces se me complica llegar a tiempo	1

7 Conclusions

The analysis of student's performance is crucial at every level of education. However, the feedback of students is also important. The analysis made in this work shows that students are more comfortable stating their opinions in their own words than in a yes or no question or in Likert-type questions. The more common responses are the teacher teaches well" in Spanish "El professor enseña bien", the most common terms are, "claro"-clear, explains-"explica", exercises-"ejercicios" among others (See the WorldCloud in Fig. 4). For example in the case of the spatial analysis students reflect that the location of where they live can affect some times their learning process. Because sometime the have less time. Because of their transportation needs. For these, we use the NLTK library to process the text written by students. Later we intended to see if there was a data abstraction for their responses. So we label the positive responses and negative responses to train a model. We found that negative responses in the courses on Numeric Method have a similar pattern where students are not willing to write a large response. Negative examples have just, no, very short answers. The spatial information is important because the students who access the courses study in a hybrid modality which means students sometimes access it at school and sometimes at home. Students that access the Campus access from several sites, but the connectivity differs from one place to another. So, it is necessary to add spatial information to the Teddi Platform in order to perform spatial reasoning to study the connectivity phenomena.

Acknowledgements. The authors would like to thank to Universidad Nacional Autónoma de México, Facultad de Estudios Superiores Acatlán and DGAPA-UNAM (PAPIME PE305523) and PAIDI/012/2023 "Ciencia de datos: aplicaciones en la investigación social" for the funds to support this work. Additionally this work was partially sponsored by Secretaría de Educación, Ciencia, Tecnología e Innovación de la Ciudad de México with the grant: "Aplicación del cómputo urbano para analizar la dinámica urbana y la sustentabilidad de las grandes ciudades", number: SECTEI/182/2023.

References

1. Kulkarni, A., Shivananda, A., Kulkarni, A.: Natural Language Processing Projects: Build Next-Generation NLP Applications Using AI Techniques. (2022)
2. Loza, E., Olguin, M., et al.: Machine learning to predict the level of approval in hybrid courses in programming and mathematics. Research in Computing Science, IPN (2023)
3. Lan, Y., Li, X., Du, H., Lu, X., Gao, M., Qian, W., Zhou, A.: Survey of Natural Language Processing for Education: Taxonomy, Systematic Review, and Future Trends (2024). arXiv preprint arXiv:2401.07518
4. Tian, X., Boyer, K.E.: A Review of Digital Learning Environments for Teaching Natural Language Processing in K-12 Education (2023). arXiv preprint arXiv:2310.01603
5. Ayaz, T.B., Uslu, M.S., Ağcabay, İ., Ahmad, F., Korkmaz, O.F., Küreksiz, M., Akbulut, F.P.: Global impact of the pandemic on education: a study of natural language processing. In: 2022 Innovations in Intelligent Systems and Applications Conference (ASYU), pp. 1–4. IEEE (2022)
6. Marutschke, D.M., White, J., Serdült, U.: WordPress and Kanban use in software engineering education evaluated by natural language processing and neural network. In: 2021 IEEE 12th International Workshop on Computational Intelligence and Applications (IWCIA), pp. 1–6. IEEE (2021)
7. What is network provisioning? (2023) Cisco. Available at: https://www.cisco.com/c/en/us/solutions/automation/what-is-network-provisioning.html. Accessed 15 May 2024
8. MapKit for Swiftui (no date) Apple Developer Documentation. Available at: https://developer.apple.com/documentation/mapkit/mapkit_for_swiftui. Accessed 15 July 2024
9. Naveen, P., Maheswar, R., Trojovský, P.: GeoNLU: Bridging the gap between natural language and spatial data infrastructures. Alex. Eng. J. **87**, 126–147 (2024)
10. Zhang, Y., et al.: BB-GeoGPT: a framework for learning a large language model for geographic information science. Inf. Process. Manage. **61**(5), 103808 (2024)
11. Calì, D., Condorelli, A., Papa, S., Rata, M., Zagarella, L.: Improving intelligence through use of Natural Language processing. A comparison between NLP interfaces and traditional visual GIS interfaces. Procedia Comput. Sci. **5**, 920–925 (2011)

Semi-automatic Construction of Knowledge Graphs on Natural Disasters in Mexico Using Large Language Models

Luis Roberto Polo-Bautista[1](✉), Sandra Dinora Orantes-Jiménez[1], Francisco Carrillo-Brenes[1], and Luis M. Vilches-Blázquez[2]

[1] Centro de Investigación en Computación, Instituto Politécnico Nacional, Mexico City, Mexico
lpolob2023@cic.ipn.mx

[2] Ontology Engineering Group, Universidad Politécnica de Madrid, Madrid, Spain
luis.vilches@upm.es

Abstract. The growing trend of developing Large Language Models (LLMs) has gained popularity due to their ability to process and generate natural language, which has applications in various industries. However, the use of LLMs to build domain-specific knowledge graphs remains challenging due to the reliance on human experts to define entities and relationships and to address problems such as information granularity, lack of timeliness, etc. This work presents a workflow that integrates three different LLMs (Llama 3, GPT-4o, and Claude 3 Sonnet) to perform a semiautomated construction of knowledge graphs from news related to natural disasters in Mexico. This ongoing work provides a preliminary assessment of the ability of LLMs to represent specific knowledge domains, with the potential to improve accessibility and retrieval of relevant data, thus facilitating future identification of associations and patterns related to natural disasters. The experiments carried out have shown that our workflow enriches the identification and relationships of entities from the news corpus. However, our current evaluation shows that the LLMs used are far from replacing human intervention.

Keywords: Large Language Models · Knowledge graphs · News · Natural Disasters · Mexico

1 Introduction

In recent years, there has been a notable increase in the frequency and intensity of natural disasters, including floods, wildfires, earthquakes, and hurricanes. These events have caused considerable damage to communities around the globe, frequently resulting in loss of life [1]. The occurrence of natural disasters is a global phenomenon, yet their impact is disproportionately greater in developing countries due to the limited resources available for disaster management and resilience programs [3].

M. F. Mata-Rivera et al. (Eds.): GIS-LATAM 2024, CCIS 2298, pp. 148–167, 2025.
https://doi.org/10.1007/978-3-031-80017-7_10

Currently, a substantial corpus of data on natural disasters is accessible via the Internet. This information is stored in a variety of databases or digital repositories, which have been designed to accommodate specific data types. However, these sources lack a comprehensive view of events, with numerous details about situations and impacts remaining obscured. In order to gather these hidden data from natural disasters, it is recognized that newspapers are among the most valuable sources of information for scholars interested in researching public opinion and how it has been shaped over time [18]. Furthermore, newspapers can offer valuable insights into the evolution, perception, and dissemination of environmental, administrative, economic, and social phenomena across different countries [12, 18]. This is particularly relevant in the context of the growing importance of collecting large amounts of hidden data [23].

Considering this scenario, we employed GDELT (Global Database of Events, Language, and Tone), a knowledge base comprising event data from media sources across the globe in a multitude of languages, to construct a knowledge graph on natural disasters in Mexico. This country is characterized by elevated risk levels, which are a consequence of a convergence of hazards and vulnerability. The specific characteristics of the ecosystem are of great importance in the occurrence of natural hazards. A substantial portion of Mexico's territory is situated in mountainous regions, which are prone to tectonic and volcanic activity. Additionally, these areas are subject to surface processes influenced by the tropical climate [2].

Knowledge graphs (KGs) represent an extension of Semantic Web practices and have been embraced by a diverse range of companies, including Google, IBM, Facebook, and Microsoft [19]. They play a significant role in numerous artificial intelligence tasks, including semantic search, recommendation systems, and question-answering systems, among others [24]. Furthermore, KGs facilitate the creation, reuse, and recovery of human- and machine-readable structured data about real-world objects using a graph-based representation [21]. These graphs integrate collections of entities connected by semantic relationships, representing structured knowledge that allows for the easy retrieval of information [11].

The conventional approach to KGs construction typically involves a collaborative effort between domain experts and computer scientists, who engage in a range of activities and tasks to construct a KG [15]. Nevertheless, this traditional approach is associated with several limitations, including the granularity and updatability of KGs [11]. Frequently, these graphs are designed for the general public and lack detailed and specific information on specific topics. Moreover, maintaining a KG in alignment with the rapidly evolving real world represents a significant challenge, particularly in the context of rapidly evolving events. Such updates frequently require considerable annotation and monitoring efforts by humans or experts. To address these limitations, some works have applied LLMs, together with domain-specialized ontological models, and diverse techniques, with the aim of dealing with the aforementioned limitations and improving the temporal representation and reasoning of the data [10, 11].

This paper presents an ongoing work that deploys a workflow that integrates LLMs and semantic tools to facilitate a semi-automatic construction a KG about natural disasters. Three different LLMs were utilized to construct a KG of events related to floods, wildfires, earthquakes, and hurricanes in Mexico between 2017 and 2022. In particular, we utilized three cutting-edge language models: Llama 3 [16], GPT-4o [20], and Claude 3 Sonnet [4]. These models demonstrate a remarkable capacity for processing vast quantities of unstructured text data and achieving results in a multitude of natural language processing tasks.

The diverse LLMs were employed to construct a multitude of KGs derived from the same news corpus. This ongoing work is a preliminary assessment of the LLMs capacity to represent discrete knowledge domains, with the potential to enhance the accessibility and retrieval of pertinent data, thereby facilitating the identification of associations and patterns related to natural disasters. Furthermore, this contribution enhances the interoperability of the original dataset, as outlined in reference [9], through the application of the Semantic Web vision.

The remainder of this article is structured as follows: Sect. 2 provides an overview of some relevant related works. Section 3 outlines our approach to semi-automated knowledge graph construction for natural disaster research. Section 4 presents the main results. Finally, Sect. 5 offers insights into the conclusions and future directions of this research.

2 Related Works

Although the integration of knowledge graphs and LLMs is a recent phenomenon, several studies have been conducted to develop knowledge graphs for specific domains. In this regard, contributions such as Ding et al. [11] developed a topic-specific knowledge graph (ThemeKG) using the unsupervised TKGCon framework. This approach was designed to address the inherent granularity and updating challenges associated with current knowledge graphs. In their study, the researchers employed the use of GPT-4 in conjunction with two data sets, each comprising 20 documents.

Bi et al., [7] aimed to enhance the construction of generative knowledge graphs through the utilization of structured code language models. This approach proved to be a more effective means of capturing structural knowledge than traditional approaches based on plain text. The researchers employed GPT-3 and three sets of labeled sentences for assessment.

In their work, Zhang and Soh [30] concentrated on the utilization of automated techniques for the construction of knowledge graphs from textual sources. The authors address the challenge of scaling models to varied texts using the Extract-Define-Canonicalize (EDC) framework, which performs open information extraction, schema definition, and post-hoc canonicalization. In their study, the researchers employed a range of models, including GPT-3.5, GPT-4, and Mistral 7B, along with three sets of labeled sentences, to assess the outcomes.

Yu et al., [28] addressed the creation of knowledge graphs in a specific domain, emphasizing the lack of open resources and the complexity of domain knowledge as primary challenges. The authors developed BEAR, a service domain knowledge graph constructed with an ontology designed to assist an LLM in knowledge extraction. In their study, they employed GPT-3.5, which resulted in the creation of BEAR, comprising 133,906 nodes, 169,159 relationships, and approximately 424,000 available facts.

Krishna et al., [15] examined the semi-automatic construction of ontologies and knowledge graphs using LLMs, contrasting this approach with the conventional one that relies heavily on human experts. Their approach entailed a process that employed competency questions to direct ontology construction and knowledge graph construction. Initially, the process drew upon deep learning methodologies derived from academic publications. In their study, they employed the use of GPT-3.5 and Mistral 7B in conjunction with a set of five scientific publications.

Trajanoska et al., [24] explored the integration of LLMs, such as ChatGPT and REBEL, with semantic technologies for reasoning and inference in entity and relationship extraction. The authors evaluated this approach through experiments using texts about sustainability, thereby demonstrating the enhanced capacity of advanced LLMs to automatically construct knowledge graphs from unstructured text.

Xue and Zou [26] provided a comprehensive review of quality management in knowledge graphs (KG), addressing quality issues, dimensions, and metrics, as well as KG evaluation, error detection, correction, and completion processes.

Ren et al., [22] provided a comprehensive review of LLMs applied to graph learning, proposing a taxonomy that categorizes the methods into four designs: GNN as a prefix, LLM as a prefix, graph integration in LLM, and LLM alone. The key methodologies, strengths, and limitations of each approach are highlighted, and future research opportunities are identified to overcome current integration challenges and explore new applications in graph learning.

3 A Workflow for the Semi-automatic Construction of Knowledge Graphs

A workflow has been developed for the semi-automatic construction of KGs on natural disasters in Mexico. The key components of this workflow are as follows: (i) selection of a news corpus, (ii) text preprocessing, (iii) topic modeling, (iv) identification of named entities and relations, (v) post-processing, and (vi) creation of KGs (see Fig. 1). The following subsections provide details associated with each stage of the process.

3.1 Selecting News Corpus

The initial phase of the study entailed the compilation of a dataset comprising news articles about natural disasters in Mexico, spanning the period from 2017 to 2022. An initial filter was applied to the GDELT database using the theme

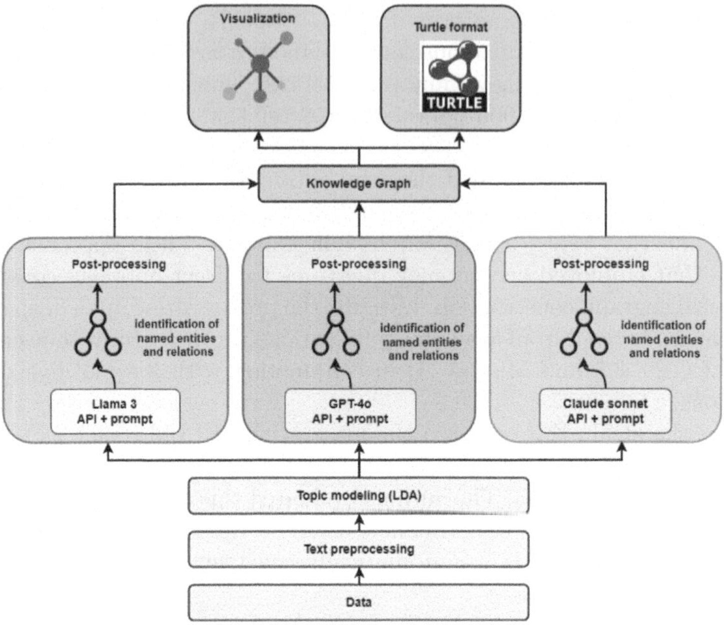

Fig. 1. Knowledge graph construction process

"NATURAL DISASTER TREMOR", which had been assigned by the GDELT team to news items related to this topic.

Taking into account the noise in the annotation of the collected news, a second filter was applied using a set of keywords that were expected to be present in the news content, to define the corpus. The GDELT API permits the download of a maximum of 250 news items per day. Consequently, the filter indicates the number of downloaded items. This approach enabled the retrieval of specific news items, which were then used to create the corpus within the selected knowledge domain. The aforementioned filters were applied through the GDELT API in Python and a web scraping process. This resulted in the collection of 4,200 news items in Spanish. Filter details are shown below:

- keyword= ['earthquake', 'tsunami', 'richter scale', 'hurricane', 'epicenter', 'flood', 'tectonic plates'],
- start date=2017, 1, 1,
- end date=2022, 12, 31,
- country="MX",
- theme='NATURAL DISASTER TREMORS',
- num records=250

3.2 Text Preprocessing

The preprocessing stage entailed the preparation and cleansing of the news content in advance of its processing by the LLMs. The tasks included in this stage were as follows, and some examples of these specific tasks can be seen in Table 1.

1. Text normalization: The text was converted to a standard form (lowercase) and punctuation marks were removed.
2. Elimination of special characters: Non-alphabetic or special characters without relevant information for the analysis were eliminated.
3. Spelling and grammar correction: Regular expressions are employed to rectify spelling or grammatical errors to enhance the quality of the processed text, for example, hyphenation.

Table 1. Examples of text preprocessing

Task	Before preprocessing	After preprocessing
1	EN CHIAPAS EL GOBERNADOR MANUEL VELASCO EMITE	en chiapas el gobernador manuel velasco emite
2	Oaxaca.-México está situado en el área conocida como Cinturón	oaxaca méxico está situado en el área conocida como cinturón
3	Investigadores de la UNAM y del ServicioSismológico	investigadores de la unam y del servicio sismológico

3.3 Topic Modeling

Topic modeling is a technique used to organize a large collection of documents into different topics. Although often associated with clustering methods, topic modeling tends to be more accurate and reliable than clustering techniques such as k-means. Clustering assumes that each document belongs to a single topic and is based on measuring the distance between documents [6].

In this stage, the unsupervised machine learning algorithm LDA (Latent Dirichlet Allocation) was used. This algorithm can identify the main themes of a collection of unlabeled texts. Each news in LDA is considered a probabilistic distribution over a set of K topics. Each topic $K \in \{1, \cdots, K\}$ is represented as a distribution ϕ_k over vocabulary words [8]. In this way, each news item of our corpus has a topic encompassed by a specific distribution of words.

Furthermore, topic modeling was employed as an additional filter to remove news items whose topics exhibited a distinctive distribution of words that was incongruent with the semantic associations associated with our knowledge domain (natural disasters). Consequently, topic modeling plays a crucial role in cleaning and refining news, allowing a more accurate and consistent news corpus. Therefore, topic modeling not only improves the quality of selected news, but also facilitates a more useful representation of the topics covered in the corpus.

3.4 Identification of Named Entities and Relations

In order to identify the named entities and relations present within our news corpus, we employed the API of three distinct models: Llama 3 [16], GPT-4o [20], and Claude 3 Sonnet [4]. These models utilize sophisticated natural language processing techniques that enable them to discern triplets of named entities within texts, following the following format: <head>, <head_type>, <relation>, <tail>, and <tail_type>.

<head> contains the head entity, <head_type> the head entity type, <relation> the relationship type, <tail> the tail entity, and <tail_type> the tail entity type. The prompt used to identify named entities and relationships was designed to maximize the accuracy and clarity of responses, as shown below:

> From this text, you must extract named entities and generate output in JSON format. Each entity and relationship must be detailed in an object with the keys 'head', 'head_type', 'relation', 'tail', and 'tail_type'. 'head' will contain the text of the main entity, 'head_type' the type of main entity, 'relation' the type of relationship in Spanish, 'tail' the text of the tail entity and 'tail_type' the type of tail entity. The model should extract as many entities and relationships as possible based on the length of the text.

Each model processed the input text and returned a JSON structure containing the identified entities and the relations between them.

3.5 Post-processing

The post-processing stage focuses on normalizing the entities and relationships discovered in the previous step. This involved mapping the different ways of mentioning a given entity and relations into a single canonical form. For example, an entity like "earthquake" can be mentioned in different ways: "the earthquake", "an earthquake", "earthquakes", etc. This normalization allows all these mentions to refer to a single entity "earthquake". Similarly, relations between entities like "occurred in" or "happened at" were also normalized.

This process was carried out by applying lemmatization techniques, word embeddings, and vector clustering using cosine similarity. A similarity parameter is used to group the defined entities, relations, and entity types. The normalization process resolved any ambiguities by identifying the correct context of the entities, thereby enhancing the accuracy of the named entities and their relations.

Furthermore, this phase entailed translating into Spanish certain entity and relation types that were generated by LLMs in another language, often English. In some cases, we included this translation step so that all collected entities and relations were written in Spanish. The translation facilitated the integration of data in multiple languages by standardizing the entities in a common language.

These techniques not only consolidate and improve the quality of information, but also ensure a more consistent and accurate representation of knowledge. Some examples of post-processing are shown in Table 2.

Table 2. Examples of post-processing

Translation	
{‘head’: ‘servicio de cartografía’, ‘head_type’: ‘organization’, ‘relation’: ‘will measure again’, ‘tail’: ‘everest’, ‘tail_type’: ‘location’}	{‘head’: ‘servicio de cartografía’, ‘head_type’: ‘organización’, ‘relation’: ‘medirá de nuevo’, ‘tail’: ‘everest’, ‘tail_type’: ‘lugar’}
Normalization	
“fondo de desastres naturales”: [“fondo de desastres naturales (fonden)”, “fondo de desastres naturales”, “fondo nacional de desastres naturales”]	“sedena”: [“secretaría de defensa nacional sedena”, “sedena”, “secretaría de defensa nacional (sedena)”]

Note: The canonical term is the first one in the normalization section, while the terms in brackets are its variants.

3.6 Creation of Knowledge Graphs

This step of our workflow transforms the output of each LLM into a KG. The RDFLib library [14] was used to convert the JSON format of entities and relations into an RDF file serialized in Turtle format. This conversion allows entities and relations to be represented in a graph model, facilitating analysis and visualization of the connections between discovered elements. Serialization in Turtle makes the knowledge graph readable by humans and machines, making it easy to query and share data between different applications and services.

For the construction of KGs, we used widely used ontologies and vocabularies such as DBpedia[1], Organization[2], FOAF[3], Time[4], and Schema.org[5], to improve the representation of entities and relations and to obtain a more complete and detailed view of our corpus.

4 Results

Using the three LLMs, a total of 6,935 unique entities were identified in our news corpus, such as places, persons, institutions, and events, among others, and 2,899

[1] https://www.dbpedia.org/resources/ontology/.
[2] https://www.w3.org/TR/vocab-org/.
[3] http://xmlns.com/foaf/spec/.
[4] https://www.w3.org/TR/owl-time/.
[5] https://schema.org/.

relationships. Figure 2 shows the number of entity types identified by each LLM, considering only the most frequent entities.

This distribution is useful to show the characteristics of the growth and decrease dynamics among the different types of entities related to each model, allowing us to observe that an LLM can perform better in identifying a specific type of entity compared to the other models.

In this case, Llama 3 identified more entities related to events and locations than the other models. In the identification of persons and organizations, the three LLMs had a similar behavior, this can be useful to use a specific model for the identification of a certain type of entity.

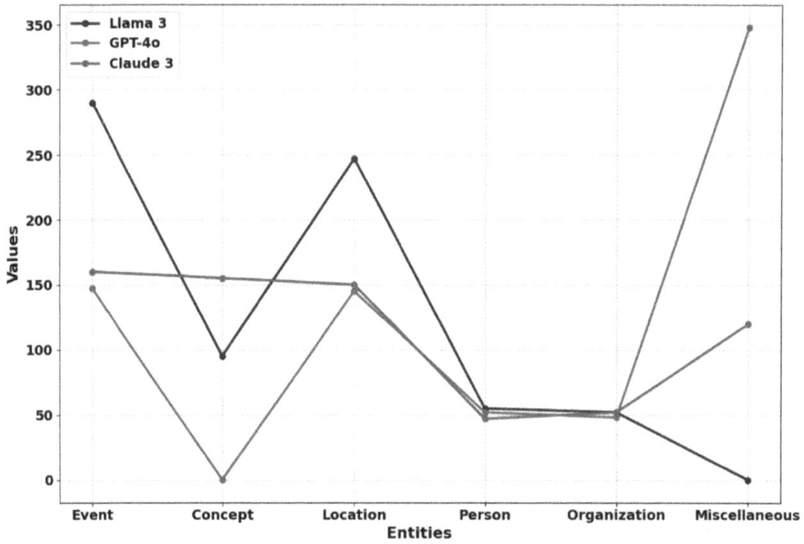

Fig. 2. Types of entities identified by each LLM

Figure 3 presents the strengths and weaknesses of three LLMs in identifying components of a KG. GPT-4o shows a clear advantage in identifying tails, suggesting its superior ability to recognize terminal elements in complex structures. Claude 3, on the other hand, excels at identifying heads, demonstrating its effectiveness in detecting principal elements. Llama 3 excels at identifying relationships, indicating its ability to understand and link interactions between entities in the network. This comparison highlights how each model has distinct areas of expertise that can be leveraged depending on the specific needs of an investigation.

To facilitate the geographic visualization of events in Mexico, the entity recognition process is used to identify the geolocation of places mentioned in our news corpus [23]. This identification is performed using the Open Cage API, which enriches the original data with latitude and longitude coordinates (see Fig. 4).

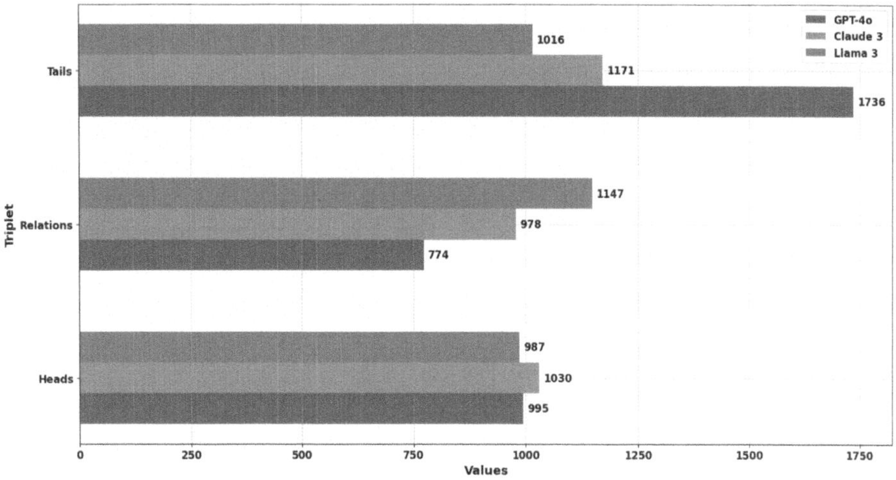

Fig. 3. Number of headss, relations and tails identified by each LLMs

This enrichment is crucial to provide a detailed representation of the spatial distribution of activities associated with natural disasters, such as earthquakes, hurricanes, or floods. Nevertheless, it is important to note that geolocation does not confirm the occurrence of these events in locations in Mexico, since the locations mentioned may refer to other contexts related to natural disaster news.

Figure 4 provides a visual approximation of the spatialization of the entities, allowing us to infer possible relations with natural disaster events based on the mentions, without establishing a direct correlation with the actual frequency of these events [23]. In the aforementioned figure, the larger circles indicate that these locations had a higher frequency compared to the others. For example, the largest circles represent Oaxaca and Chiapas, with 25 and 20 mentions, respectively, while other places such as Mexico City and the State of Mexico are mentioned 15 times.

Figure 5 shows a word cloud visualizing the frequency of entities associated with types of events, where the most present news terms reflect larger size and vice versa [25]. This representation simplifies the visualization of the entities associated with the most relevant and recurrent events in the analyzed news set. The colors and sizes of the entities help to highlight the main trends and patterns, providing a clear and concise view of the distribution of terms. The most representative entities related to events are earthquakes, tremors, magnitude, avalanches, elections, etc.

Below is an example of a newspaper article from our corpus, in which entities (highlighted in bold) have been manually identified. These entities belong to the following types: quantities, places, events, time, geographic coordinates and organizations.

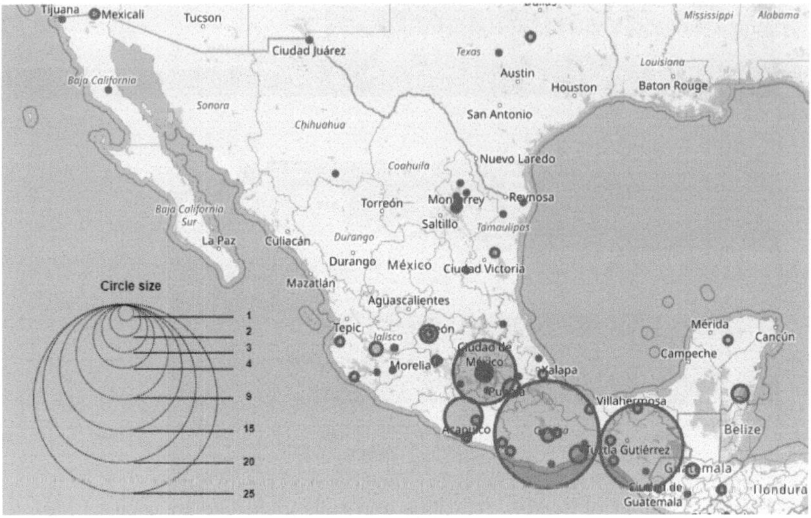

Fig. 4. Mentions of places related to natural disasters

Fig. 5. Word cloud of entities associated with events

Un **sismo** de **4.0** grados sacudió la madrugada de este **jueves** la **Reserva de la Biosfera El Abra - Tanchipa** a la altura del ejido **Laguna del Mante** sin que se reporten daños hasta el momento. La **sacudida** ocurrió a la **01 07 minutos 30** kilómetros al Norte de la cabecera municipal en la **latitud 22.26** y **longitud -98.94** de acuerdo con el **Servicio Sismológico Nacional (SSN)**. Debido a la hora pocas personas sintieron el **movimiento de tierra** tanto en **Laguna del Mante** como en el ejido **Gustavo Garnendia** y el poblado **Buena Vista** ubicados en el área. Anualmente ocurren en **México** de **10 mil** a **15 mil temblores** de **4.0** grados en la escala de Ritcher; la ocurrencia de **sacudidas** de tierra en ese sector de la reserva ha sido en varias ocasiones pero sin afectar a la población. Cabe señalar que en **Laguna del Mante** se ubica la **presa La Lajilla**, la cuarta mayor del estado de **San Luis Potosí** y los **temblores** representarían un riesgo de fracturas.[a]

[a] An example from our news corpus

In the news corpus example, a total of 23 entities are identified by manual analysis. Table 3 presents a comparative analysis of the header and tail entities identified by different LLMs applied to the corpus example. The table illustrates the discrepancies in the performance of each model and highlights the importance of selecting an appropriate model based on the context and complexity of the task. In the example considered, the model that identified the same number of entities was Claude 3 (see Fig. 6), while Llama 3 (see Fig. 7) identified 13 entities and GPT-4 (see Fig. 8) identified a total of 20 entities.

Table 3. Heads and tails identified by LLMs in the news example

Triplet	Llama 3	GPT -4o	Claude 3
Heads	7	7	8
Relations	5	11	16
Tails	6	13	15

As can be seen in Fig. 6, 7 and 8, each of the graphs has a defined structure and types of relations. The color of the nodes and edges determines the groupings within the graph, indicating that these nodes are semantically more similar and have a higher relations weight. A machine learning algorithm for graphs, known as community identification, was used to perform the clustering of nodes through node embedding. Thus, the more clustering the graphs have, the fewer relationships they have, since the nodes are isolated from most of the other nodes. For example, Llama 3 and Claude 3 have five groupings, unlike GPT-4o, whose nodes contain structurally few relationships.

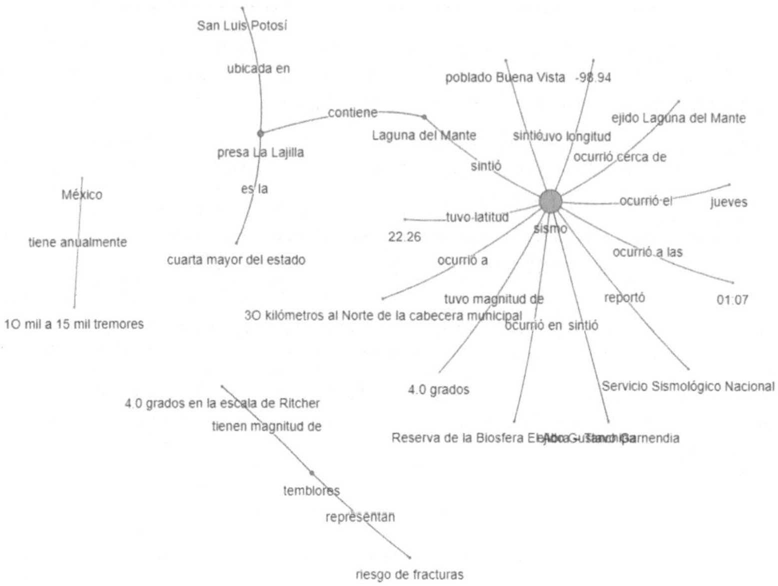

Fig. 6. Knowledge graph obtained using Claude 3

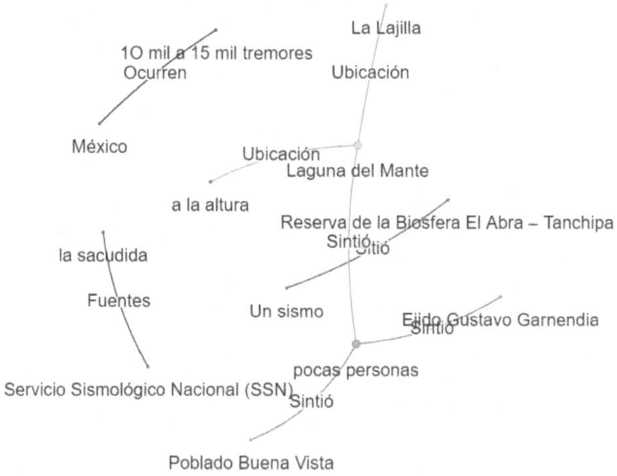

Fig. 7. Knowledge graph obtained using Llama 3

On the other hand, Llama 3 does not have a defined central node where most of the relationships are identified, whereas GPT-4o and Claude do; in both cases it is the "sismo" node where most of the relationships are centered. This variability may be due to several factors, including differences in the algorithms used by each model, the quality and diversity of the training data, and the fine-tuning techniques used [17].

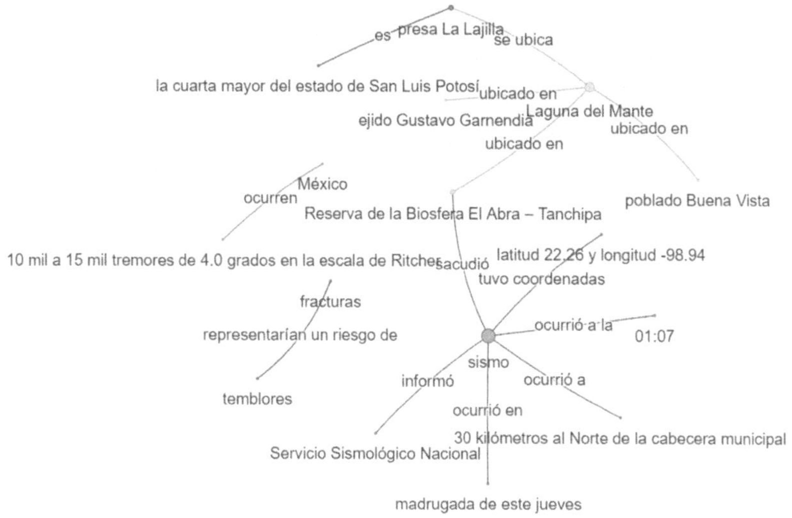

Fig. 8. Knowledge graph obtained using GPT-4o

In addition, the context in which these LLMs are used can also affect their performance. In some cases, a model may be optimized for a specific type of text or knowledge domain, which may improve its performance in these specific areas, but limit its applicability in other contexts.

Finally, an RDF file was created in turtle format where the semantic tools and prefixes used to enrich the model were defined, such as FOAF, Dbpedia, Schema.org, XMLSchema, and Dublin Core. This data serialization allows specific knowledge domains to be represented, improving their accessibility and information retrieval through interoperability. Figure 9 illustrates a particular example of our knowledge graph serialized in turtle format.

5 Evaluation

In order to ascertain the relative efficacy of Llama 3, GPT-4o, and Claude 3 Sonnet in the identification of entities, the models were subjected to evaluation based on the criteria of precision, recall, and F1 score, utilizing a representative dataset. To this end, a random sample of 40 news items from the corpus, which had been previously annotated by experts, was selected to create a reference dataset for evaluation purposes. This dataset contains detailed annotations of key entities related to natural disasters, including the names of places, organizations, and people.

- Precision is the number of positive cases correctly predicted by the algorithm [5]. It is calculated as shown in Formula 1.

$$\text{Precision} = \frac{TP}{TP + FP} \tag{1}$$

```
@prefix ex: <http://example.org/> .
@prefix dbo: <http://dbpedia.org/ontology/> .
@prefix xsd: <http://www.w3.org/2001/XMLSchema#> .
@prefix schema: <http://schema.org/> .
@prefix foaf: <http://xmlns.com/foaf/0.1/> .
@prefix org: <https://www.w3.org/ns/org#> .  # Organization Ontology
@prefix time: <http://www.w3.org/2006/time#> .  # Time Ontology

ex:Oaxaca a schema:Place ;
    ex:registra ex:22_sismos .
ex:22_sismos a dbo:Thing .

ex:México a schema:Place ;
    ex:registra ex:73_movimientos_telúricos .
ex:73_movimientos_telúricos a dbo:Thing .

ex:Oaxaca a schema:Place ;
    ex:tiene ex:Primer_lugar_nacional .
ex:Primer_lugar_nacional a dbo:Thing .

ex:Guerrero a schema:Place ;
    ex:registra ex:27_sismos .
ex:27_sismos a dbo:Thing .

ex:Chiapas a schema:Place ;
    ex:registra ex:136_sismos .
ex:136_sismos a dbo:Thing .

ex:Tlacolula a schema:Place ;
    ex:es_epicentro_de ex:Sismo .
ex:Sismo a dbo:Thing .
```

Fig. 9. An excerpt of our knowledge graph in Turtle format

- Recall. Completeness is calculated by taking the proportion of positive entries correctly identified as positive [5]. It is calculated as shown in Formula 2.

$$\text{Recall} = \frac{TP}{TP + FN} \tag{2}$$

We define the elements to calculate precision and recall in the following way:

  - TP (True Positive): Number of entities that have been correctly identified by the model.
  - TN (True Negative): Number of entities not correctly identified by the model when they did not correspond to any entity.
  - FP (False Positive): Number of entities incorrectly identified by the model as belonging to an entity when in fact they are not.
  - FN (False Negative): Number of entities that were not identified by the model, but did correspond to an entity.

- F1 Score. It is defined as a weighted average of accuracy and completeness [5]. This metric has its maximum value at 1 and the worst at 0. It is calculated as shown in Formula 3.

$$\text{F1} = \frac{2 \cdot \text{Precision} \cdot \text{Recall}}{\text{Precision} + \text{Recall}} \tag{3}$$

Based on the metrics described above, Table 4 presents the performance results of the three language models (LLMs) evaluated, compared to our benchmark data. The results indicate that Llama 3 exhibits the highest precision, meaning that it correctly identifies a higher percentage of entities in the dataset. However, GPT-4o demonstrates better recall, meaning that it is able to identify a higher proportion of relevant entities overall.

In terms of the F1 score, which provides a balance between precision and recall, GPT-4o and Llama 3 obtain equivalent scores. These results suggest that for tasks that require a balance between entity identification precision and the ability to identify as many relevant entities as possible, GPT-4o is the most suitable choice.

Table 4. Precision, Recall and F1 for each model

LLM	Precision	Recall	F1
Llama 3	0.46	0.50	0.48
Claude 3	0.34	0.32	0.33
GPT-4o	0.42	0.55	0.48

As can be seen in Table 4, the values obtained are not optimal. However, a more detailed and qualitative analysis of the results shows that the few differences observed have an important impact on the evaluation of the precision and recall metrics. For example, while the manual annotation identified entities in a specific way, the models identified the same entities with small variations. These differences in specificity led the metrics to classify the entities as different, which negatively affected the evaluation of the models' performance. In addition, a discrepancy was found in the total number of entities identified by the models compared to manual annotation, increasing the number of true negatives and decreasing precision. This variability in the identification and classification of entities highlights the need to refine models and evaluation criteria to improve the consistency and precision of the results.

6 Discussion

The construction of domain-specific knowledge graphs has recently been the subject of considerable attention in the literature [29]. Traditional methods entail the extraction of information from disparate sources [27], which is costly in terms of human annotations and the construction of ontologies to build KGs. In contrast, recent advances have begun to leverage LLMs for automatic entity and relationship recognition [11], which streamlines the process by reducing the reliance on direct human intervention and improving the efficiency of KG generation. This facilitates a more accurate and comprehensive representation of the domain in question.

This ongoing work provides a workflow that integrates LLMs and various natural language processing techniques to identify and improve the quality of named entity and relation extraction, with the objective of building a KG on natural disasters in Mexico. The principal benefit of employing LLMs as assistants to human experts in the construction of KGs is reflected in the substantial reduction in the effort and expertise required in specific domains and on the Semantic Web [15].

However, several issues have been identified in the existing literature on the use of LLMs for the construction of KGs. These include hallucination, reasoning ability, and a lack of updating in large language models [13]. While several of these issues are part of our future work, we have observed in our current work that some issues associated with LLMs often result in the identification of parent and child entities consisting of very long chains, which can result in incorrect or inconsistent information. Additionally, LLMs occasionally fail to identify complete triplets, necessitating the incorporation of graph completion techniques, such as link or relationship prediction.

In comparison to previous contributions [7,11,15,24,30], this study is distinguished by considering a significantly larger dataset for processing, which is not limited to previous training or annotation data. Furthermore, a selection of three state-of-the-art LLMs has been deployed, thus enabling a more comprehensive evaluation of their capabilities in identifying entities and relations. This approach has enhanced the construction of three different KGs by capitalizing on the distinctive strengths of each LLM and addressing their shortcomings.

The construction of domain-specific knowledge graphs is a costly process in terms of the input from human annotators and is challenging to generalize to other domains [11]. Nevertheless, our proposed workflow for the semi-automatic construction of specific KGs can be readily adapted to other knowledge domains. Furthermore, it facilitates the maintenance and updating of KG information by allowing the continuous integration of new data and the automatic identification of existing entities and relations. This allows for the overcoming of issues related to the updatability of KGs. With respect to the granularity problem, it was identified that there is a necessity to include more specific domain ontologies in order to capture all the fine details about natural disasters, such as event-specific details, affected locations, or actors involved.

A further limitation is the high computational cost associated with information processing. These costs encompass not only the computational time necessary to process the information but also the consumption of hardware resources, which can impede the scalability and accessibility of these techniques. These limitations present scientific challenges to the further development of LLMs for the construction of KGs.

7 Conclusions and Future Work

In this article, a method based on integrating LLMs was presented to build KGs on the topic of natural disasters in Mexico using raw news articles available in the GDELT (Global Database of Events, Language, and Tone) database.

The proposed process demonstrated that significant information can be extracted from unstructured data through a semi-automated process and showed the potential of LLMs as assistants in building knowledge representation models. Although the results are far from replacing human intervention, our ongoing work has demonstrated that LLMs can support the creation of KG, reducing efforts and allowing for the collection and organization of heterogeneous information on the topic of natural disasters in Mexico, giving it meaning to allow its use, access, and retrieval in the development of the Semantic Web.

As part of our future work, we will extend the information processing capacity of LLMs, improve the accuracy in detecting and recognizing entities and relations within the news corpus, implement more consistent and appropriate normalization and alignment of entities and relations, and enrich the use of vocabularies and ontologies associated with specific knowledge domains.

References

1. Abraham, K., Abdelwahab, M., Abo-Zahhad, M.: Classification and detection of natural disasters using machine learning and deep learning techniques: a review. Earth Sci. Inform. **17**, 869–891 (2024). https://doi.org/10.1007/s12145-023-01205-2
2. Alcántara-Ayala, I.: Disasters in Mexico and Central America: a little bit more than a century of natural hazards. Dev. Earth Surface Process. **19**, 75–97 (2009). https://doi.org/10.1016/S0928-2025(08)10004-9
3. Alcántara-Ayala, I.: Geomorphology, natural hazards, vulnerability and prevention of natural disasters in developing countries. Geomorphology **47**(2–4), 107–124 (2002). https://doi.org/10.1016/S0169-555X(02)00083-1
4. Anthropic: Introducing the next generation of Claude. https://www.anthropic.com/news/claude-3-family. Accessed 03 July 2024
5. Arjaria, S., Abhishek, S., Jincy, C.: Kidney disease prediction using a machine learning approach: a comparative and comprehensive analysis. In: Demystifying Big Data, Machine Learning, and Deep Learning for Healthcare Analytics, pp. 307–333. Elsevier, London (2021). https://doi.org/10.1016/B978-0-12-821633-0.00006-4
6. Batool, A., Byun, Y.-C.: Enhanced sentiment analysis and topic modeling during the pandemic using automated latent Dirichlet allocation. IEEE Access **12**, 81206–81220 (2024). https://doi.org/10.1109/ACCESS.2024.3411717
7. Bi, Z., et al.: CodeKGC: code language model for generative knowledge graph construction. arXiv (2024). https://arxiv.org/abs/2304.09048
8. Blei, D.M., Ng, A.Y., Jordan, M.I.: Latent Dirichlet allocation. J. Mach. Learn. Res. **3**, 993–1022 (2003). https://www.jmlr.org/papers/volume3/blei03a/blei03a.pdf
9. Carrillo-Brenes, F., Vilches-Blázquez, L.M., Mata, F.: A proposal for semantic integration of crime data in Mexico City. In: Mata-Rivera, M.F., Zagal-Flores, R., Arellano Verdejo, J., Lazcano Hernandez, H.E. (eds) GIS LATAM. Communications in Computer and Information Science, pp. 30–48. Springer, Cham (2020). https://doi.org/10.1007/978-3-030-59872-3_3
10. Dikeoulias, I., Amin, S., Neumann, G.: Temporal knowledge graph reasoning with low-rank and model-agnostic representations. In: Proceedings of the 7th Workshop

on Representation Learning for NLP, pp. 111–120. Association for Computational Linguistics, Dublin, Ireland (2022). https://aclanthology.org/2022.repl4nlp-1.12.pdf
11. Ding, L., Zhou, S., Xiao, J., Han, J.: Automated construction of theme-specific knowledge graphs. arXiv (2024). https://arxiv.org/abs/2404.19146
12. Gesler, W.: A place in history: a guide to using GIS in historical research. J. Interdisc. Hist. **35**, 283–283 (2004). https://doi.org/10.1162/0022195041742436
13. Kau, A.: Automated Knowledge Graph Construction with Large Language Models. https://n9.cl/xsmet. Accessed 07 Aug 2024
14. Krech, D., et al.: RDFLib (Version 7.0.0) [Software]. https://doi.org/10.5281/zenodo.6845245. Accessed 04 July 2024
15. Krishna, V., König-Ries, B., Samuel, K.: From human experts to machines: an LLM supported approach to ontology and knowledge graph construction. arXiv (2024). https://arxiv.org/abs/2403.08345
16. Meta LLaMA Team: Introducing Meta Llama 3: The most capable openly available LLM to date. https://ai.meta.com/blog/meta-llama-3/. Accessed 03 July 2024
17. Naveed, H., et al.: A comprehensive overview of large language models. arXiv (2023). https://arxiv.org/abs/2307.06435
18. Neudecker, C., Antonacopoulos, A.: Making Europe's historical newspapers searchable. In: 2016 12th IAPR Workshop on Document Analysis Systems (DAS), pp. 405–410. IEEE (2016). https://doi.org/10.1109/DAS.2016.83
19. Noy, N., Gao, Y., Jain, A., Narayanan, A., Patterson, A., Taylor, J.: Industry-scale knowledge graphs: lessons and challenges: five diverse technology companies show how it's done. Queue **17**, 48–75 (2019). https://doi.org/10.1145/3329781.3332266
20. OpenAI: Hello GPT-4o. https://openai.com/index/hello-gpt-4o/. Accessed 03 July 2024
21. Paulheim, H.: Knowledge graph refinement: a survey of approaches and evaluation methods. Semant. Web **8**, 489–508 (2017). https://doi.org/10.3233/SW-160218
22. Ren, X., Tang, J., Yin, D., Chawla, N., Huang, C.: A survey of large language models for graphs. arXiv (2024). https://arxiv.org/abs/2405.08011
23. Saquicela, V., Vilches-Blázquez, L.M., Espinoza, M.: Building a knowledge graph from historical newspapers: a study case in Ecuador. In: Narváez, F.R., Urgilés, F., Bastos-Filho, T.F., Salgado-Guerrero, J.P. (eds) Smart Technologies, Systems and Applications. SmartTech-IC 2022. Communications in Computer and Information Science, vol. 1705. Springer, Cham (2023). https://doi.org/10.1007/978-3-031-32213-6_10
24. Trajanoska, M., Stojanov, R., Trajanov, D.: Enhancing knowledge graph construction using large language models. arXiv (2023). https://arxiv.org/abs/2305.04676
25. Vilches-Blázquez, L.M., Comesaña, D., de Arrieta Moreno, L.J.: Construcción de una red de ontologías sobre eventos meteorológicos a partir de periódicos históricos. Transinformação **32** (2020). https://doi.org/10.1590/1678-9865202032e180077
26. Xue, B., Zou, L.: Knowledge graph quality management: a comprehensive survey. IEEE Trans. Knowl. Data Eng. **35**(5), 4969–4988 (2023). https://doi.org/10.1109/TKDE.2022.3150080
27. Yao, Z., et al.: Schema-aware reference as prompt improves data-efficient knowledge graph construction. arXiv (2022). https://arxiv.org/abs/2210.10709#
28. Yu, S., Huang, T., Liu, M., Wang, Z.: BEAR: revolutionizing service domain knowledge graph construction with LLM. In: Monti, F., Rinderle-Ma, S., Ruiz Cortés, A., Zheng, Z., Mecella, M. (eds) Service-Oriented Computing. ICSOC 2023. Lecture Notes in Computer Science, vol. 14419. Springer, Cham (2023). https://doi.org/10.1007/978-3-031-48421-6_23

29. Zaratiana, U., Tomeh, N., Holat, P., Charnois, T.: An autoregressive text-to-graph framework for joint entity and relation extraction. arXiv (2024). https://arxiv.org/abs/2401.01326
30. Zhang, B., Soh, H.: Extract, define, canonicalize: an LLM-based framework for knowledge graph construction. arXiv (2024). https://arxiv.org/abs/2404.03868

Spatial and Seasonal Patterns of Rainfall Climate Teleconnections in Three Hydropower Generation Basins in Tropical Ecuador

Daniela Ballari, Paul Bravo-López(✉), and Omar Delgado-Inga

Institute for the Study of the Sectional Regime of Ecuador (IERSE), University of Azuay, Av. 24 de Mayo 7-77 y Hernán Malo, Cuenca, Ecuador
{dballari,pbravo,odelgado}@uazuay.edu.ec

Abstract. Renewable energy, such as solar, wind, or hydro, is derived from natural processes where the replacement rate is faster than the consumption rate. In Ecuador, hydropower is the predominant source of renewable energy, but its intermittency is largely driven by climate variability, including climate teleconnections like the El Niño Southern Oscillation (ENSO). Previous studies have primarily focused on detecting climate teleconnections using data from sparse weather stations, neglecting the spatial and seasonal influences of these teleconnections. This study identifies climate teleconnections that are spatially and seasonally related to rainfall in three hydropower basins of Ecuador: Jubones, Paute, and Napo. Twelve climate indices from the Pacific and Atlantic Oceans were correlated with monthly CHIRPS satellite rainfall estimates (1981–2019). The results showed a predominant influence from the Pacific Ocean in all three basins, with most indices being positively correlated with ENSO. In Jubones, most indices showed positive teleconnections in the April-May-June (AMJ) season, and both positive and negative teleconnections in the July-August-September (JAS) season. Similarly, in Paute, positive teleconnections were observed in AMJ and JAS, while negative teleconnections were noted in January-February-March (JFM) and JAS. In Napo, positive influences were observed in JAS, while negative influences were observed throughout the year. This study provides valuable insights for the future development of monitoring and prediction systems for hydropower generation.

Keywords: Ecuador · renewable energy · climate variability · remote sensing · climate teleconnection

1 Introduction

Energy is a fundamental element for the development of society. In fact, sustainable energy is one of the central pillars of the 2030 Agenda. Although there is a Sustainable Development Goal (SDG) specifically dedicated to energy (SDG 7), several linkages have been found with other SDG targets [1], such as life on land, climate action, sustainable cities, and clean water. By advocating for renewable energies, the aim is to provide an alternative to the environmental and climate impacts associated with the use of fossil fuels, facilitating a transition in the energy sector aimed at reducing environmental

M. F. Mata-Rivera et al. (Eds.): GIS-LATAM 2024, CCIS 2298, pp. 168–184, 2025.
https://doi.org/10.1007/978-3-031-80017-7_11

impact. Renewable energy is one of the most efficient and effective solutions for this purpose [2]. In recent years, there has been an increase in the use of these energy sources. For instance, by 2016 about 17% of the world's electricity generation came from hydropower [3], and by 2019, according to the latest SDG report, this value increased to 26% [4]. In South America, the most widespread renewable energy source is hydropower. And particularly in Ecuador, a tropical country in northern-South America, about 50% of effective power generation comes from hydropower [5]. In the last two decades, several hydroelectric projects, such as Coca Codo Sinclair, Sopladora, Manduriaco, and Toachi Pilatón, have been built in Ecuador, helping to produce around 73% of the total renewable energy generated in the country [6]. Thus, most economic and social activities in Ecuador are currently highly dependent on hydropower generation.

According to the International Energy Agency (IEA), renewable energies are derived from natural processes where the replacement rate is faster than the consumption rate [7]. Regarding the source, renewable energies can be intermittent or non-intermittent, with intermittency largely driven by the natural variability of climate [8]. This is why they are also known as Climate-Related Energy (CRE), which includes solar, wind, and hydropower energies [9, 10]. Hydropower energy, however, is influenced not only by climate and atmospheric processes but also by earth surface processes such as landscape, basin geometry, and properties, which are essential for generating flow [9]. Nevertheless, the main driver for hydropower generation is the hydrological cycle and climate variability [11]. Hydropower and CRE in general may fluctuate on different temporal and spatial scales due to their relation to climate variables such as wind speed, solar radiation, rainfall, and temperature [10]. For instance, during severe droughts or heavy rains, average hydroelectric generation can vary substantially, and the effects of rainfall can persist for long periods [12]. Therefore, understanding the relationship of hydropower production in response to climate variability is a fundamental step in assessing its potential and resource availability over time.

Climate variability can occur at high temporal frequencies from seconds to hours, intermediate frequencies from hours to seasonal cycles, and low frequencies from years to decades. The intermediate (month and seasons) and low temporal frequency (years and decades) has been related to climate teleconnections such as the El Niño Southern Oscillation (ENSO) in tropical regions, or the North Atlantic Oscillation (NAO) in North America and Europe [10]. Climate teleconnections represent remote and large-scale connections between distant points on Earth, leading to climate anomalies and variability [13, 14]. They are monitored through climate indices [15, 16] that measure different characteristics (e.g., sea surface temperature or pressure) in specific geographic areas. Identifying the influence of climatic teleconnections, such as ENSO, on climate variables related to water availability and hydropower generation is very useful for prediction, analysis, and modeling the behavior of energy generation. To detect such influence in a specific location and on a specific climate variable such as rainfall, correlation methods are generally applied to show the degree of association between rainfall and climate indices [17, 18].

Climate teleconnections in Ecuador have been previously explored using weather station networks [19–24] and remote sensing rainfall images [25, 26]. It was reported for both Pacific and Atlantic Ocean teleconnections that significantly influence rainfall. For instance, Pacific Ocean teleconnections (by the increase of the sea surface temperature (SST) in the tropical Pacific Ocean) showed rainfall increases in the coastal basins, while decreases in the Andean and Amazonian regions [21]. In this context, and from a mythological perspective, Mendoza et al. (2019, 2020) identified climatic teleconnections by integrating rainfall from weather stations into a modeling framework for the Paute river basin. Hasan and Wyseure [28] and Carvajal et al. [29, 30] identified the influence that climate change will have on hydroelectric power generation through climate projection scenarios. These studies showed that the effects of climate variability and climate change on water resources can modify hydroelectric potential. However, these studies focus only on the temporal influence and at the locations of very scarce weather stations, without accounting for the spatial distribution of such influence. Other works used rainfall estimates from satellite sources for representing the spatial distribution of the influences of climatic indices [25, 26, 31, 32]. This source of information, instead of providing a point-based representation like weather stations, provides a continuous representation of rainfall. Despite these previous works, the temporal and spatial relationships rainfall as main natural resource of hydroelectric power generation in response to climatic indices have been scarcely explored.

Therefore, this study identified the climate teleconnections that spatially and seasonally influence rainfall in the three main hydropower basins in Ecuador, namely Paute, Napo, and Jubones river basins. For the period 1981–2019, it was used CHIRPS satellite rainfall estimates, climate indices, and correlation methods. Spearman correlation analysis was applied pixel-wise on detrended time series and mean aggregated seasonality for January-February-March (JFM), April-May-June (AMJ), July-August-September (JAS), and October-November-December (OND). This work contributes with a better knowledge about climate teleconnections through climatic indices and local variability across the whole basin from satellite images.

2 Methods

2.1 Study Area

Ecuador's climate presents high spatial-temporal variability, as the Andes mountains act as a climate barrier and modulate rainfall regimes [33]. Three main factors characterize Ecuador's climate regimes (Pourrut et al., 1995, cited in [34]: first, the movement of the Intertropical Convergence Zone (ITCZ) north or south determines the entry of air masses with different temperature and humidity conditions; second, the topographic influence on the production of orographic rainfall; and third, the Pacific Ocean and its marine currents, such as the Humboldt Current, which brings masses of fresh and dry air from the south that affect the eastern slopes of Ecuador and Peru [35], and the El Niño Current, which brings air masses with high moisture content from the north.

Due to these characteristics, three hydrographic basins located in different climatic regions of Ecuador have been selected for our study: 1) the Jubones river basin, located in the coastal region, which is a Pacific Ocean basin; 2) the Paute river basin, in the Andean region, which is an Amazon basin with high mountain as well as Amazon regimes; and 3) the Napo river basin, which is an Amazon basin with an Amazonian regime (Fig. 1).

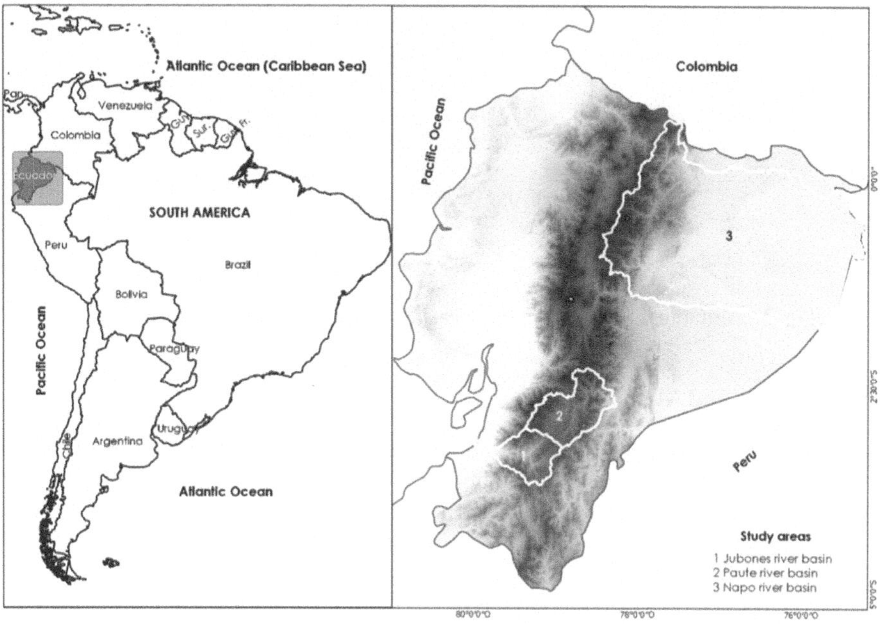

Fig. 1. Study area. Hydropower basins of Jubones (1), Paute (2) and Napo (3) rivers.

The Jubones river basin is located in the southwestern part of Ecuador, on the western slope of the Andes mountains, with an area of 4,362 km^2 (Figs. 1 and 2.a). Its climate conditions are extremely variable due to the presence of the Andes, trade winds, and ocean currents [28]. The climate ranges from humid to arid, and the rainy season extends from January to May, with annual rainfall between 290 and 925 mm. The Minas-San Francisco hydroelectric plant, with a capacity of 275 MW, is located in this basin [28].

The Paute river basin is located in the southern Andes of Ecuador, in the Inter-Andean Depression, a tectonic depression that separates the Eastern and Western Cordilleras in the Andes [36] (Figs. 1 and 2.b). The basin covers approximately 5,069 km^2 [34]. In this basin is located the Paute Integral System, which consists of three hydroelectric plants: Mazar, Molino, and Sopladora. This project originated in 1961 thanks to the great flow of the Paute river, reservoirs, and tunnel systems. It contributes with an approximate power of 1,757 MW.

The Napo river basin is located on the eastern slope of the Andes Mountains in the northwestern zone of the Amazon basin (Figs. 1 and 2.c). Due to its extension, this basin is located between Ecuador and Peru; however, in this study, the analyses were conducted only in Ecuadorian territory. With a total area of approximately 100,518 km^2, this zone has an average annual rainfall that varies from 2,700 to 4,100 mm. In this basin is located the hydroelectric plant Coca Codo Sinclair. Its power is 1,500 MW and supplies approximately 30% of the national demand.

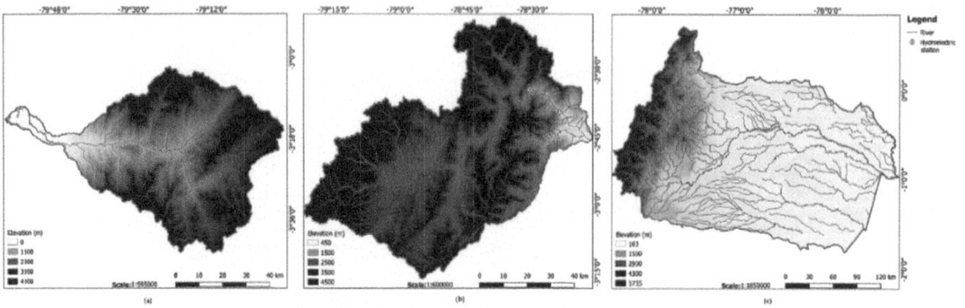

Fig. 2. Altitudinal levels of the study basins: a) Jubones, b) Paute and c) Napo.

2.2 Materials and Methods

We made use of two types of data: 1) rainfall satellite estimates and 2) climate indices for teleconnections. Regarding the methods, they consisted of: 1) seasonal correlation maps and 2) explorative pixel-wise interaction among teleconnections. Figure 3 shows a schema of the methods.

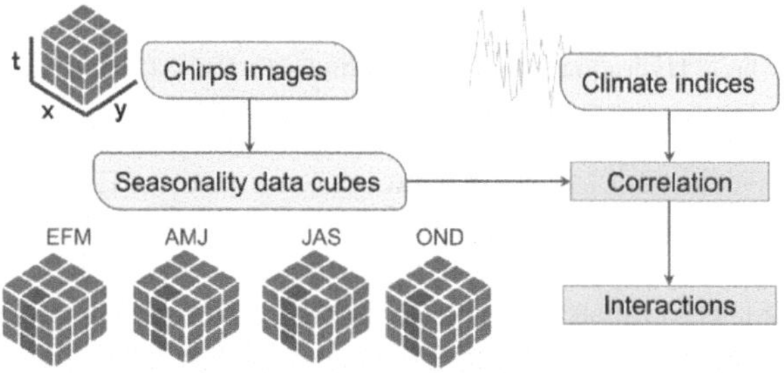

Fig. 3. Schema for methodological steps.

Rainfall Satellite Estimates. Obtaining reliable data at high spatial resolutions remains a challenge, especially in regions with high rainfall variability and poor monitoring [37]. In poorly monitored regions, spatially continuous data from satellite images are an important source of information for rainfall analysis. In this study, we used the Climate Hazards Group Infrared Rainfall with Stations (CHIRPS V2.0), with a spatial resolution of $0.05^\circ \times 0.05^\circ$ and monthly temporal resolution [38]. This product was selected because of its high spatial resolution and long temporal period. The temporal period of monthly images selected for this study was from 1981 to 2019. Before using the images, the linear trend was removed without affecting the mean (R environment: Detrend from SpecsVerification; [39]). Data were structured as a spatio-temporal data cube of satellite images (R environment: rasterbrick from raster; [40]). In this way, each cube pixel contained a monthly time series. CHIRPS data were downloaded from https://www.chc.ucsb.edu/data/chirps.

This product was selected after the validation provided by Vázquez-Patiño et al. [41] with 10 rain gauges from 1981 to 2014. The validation covered the entire country using a pixel-wise approach. Of the 10 rain gauges, 2 were located in the Jubones river basin, 2 in Paute, and 6 in Napo. The results showed a median RMSE value of 89.54 mm/month, a median PBIAS% of −0.28%, and a median Spearman correlation coefficient of 0.81. This product was also used in other research for Ecuador [32].

Climate Indices for Teleconnections. The indices were selected following previous research [16, 17, 21, 26, 42] (Table 1). Similar to the rainfall images, the temporal period for monthly indices was also from 1981 to 2019, and the linear trend was removed. The indices were obtained from https://www.esrl.noaa.gov/psd/data/climateindices/list/.

Table 1. Climate indices for climate teleconnections.

Region	Index	Description
Pacific Ocean	Niño1 + 2	It measures the SST in the region 0-10S, 90W-80W eastern Pacific (close to Ecuador and Peru)
	Niño3	It measures the SST in the region 5N-5S, 150W-90W in Pacific Ocean
	Niño3.4	It measures the SST in the region 5N-5S, 170W-120W in Pacific Ocean
	Niño4	It measures the SST in the region 5N-5S, 160E-150W in Pacific Ocean
	ONI	Oceanic Niño Index located in 5N-5S, 170W-120W Pacific Ocean (same region as Niño3.4)
	PDO	Pacific Decadal Oscillation is the leading PC of monthly sea surface temperature anomalies in the North Pacific Ocean
	TNI	Trans Niño Index is the difference in normalized SST anomalies between Niño1 + 2 and Niño4 regions
	PNA	Pacific North American teleconnection index is one of the most prominent modes of low frequency variability in the Northern Hemisphere extra-tropics
		Southern Oscillation Index is based on the atmospheric pressure difference between Tahiti and Darwin
Atlantic Ocean	Ammsst	Atlantic Meridional Mode describes SST in the meridional variability in tropical Atlantic Ocean
	TNA	Tropical Northern Atlantic Index is an anomaly of the monthly SST from 5.5N-23.5N and 15W-57.5W
	TSA	Tropical Southern Atlantic Index is an anomaly of monthly average SST, Eq-20S and 10E-30W

Seasonal Correlation Maps. Spearman correlation was calculated between the climate indices and rainfall for each pixel of the spatio-temporal data cube (i.e., time series of rainfall stored in each pixel). Spearman correlation is a non-parametric method to measure the strength and direction of association between two variables [43]. Individual values of correlation coefficient were obtained for each pixel, allowing correlation maps to be plotted for each climate index.

To observe the intra-annual and seasonality variability of teleconnections, this analysis was performed seasonally according to January-February-March (JFM), April-May-June (AMJ), July-August-September (JAS), and October-November-December (OND). The seasonality maps were obtained as the mean of the monthly images for a specific season. As a result, correlation maps for the four seasons and each climate index were obtained. Teleconnections were identified as moderate correlations with values larger than +0.3 and smaller than −0.3, and the percentage of spatial coverage per climate index in each map was computed.

The cartographic representation of the resulting maps showed positive associations in blue and negative associations in red. Intensities in this diverging color palette indicated the strength of the association.

Explorative Pixel-Wise Interaction Among Teleconnections. The interaction among teleconnections was visualized pixel-wise as the frequency of climate indices with correlations larger than +0.3 or smaller than −0.3. Thus, the higher the frequency of indices influencing a pixel, the more interaction among teleconnections could be expected. The aim of this explorative and straightforward approach was to detect hotspot areas of high teleconnection interactions, which might be related to complexities of climate processes.

The computational implementation was done in R using libraries such as raster, SpecsVerification and ggplot2.

3 Results and Discussion

3.1 Seasonal and Spatial Patterns of Teleconnections

This section shows the spatially aggregated mean for the whole basins (Table 2). Table 2 reports only the correlation values that were larger than +0.3 (blue) and lower than − 0.3 (red). The table is organized as follows: in the rows, there are the climate indices related to the Pacific and Atlantic Oceans. In the columns, there are the three hydropower basins and the four intra-annual seasons (JFM, AMJ, JAS, and OND). In the cells, the mean correlation value for a given index, season, and basin is reported first, followed by the spatial coverage of the teleconnection in percentage. The table shows different directions (red for negative and blue for positive) as well as strengths in the associations according to the climate index and the seasons. The following subsections provide maps with the spatial distribution (pixel-wise correlations) by basin. The Table 2 will be further discussed along with the correlation maps by season for Jubones in Fig. 4, Paute in Fig. 5, and Napo in Fig. 6.

Jubones River Basin. In the Jubones river basin, most of the Pacific teleconnections were positive in JFM and AMJ, while most were negative in JAS (Table 2 and Fig. 4). This pattern is consistent with the intra-annual variability of rainfall in the region, where the rainy season is concentrated from January to May, and the dry season extends from June to December. This seasonality is similar to the C.2 region reported by [44] and the R3 (lowlands) and R9 (highlands) regions reported by [45]. Additionally, no teleconnections

Table 2. Summary of the spatially aggregated mean for the teleconnections by basin, season and climate index.

Index	Jubones				Paute				Napo			
Pacific Ocean	JFM	AMJ	JAS	OND	JFM	AMJ	JAS	OND	JFM	AMJ	JAS	OND
Niño 1+2	0,50 100%	0,68 100%			0,38 45%	0,47 78%	-0,37 74%		-0,35 6%	-0,34 32%	-0,42 47%	-0,32 4%
Niño3		0,52 100%	-0,35 72%		-0,32 22%	0,42 40%	-0,58 100%		-0,41 44%	-0,35 61%	-0,49 47%	-0,33 47%
Niño34		0,38 69%	-0,42 91%		-0,38 47%	0,32 12%	-0,68 100%		-0,44 64%	-0,41 85%	-0,54 47%	-0,35 56%
Niño4			-0,51 94%		-0,44 83%		-0,70 100%		-0,49 91%	-0,41 66%	-0,53 50%	-0,35 57%
ONI		0,38 69%	-0,42 89%		-0,38 49%	0,30 14%	-0,67 100%		-0,46 62%	-0,41 86%	-0,57 48%	-0,35 57%
PDO			-0,33 40%		-0,32 8%		-0,43 99%		-0,35 33%	-0,35 35%	-0,4 33%	-0,38 23%
TNI	0,57 100%	0,58 100%	0,32 38%		0,63 100%	0,54 100%	0,33 40%		0,45 95%			0,34 35%
PNA			-0,34 36%						-0,41 60%	-0,32 11	-0,37 15%	
SOI			0,48 93%		0,38 35%		0,6 100%		0,42 49%	0,36 52%	0,48 50%	0,35 41%
Atlantic Ocean	JFM	AMJ	JAS	OND	JFM	AMJ	JAS	OND	JFM	AMJ	JAS	OND
Ammsst			0,36 54%				0,33 59%				0,37 39%	0,33 31%
TNA			0,35 34%	0,33 40%			0,33 68%		-0,32 24%		0,33 26%	
TSA			0,39 61%			0,36 11%	0,46 100%	0,34 32%		0,36 21%	0,35 35%	

were observed from the Pacific in OND. Meanwhile, teleconnections from the Atlantic were positive in JAS and OND (dry season).

The strongest (i.e., larger than 0.5) and most spatially extended teleconnections were related to Niño 1 + 2, Niño 3, and TNI, covering the whole basin (Fig. 4). Niño 1 + 2 and TNI had positive associations in JFM and AMJ over the whole basin, and Niño 3 only in AMJ. TNI had a lower positive association in JAS than in JFM. Niño 3, Niño 3.4, and ONI showed similar behavior with positive correlations in AMJ (central west region of the basin) and negative in JAS (central east region). Regarding Niño 4, PDO, and PNA, they showed negative associations in JAS. Niño 4 was present in the whole basin, PDO in the central east region, and PNA in the west region. Finally, SOI showed positive correlation in most of the basin in JAS.

Associations from the Atlantic Ocean (AMMSST, TNA, and TSA; between 0.33 and 0.30) were found in JAS. Such associations did not cover the whole basin but instead

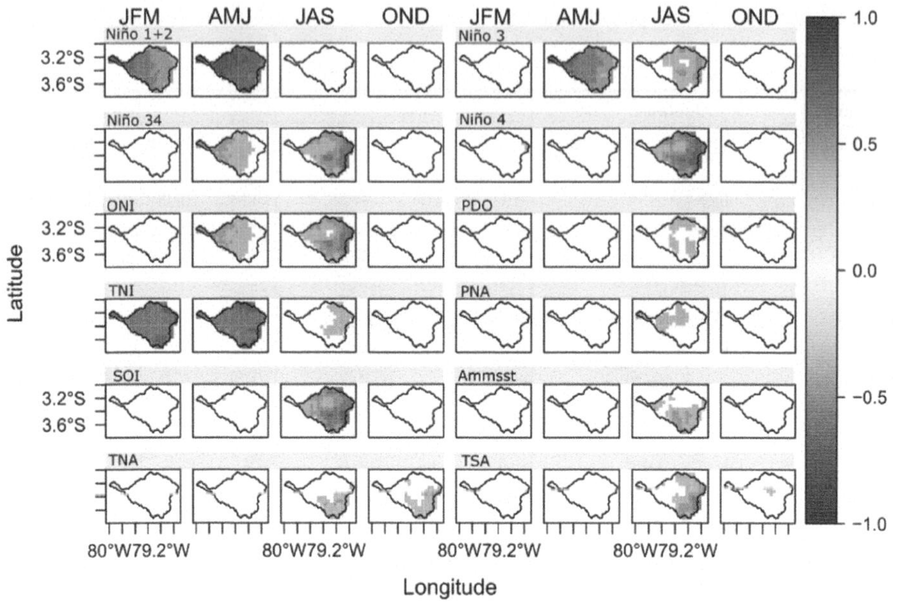

Fig. 4. Climate Teleconnection in the Jubones river basin: Spatial and seasonal distribution of teleconnection maps. The maps show Spearman correlation values larger than +0.3 (blue) or smaller than −0.3 (red).

certain regions of it. AMMSST was present mainly in the central-south, TNA in the south, and TSA in the east region. The only relation found for OND was related to TNA in the southeast region.

Few related studies addressed climate teleconnections in the Jubones river basin, and they mainly analyzed ENSO. In this sense, Thielen et al. [32] reported that ENSO is one of the main forces in rainfall from December to April in most of the coastal regions of Ecuador. Ilbay-Yupa et al. [45], in their regionalization for the whole country, found that regions R3 (lowlands) and R9 (highlands) are linked to ENSO modes. The negative association with PDO was also found by Oñate-Valdivieso et al. [46], although they focused only on specific drought events. Finally, TNI was also found to have an influence all over Ecuador [47]. Although these similitudes, our work also provides the intra-annual and the spatial variation of such relations.

Paute River Basin. In the Paute river basin, most of the Pacific teleconnections were negative in JFM and JAS, while positive in AMJ (Table 2 and Fig. 5). No teleconnection was observed from the Pacific in OND. The Atlantic influence was observed as positive correlation in AMJ, JAS, and OND.

From the Pacific Ocean, the strongest (larger than 0.5) and most spatially extended teleconnections with negative influence were related to Niño 3, Niño 3.4, Niño 4, and ONI. All of them had negative influences (around -0.6) in JAS, covering the whole basin. Additionally, these four indices, Niño 3, Niño 3.4, Niño 4, and ONI, shared similar spatial patterns throughout the year. They had a negative influence in JFM (east region), positive influence in AMJ (west region), and negative in JAS (whole basin).

Moreover, TNI had a strong teleconnection in the whole basin in JFM and AMJ, with a less strong influence in JAS. Niño 1 + 2 had positive correlation in JFM and AMJ (west and center regions of the basin) and negative in JAS (center and east regions). Finally, SOI had positive influence in JFM (east region) and JAS (whole basin).

The influences from the Atlantic Ocean (AMM SST, TNA, and TSA) were positive in JAS and in most of the basin extension. The only relations found for AMJ and OND were related to TSA in the east region of the basin.

In central weast of the Paute river basin, the main rainfall seasonality occurs from January to May, with JAS as the dry season and a second rainy season in October [34]. From our results, it can be observed that this seasonality pattern is in concordance with the teleconnections from the Pacific Ocean, which showed positive influences in AMJ and some positives in JFM, while mainly negatives in JAS. Nevertheless, the only evidence related to the second rainy season in October seems to be related to the Atlantic driver of TSA in the east of the basin. In the east of the basin, the main rainy season is from April to August, with a peak in June-July. In this season, it was found negative correlations with the Pacific indices, as well as positive with the Atlantic ones.

Ilbay-Yupa et al. [45] found that, although the regions for highlands (R9) and for lowlands (R3) were linked to ENSO modes, the ENSO's impact on rainfall in the central Andes and Amazonia (see next section) was much less conclusive. Our results contribute to this in the sense that ENSO-index correlations showed lower values in Paute than in Jubones river basin. Additionally, they argued that cooling in the central Pacific could impact increased rainfall in some regions of the Andes and the Amazon. In our study, this is supported by the increase of negative correlations of the Pacific indices in the Paute and Napo river basin (see next section).

The high correlation to TNI suggest that the rainfall in the Paute river basin obey to a process from the entire Pacific ENSO, rather than specific ENSO areas [21]. The positive TSA relation was also reported by [21]. Although our results shower a larger spatial coverage, Campozano et al., [47] also detected positive correlation to TNI. Similarly, they also reported the positive correlation to TSA. Our work also showed a positive influence of TNA in JAS.

Napo River Basin. In the Napo river basin, most of the Pacific teleconnections were negative throughout the year (Table 2 and Fig. 6). An exception was SOI, which had a positive influence in all four seasons, and TNA in JFM and OND. The Atlantic influence was observed as negative for TNA in JFM and positive in JAS, and positive for TSA in AMJ and JAS.

From the Pacific Ocean, the strongest (larger than 0.5) teleconnections with negative influence were related to Niño 3.4, Niño 4, and ONI, all of which had negative influences (around −0.6) in JAS. Most of the teleconnections from both the Pacific and the Atlantic were present in the west and central regions of the basin.

In the Napo river basin, the main rainfall seasonality occurs from April to June and from October to December, with January and August as dry months [45]. The Napo river basin coincides with R21 and R22 in [45], and similarly to this work, ENSO relation was less conclusive than in other parts of the country. This is because the ENSO indices showed similar moderate to low correlation values (close to the threshold of -0.3). However, for the lower rainy season around August, it was observed a strong negative relation to Niño 34, Niño4 and ONI.

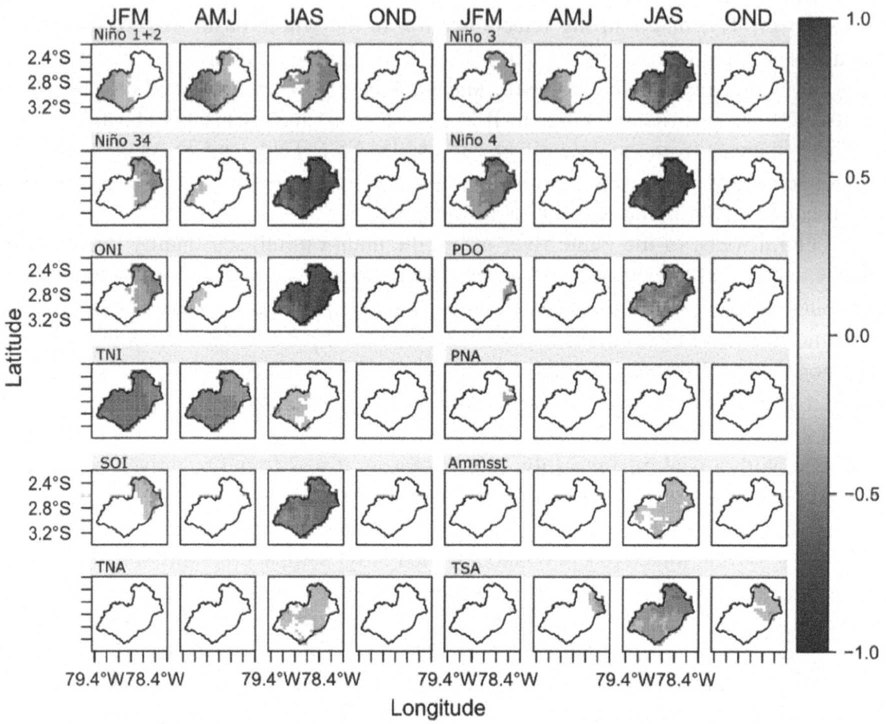

Fig. 5. Climate teleconnection in Paute river basin. Spatial and seasonal distribution of teleconnection maps. The maps show spearman correlation values larger than +0.3 (blue) or smaller than −0.3 (red).

3.2 Explorative Pixel-Wise Interaction

Figure 7 shows an alternative spatial visualization to Table 2, allowing for the visual exploration of pixel-wise spatial interactions among teleconnections. This method of exploring interactions needs to be carefully interpreted since there might be association or correlation among climate indices. For instance, Niño 1 + 2 and Niño 3 are highly correlated. Additionally, the visualization is dependent on the indices used in this study, meaning that most of the indices were ENSO-related.

In the Jubones river basin, AMJ and JAS were the seasons with the most pixel-wise teleconnection interactions, with positive associations in AMJ and negative associations in JAS. In JFM, there was a low teleconnection interaction with only two climate indices having positive influences in most of the basin; however, both indices showed strong associations with rainfall. These indices were Niño 1 + 2 and TNI (Table 2). In AMJ, the number of climate indices with positive influence increased to five in the west and center of the basin (strong association: Niño 1 + 2, Niño 3, TNI; moderate association: Niño 3.4 and ONI). In JAS, there were both positive and negative associations. Positive associations were located in the southeast with TNI, SOI, AMM SST, TNA, and TSA. Negative associations were located in most of the basin with Niño 3, Niño 3.4, Niño 4, ONI, PDO, and PNA. In OND, there were neither positive nor negative associations.

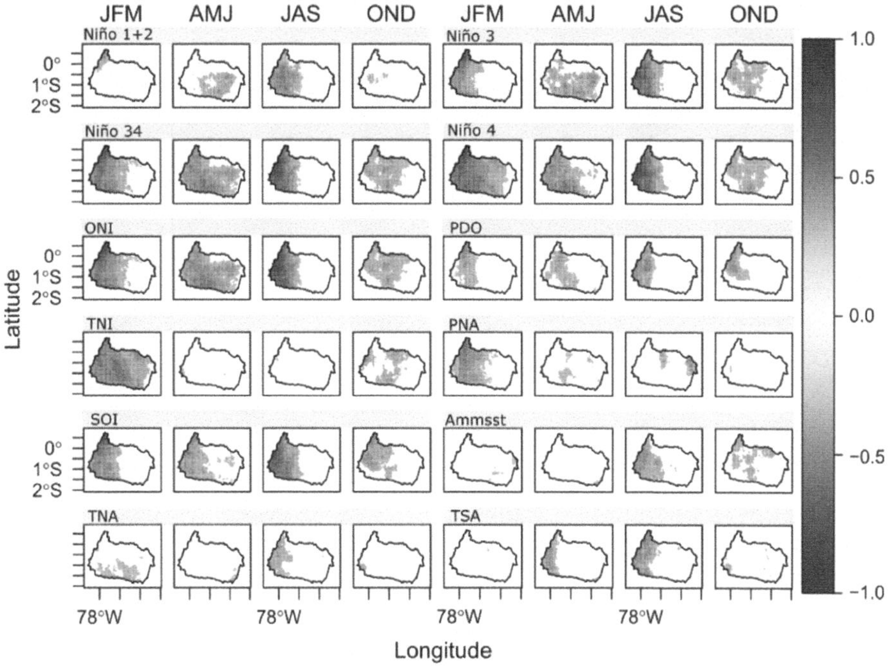

Fig. 6. Climate teleconnection in Napo river basin. Spatial and seasonal distribution of teleconnection maps. The maps show spearman correlation values larger than +0.3 (blue) or smaller than −0.3 (red).

In the Paute river basin, in JFM there was a low spatial teleconnection interaction with only two climate indices having positive influences. TNI was present in the whole basin, while Niño 1 + 2 was in the west and SOI in the east (Fig. 6 and Table 2). An increased number of negative influences were observed in JFM for Niño 3, Niño 3.4, Niño 4, ONI, and PDO. This interaction was stronger in the east of the basin. In AMJ, there were only positive influences with Niño 1 + 2, Niño 3, Niño 3.4, ONI, TNI, and TSA in the east of the basin. In JAS, there were both positive and negative influences in most of the basin. Positive influences included TNI, SOI, AMM SST, TNA, and TSA. Negative influences, located mainly in most of the basin, included Niño 1 + 2, Niño 3, Niño 3.4, Niño 4, ONI, and PDO. In OND, there were neither positive nor negative influences. For JAS and OND, very similar influences were observed in the Jubones and Paute river basins.

In the Napo river basin, in JFM there was a low spatial teleconnection interaction with only two climate indices having positive influences: TNI and SOI in the west of the basin (Fig. 7 and Table 2). Regarding negative influences in this season, there was a more complex interaction (Niño 1 + 2, Niño 3, Niño 3.4, Niño 4, ONI, PDO, PNA, and TNA). In AMJ, there were only positive influences for SOI and TSA, while negative influences were the same as in JFM, with the exception of TNA, although with a larger spatial extension. In JAS, both positive (SOI, AMM SST, TNA, and TSA) and negative

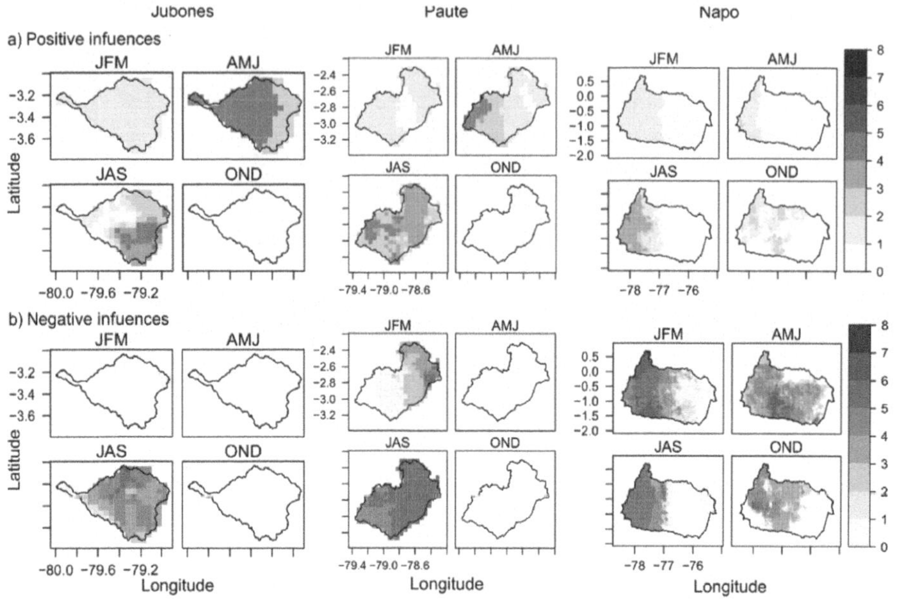

Fig. 7. Explorative interaction among teleconnections. a) Positive influences (in purple) and b) Negative influences (in orange). Frequency is the amount of climate indices with positive and negative correlation with values larger than +0.3 or smaller than −0.3.

interactions (Niño 1 + 2, Niño 3, Niño 3.4, Niño 4, ONI, PDO, and PNA) were observed in the west region of the basin.

4 Conclusions

In this study, a non-parametric Spearman correlation analysis was applied to three hydropower basins located in the three climatic regions of continental Ecuador (Coast, Andes, and Amazon). The correlation analysis was conducted between CHIRPS satellite rainfall estimates and climate indices across four intra-annual seasons (JFM, AMJ, JAS, OND). The use of the satellite-based rainfall estimates allowed the analysis of the spatial variability in regions with scarce (or none) weather stations. Additionally, they provide comparable temporal periods, which is usually a challenge with weather station that are installed at different times. The results were shown as pixel-wise correlation maps, allowing a continuous representation of the teleconnections that influence the basins. It extends the previous teleconnections' knowledge in the region by providing a continuous map, instead of a point-based map (weather station locations). Additionally, it provides seasonal representation showing how the influences vary along the year.

The results showed a stronger teleconnection influence related to the Pacific Ocean in all basins. Moreover, the majority of climate indices with positive correlation values were related to ENSO; however, the influence of specific indices related to the Atlantic Ocean in each basin was also evident. In the Jubones river basin, most of the climate indices showed positive teleconnections in AMJ and negative in JAS. Similarly, in the

Paute river basin, most of the climate indices showed positive teleconnections in AMJ and negative in JFM and JAS. Finally, in the Napo river basin, positive influences were observed in JAS, while negative influences were observed throughout the year.

Regarding the discussion, it must be noted that, of the three basins, Paute has received more attention from the scientific community regarding the identification of climate teleconnections. Therefore, more related works were found for this basin. However, for the Jubones and Napo river basins, only a few works were found. Additionally, the ENSO-Pacific-related teleconnections were the most explored ones. The Atlantic-related teleconnections, although with fewer studies, were also previously reported. Finally, the comparison of findings needs to be carefully understood since previous studies applied different methodologies, time periods, and data sources (mainly from in-situ weather stations). Therefore, the discussion is based solely on the identification of similar teleconnections and their trends.

Limitations of our study are related to the spatial resolution of the rainfall images, which is still coarse (5 km) for the highly rainfall variability, and prevents properly detecting local variability and micro-climates, which are frequent in the Andean region. In this regard, it is needed to explore downscaling methods for more detailed spatial resolutions. Additionally, we applied simple correlation analysis, which prevents detecting temporal lags of teleconnections, and the explorative visual interaction among teleconnections can to be complemented with more robust approaches. The Spearman correlation detects monotonic relations, omitting other possible types of non-linear or non-monotonic relations. The results are specific to the selected indices and the atmospheric patterns present in the index´s calculation. This means that the extension of the analyzed indices might be of interest, as well as the development of customized local indices. Results could differ based on the used satellite product and the temporal period, therefore it is advisable to intercomparing other rainfall products and to update the temporal period of the analysis. Finally, further indices from the Atlantic Ocean are worthwhile to be studied, as well as further methods to deeper the interaction analysis.

This study, by using the satellite-based CHIRPS data, identified the main climate teleconnections that are spatially and seasonally related to rainfall. It allows to better understand where and when a teleconnection has a stronger influenced on the rainfall, supporting the future development of robust monitoring and prediction systems for hydropower generation. By knowing the spatial variability, a more suitable spatial monitoring of rainfall can be designed in order to contribute with accurate early warnings and predictions of extreme rainfall events. Accounting for this knowledge, and mainly extreme events such as flows and droughts, will allows appropriately managing hydroelectric plant operation.

Acknowledgments. This research was funding has been financed by the Corporación Ecuatoriana para el Desarrollo de la Investigación y la Academia (CEDIA) through the project CEPRA XII "Spatial representation of climatic teleconnections in the precipitation of Ecuador", and by Corporación Eléctrica del Ecuador (CELEC) and Universidad del Azuay through project "Spatio-temporal applications as decision-making support for renewable energies and climate change" under the grant number 2023 – 0221.

Disclosure of Interests. The authors have no competing interests to declare that are relevant to the content of this article.

References

1. Nerini, F.F., et al.: Mapping synergies and trade-offs between energy and the Sustainable Development Goals. Nat. Energy **3**(1), 10–15 (2017). https://doi.org/10.1038/s41560-017-0036-5
2. Yüksel, I.: Hydropower for sustainable water and energy development. Renew. Sustain. Energy Rev. **14**, 462–469 (2010). https://doi.org/10.1016/j.rser.2009.07.025
3. Van Vliet, M.T.H., Sheffield, J., Wiberg, D., Wood, E.F.: Impacts of recent drought and warm years on water resources and electricity supply worldwide. Environ. Res. Lett. **11**, 124021 (2016). https://doi.org/10.1088/1748-9326/11/12/124021
4. UN. The Sustainable Development Goals Report 2022. New York, USA. https://unstats.un.org/sdgs/report/2022/ (2022). Last accessed 04 July 2024
5. Cevallos-Sierra, J., Ramos-Martin, J.: Spatial assessment of the potential of renewable energy: the case of Ecuador. Renew. Sustain. Energy Rev. **81**, 1154–1165 (2018). https://doi.org/10.1016/j.rser.2017.08.015
6. Ministerio de energía y recursos naturales no renovables. Plan Maestro de Electricidad. Ecuadror. https://www.recursosyenergia.gob.ec/plan-maestro-de-electricidad/. (2018). Last accessed 4 July 2024
7. IEA. Renewable energy into the mainstream. Sittard Novem, Netherlands. 54 p. (2002)
8. Resch, G., Held, A., Faber, T., Panzer, C., Toro, F., Haas, R.: Potentials and prospects for renewable energies at global scale. Energy Policy **36**, 4048–4056 (2008). https://doi.org/10.1016/j.enpol.2008.06.029
9. Engeland, K., Borga, M., Creutin, J.-D., François, B., Ramos, M.-H., Vidal, J.-P.: Space-time variability of climate variables and intermittent renewable electricity production–A review. Renew. Sustain. Energy Rev. **79**, 600–617 (2017). https://doi.org/10.1016/j.rser.2017.05.046
10. François, B.: Influence of winter North-Atlantic oscillation on climate-related-energy penetration in Europe. Renew. Energy **99**, 602–613 (2016). https://doi.org/10.1016/j.renene.2016.07.010
11. Peláez, M.R., Espinoza, J.L., et al.: Energias renovables en el Ecuador. Situación actual, tendencias y Perspectivas (2015). https://biblioteca.olade.org/opac-tmpl/Documentos/cg00214.pdf. Last accessed 4 July 2024
12. Munoz, J.R., Sailor, D.J.: A modelling methodology for assessing the impact of climate variability and climatic change on hydroelectric generation. Energy Convers. Manag. **39**, 1459–1469 (1998). https://doi.org/10.1016/S0196-8904(98)00017-X
13. Carleton, A.M.: Atmospheric teleconnections involving the Southern Ocean. J. Geophys. Res: Oceans (2003). https://doi.org/10.1029/2000JC000379
14. Liu, Z., Alexander, M.: Atmospheric bridge, oceanic tunnel, and global climatic teleconnections. Rev. Geophys. (2007). https://doi.org/10.1029/2005RG000172
15. Hanley, D.E., Bourassa, M.A., O'Brien, J.J., Smith, S.R., Spade, E.R.: A quantitative evaluation of ENSO indices. J. Clim. **16**, 1249–1258 (2003). https://doi.org/10.1175/1520-0442(2003)16%3c1249:AQEOEI%3e2.0.CO;2
16. Kiem, A.S., Franks, S.W.: On the identification of ENSO-induced rainfall and runoff variability: a comparison of methods and indices. Hydrol. Sci. J. **46**, 715–727 (2001). https://doi.org/10.1080/02626660109492866
17. Fierro, A.O.: Relationships between California rainfall variability and large-scale climate drivers. Int. J. Climatol. **34**, 3626–3640 (2014). https://doi.org/10.1002/joc.4112

18. Liu, Y.-C., Di, P., Chen, S.-H., DaMassa, J.: Relationships of rainy season precipitation and temperature to climate indices in California: long-term variability and extreme events. J. Clim. **31**, 1921–1942 (2018). https://doi.org/10.1175/JCLI-D-17-0376.1
19. Bendix, A., Bendix, J.: Heavy rainfall episodes in Ecuador during El Nino events and associated regional atmospheric circulation and SST patterns. Adv. Geosci. **6**, 43–49 (2006). https://doi.org/10.5194/adgeo-6-43-2006
20. Bendix, J., et al.: El niño meets la niña—anomalous rainfall patterns in the" traditional" el niño region of southern Ecuador. Erdkunde 151–167 (2011). https://www.jstor.org/stable/23030663
21. Mendoza, D.E., Samaniego, E.P., Mora, D.E., Espinoza, M.J., Campozano, L.V.: Finding teleconnections from decomposed rainfall signals using dynamic harmonic regressions: a Tropical Andean case study. Clim. Dyn. **52**, 4643–4670 (2019). https://doi.org/10.1007/s00382-018-4400-3
22. Morán-Tejeda, E., et al.: Climate trends and variability in Ecuador (1966–2011). Int. J. Climatol. (2015). https://doi.org/10.1002/joc.4597
23. Pineda, L., Ntegeka, V., Willems, P., Fermi, E.: Rainfall variability related to sea surface temperature anomalies in a Pacific -Andean basin into Ecuador and Peru. Adv. Geosci. (2013). https://doi.org/10.5194/adgeo-33-53-2013
24. Vuille, M., Bradley, R.S., Keimig, F.: Interannual climate variability in the Central Andes and its relation to tropical Pacific and Atlantic forcing. J. Geophys. Res. Atmos. **105**, 12447–12460 (2000). https://doi.org/10.1029/2000JD900134
25. Ávila, R., Ballari, D.: A Bayesian Network Approach to Identity Climate Teleconnections within Homogeneous Precipitation Regions in Ecuador. In: Efrain Fosenca, C., Rodríguez Morales, G., Cordero, M.O., Botto-Tobar, M., Martínez, E.C., León, A.P. (eds.) Information and Communication Technologies of Ecuador (TIC.EC), pp. 21–35. Springer International Publishing, Cham (2020). https://doi.org/10.1007/978-3-030-35740-5_2
26. Ballari, D., Campozano, L., Samaniego, E., Orellana, D.: Spatial association to characterize the climate teleconnection patterns in ecuador based on satellite precipitation estimates. In: 2020 IEEE Latin American GRSS & ISPRS Remote Sensing Conference (LAGIRS), pp 219–224. (2020). https://doi.org/10.1109/LAGIRS48042.2020.9165647
27. Mendoza, D.E., Samaniego, E.P., Mora, D.E., Espinoza, M.J., Pacheco, E.A., Avilés, A.M.: Local rainfall modelling based on global climate information: a data-based approach. Environ Model Softw. **131**, 104786 (2020). https://doi.org/10.1016/j.envsoft.2020.104786
28. Hasan, M.M., Wyseure, G.: Impact of climate change on hydropower generation in Rio Jubones Basin. Ecuador. Water Sci Eng. (2018). https://doi.org/10.1016/j.wse.2018.07.002
29. Carvajal, P.E., Li, F.G.N., Soria, R., Cronin, J., Anandarajah, G., Mulugetta, Y.: Large hydropower, decarbonisation and climate change uncertainty: modelling power sector pathways for Ecuador. Energy Strateg. Rev. **23**, 86–99 (2019). https://doi.org/10.1016/j.esr.2018.12.008
30. Carvajal, P.E., Anandarajah, G., Mulugetta, Y., Dessens, O.: Assessing uncertainty of climate change impacts on long-term hydropower generation using the CMIP5 ensemble—the case of Ecuador. Clim. Change **144**, 611–624 (2017). https://doi.org/10.1007/s10584-017-2055-4
31. Thielen, D.R., et al.: Effect of extreme El Niño events on the precipitation of Ecuador. Nat. Hazards Earth Syst. Sci. **23**, 1507–1527 (2023). https://doi.org/10.5194/nhess-23-1507-2023
32. Thielen, D., et al.: Hydroclimatological extreme events affecting the Daule-Peripa Reservoir (Coast of Ecuador)-Historical dynamics and teleconnections. Rev. Climatol 21 (2021). https://rclimatol.eu/wp-content/uploads/2021/09/Articulo21k.pdf. Last accessed 4 Jul 2024
33. Campozano, L., et al.: Climatology and teleconnections of mesoscale convective systems in an Andean basin in southern Ecuador: the case of the Paute basin. Adv. Meteorol. **2018**, 1–13 (2018). https://doi.org/10.1155/2018/4259191

34. Celleri, R., Willems, P., Buytaert, W., Feyen, J.: Space-time rainfall variability in the paute basin. Ecuadorian Andes. Hydrol Process **21**, 3316–3327 (2007). https://doi.org/10.1002/hyp.6575
35. Sarmiento, G.: Ecological features of climate in high tropical mountains. High Alt Trop Biogeogr **11**, 45 (1986). https://www.ciens.ula.ve/icae/publicaciones/paramo/pdf/sarmiento_g1986.pdf. Last accessed 4 Jul 2024
36. Coltorti, M., Ollier, C.D.: Geomorphic and tectonic evolution of the Ecuadorian Andes. Geomorphology **32**, 1–19 (2000). https://doi.org/10.1016/S0169-555X(99)00036-7
37. Ulloa, J., Ballari, D., Campozano, L., Samaniego, E.: Two-Step Downscaling of Trmm 3b43 V7 precipitation in contrasting climatic regions with sparse monitoring: the case of Ecuador in Tropical South America. Remote Sens. **9**, 758 (2017). https://doi.org/10.3390/rs9070758
38. Funk, C., et al.: The climate hazards infrared precipitation with stations—a new environmental record for monitoring extremes. Sci. Data (2015). https://doi.org/10.1038/sdata.2015.66
39. Siegert, S.: SpecsVerification: Forecast Verification Routines for Ensemble Forecasts of Weather and Climate. R package version 0.5-2. (2017). https://cran.r-project.org/web/packages/SpecsVerification/SpecsVerification.pdf. Last accessed 4 July 2024
40. Hijmans, R.J.: raster: Geographic Data Analysis and Modeling. R package version 2.6-7. (2017). https://cran.r-project.org/web/packages/raster/raster.pdf. Last accessed 4 Jul 2024
41. Vázquez-Patiño, A., Campozano, L., Ballari, D., Córdova, M., Samaniego, E.: Virtual control volume approach to the study of climate causal flows: identification of humidity and wind pathways of influence on rainfall in Ecuador. Atmosphere **11**(8), 848 (2020). https://doi.org/10.3390/atmos11080848
42. Córdoba-Machado, S., Palomino-Lemus, R., Gámiz-Fortis, S.R., Castro-Diez, Y., Esteban-Parra, M.J.: Seasonal streamflow prediction in Colombia using atmospheric and oceanic patterns. J. Hydrol. **538**, 1–12 (2016). https://doi.org/10.1016/j.jhydrol.2016.04.003
43. Hauke, J., Kossowski, T.: Comparison of values of Pearson's and Spearman's correlation coefficients on the same sets of data. QUAGEO **30**(2), 87–93 (2011). https://doi.org/10.2478/v10117-011-0021-1
44. Ballari, D., Giraldo, R., Campozano, L., Samaniego, E.: Spatial functional data analysis for regionalizing precipitation seasonality and intensity in a sparsely monitored region: unveiling the spatio-temporal dependencies of precipitation in Ecuador. Int. J. Climatol. **38**, 3337–3354 (2018). https://doi.org/10.1002/joc.5504
45. Ilbay-Yupa, M., Lavado-Casimiro, W., Rau, P., Zubieta, R., Castillón, F.: Updating regionalization of precipitation in Ecuador. Theor. Appl. Climatol. **143**, 1513–1528 (2021). https://doi.org/10.1007/s00704-020-03476-x
46. Oñate-Valdivieso, F., Uchuari, V., Oñate-Paladines, A.: Large-scale climate variability patterns and drought: a case of study in South – America. Water Resour. Manag. **34**, 2061–2079 (2020). https://doi.org/10.1007/s11269-020-02549-w
47. Campozano, L., Ballari, D., Célleri, R., et al.: Imágenes TRMM para identificar patrones de precipitación e Índices ENSO en Ecuador, pp. 185–191 (2014). http://dspace.ucuenca.edu.ec/handle/123456789/21368

Implementation of Spatial Correlations and Kernel Densities to Identify Deficiencies in the Coverage of Public Health Infrastructure

Maria Carolina Quintana Noriega(✉)

Tecnologico de Monterrey, Monterrey, Mexico
quintanamariacarolina@hotmail.com

Abstract. There is a justified perception of shortage of public health infrastructure on the outskirts of cities. This deficiency in urban planning is aggravated in the peri-urban settlements inhabited by population living in poverty conditions, which unlike the suburbs for the middle and upper classes, planned according to the North American model and the Garden City theory, they show distinct conditions of precariousness, deprivation and a worrying limitation for accessing to urban services. In order to mitigate this lag in urban planning, it is important to first identify the lack of coverage of urban health facilities and understand the spatial correlations that intervene in the access of the population living at the edges of the urban growth to the benefits of a consolidated city. Thus, this research proposes an exploratory spatial data analysis (ESDA), which reviews the spatial correlations based on the number of active cases of people with COVID-19 per neighborhood for Mexico City, as a local indicator of spatial association (LISA). Afterwards, it compares them with heat maps using public health facilities as origins and weighted by the saturation of their intensive care units, to finally integrate them cartographically through the implementation of kernel densities, generated from hospital capacity and coverage. This methodology shows patterns of deficiencies in the coverage of public health infrastructure that corroborates the perception of abandonment of popular neighborhoods which in the context of the SARS-CoV-2 virus pandemic, have shown a higher incidence of cases, thus highlighting the precarious conditions in which they find themselves. Through the identification of these spatial arrangements, it is possible to plan urban development policies that improve the conditions of Latin American cities in the face of an accelerated urban expansion.

Keywords: Urban health · urban inequity · land use planning · socio-spatial vulnerability · kernel densities · spatial correlations

1 Introduction

The accelerated growth of Mexican cities has resulted in a lack of infrastructure coverage in peripheral urban areas, especially in those irregular settlements whose occupation consequently presents notorious lags in education and health. This scenario is particularly notorious in Mexico City.

M. F. Mata-Rivera et al. (Eds.): GIS-LATAM 2024, CCIS 2298, pp. 185–192, 2025.
https://doi.org/10.1007/978-3-031-80017-7_12

At a federal level, Mexico developed the concept of Urban Containment Perimeters (CONAVI, 2018) as a figure of territorial planning. These instruments for regulating urban growth offer a reading of the quality of services provided in different areas of cities, since they distribute urban areas into three contours, according to the degree of urban services available in each area. The perimeters were defined not only for metropolitan areas but for the entire National Urban System, and are based on variables such as sources of employment and services in housing, for example water and drainage, but use a quantitative analysis of facilities and their installed capacity to differentiate one urban area from another (CONAVI, 2018).

Thus, the first containment perimeter occupies the consolidated central city, as it has very good infrastructure coverage. The second perimeter is the area of the city that, despite having good coverage, is beginning to show deficiencies. Perimeter three of urban containment, defined as "the growth areas contiguous to the consolidated urban area" (CONAVI, 2018), represents an envelope that seeks to buffer urban sprawl. Although these tools are designed to guide the growth of cities through housing subsidies, based on a more favorable location for socio-economic development, they are in turn a parameter of infrastructure coverage and consequently of social backwardness. In this sense, this research intends to validate the implementation of Urban Containment Perimeters as a State recognition of those urban areas with more or less urban services and therefore as a measure of evaluation of gaps in the coverage of urban facilities. Consequently, and in the face of the COVID-19 pandemic, this research will review the simple and geo-spatial correlation between the lack of health facilities in the peripheries of Mexico City and an increase in registered cases, which form patterns of coverage/non-coverage in Mexican cities.

As a starting point for this research work, public health facilities dependent on the State were located and differentiated according to their location with respect to each urban containment perimeter (see Fig. 1). Within the first containment perimeter there are 55 health units, equivalent to 57.29% of the total number of public health facilities in Mexico City. This figure is significantly higher than the 38 units in the second perimeter, which represent 39.58%. And it is precisely in the third peripheral contour where the greatest deficiencies in health facilities are found, with only 3 units that barely reach 3.23% of the supply for the entity. From this simple quantitative exercise of cartographic representation, the feasibility of the Urban Containment Perimeters as a parameter of evaluation of urban infrastructure coverage deficiencies can be verified.

The seriousness of this logic of location of health facilities is evident in the face of the poverty conditions of the population living in these peripheral areas of the city. A second spatial exploration based on poverty measurements by AGEB for Mexico City, from the Consejo Nacional de Evaluación de la Política de Desarrollo Social (CONEVAL, 2018), compared with health facilities, located within Urban Containment Perimeters 2 and 3, allows us to observe a possible correlation between the location of these and the highest ranks of urban poverty in Mexico City (see Fig. 2). These observations should not be strange, since they are precisely in line with the alternative use proposed for the Urban Containment Perimeters as a pattern of urban service deficiencies.

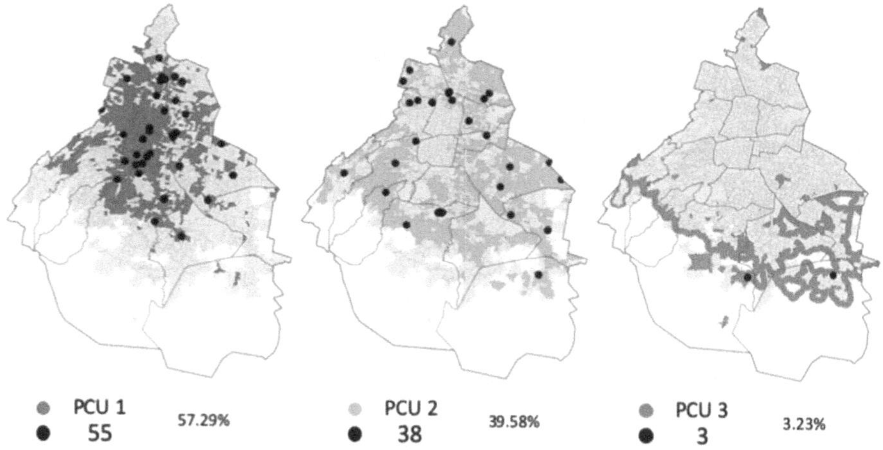

Fig. 1. Health facilities by urban containment perimeter (UCP), Mexico City. Source: Own elaboration based on Perímetros de Contención Urbana, Comisión Nacional de Vivienda (CONAVI, 2018)/Secretaría de Desarrollo Agrario, Territorial y Urbano (SEDATU), Mexico City health equipment (Salud, 2020) and Sistema para la Consulta de la Información Censal (SCINCE), INEGI (2016).

If we refer to the essence of the concept of the right to the city, embodied by Henri Lefebvre (1967) and in tune with goal eleven of the 2030 Agenda for Sustainable Development (ONU, 2015) reiterated in the New Urban Agenda (ONU, 2017), which identifies equal access to urban services as the first obstacle to achieving an adequate standard of living for the poor population living in the peripheries. Mexico City and its Metropolitan Area, like many Latin American cities, faces an important urban planning challenge that has become evident in the context of the COVID-19 pandemic.

Despite the existence of a notion of these deficiencies, it is necessary to have a territorial identification of urban areas with low hospital coverage, beyond the simple perception of the inhabitants who suffer from it. For this reason, this research proposes a methodology for identifying these areas, which will also help to determine the effects of this deficiency on urban planning.

2 Methodology

To achieve these objectives, an exploratory spatial data analysis (ESDA) was followed, according to the principle of auto-correlation, which considers that "every activity located in physical space [...] develops a complex network of bidirectional relationships [...] with the surrounding environment [...]" (Camagni, 2005: 79).

Based on the data of daily active cases per colony for Mexico City, from the Sistema de Vigilancia de Enfermedades Respiratorias (SINAVE, 2020) of the Ministry of Health, it was possible not only to locate the active cases reported, but also, based on the first law of geography, formulated by Waldo Tobler (1970) and by means of a geospatial analysis based on Moran's I (1950) as a local indicator of spatial association, LISA (Anselin,

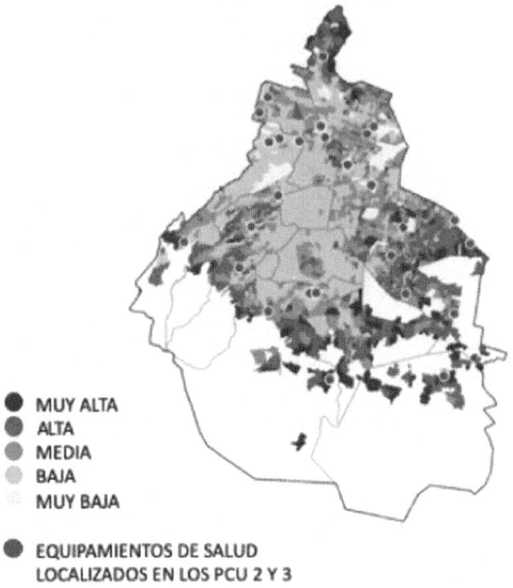

Fig. 2. Urban population living in poverty by AGEB and health facilities located in Urban Containment Perimeters 2 and 3. Source: Own elaboration based on average population in conditions of urban poverty by AGEB for Mexico City (CONEVAL, 2018), Perímetros de Contención Urbana, Comisión Nacional de Vivienda (CONAVI, 2018)/Secretaría de Desarrollo Agrario, Territorial y Urbano (SEDATU), Mexico City health infrastructure (Salud, 2020) and Sistema para la Consulta de la Información Censal (SCINCE), INEGI (2016).

1995), those groups of neighborhoods with a high significance in their ratio of active cases were identified (see Fig. 3).

Since SARS-CoV-2 is a virus of direct transmission among the population, an analysis of spatial correlations based on active cases becomes relevant because it allows us to locate the most significant clusters of urban areas, in this case of infections and non-contagions by COVD-19. This same correlation can be used to identify localities of priority attention not only during the pandemic, but also for a review of urban planning of health facilities.

Once these grouping patterns were identified, public health facilities were located, and attention was paid to the hospital capacity of their intensive care units (Salud, 2020). This mapping exercise shows a linear concentration of hospitals whose units are saturated with COVID-19 cases, towards the center of the entity, in the Benito Juárez district and with a concentration towards the north of the city, between the Cuauhtémoc and Gustavo A. Madero districts. To dimension this saturation, heat maps were elaborated based on the hospital capacity of intensive care units (Salud, 2020) for this federative entity (see Fig. 4). The territorial visualization of these elements makes it possible to identify the areas with saturation in hospital capacity and the areas with availability, but it also makes it possible to know the groupings of health facilities that, although they are at critical levels of care capacity, represent those areas of the city where the greatest care is being provided. When comparing this territorial trend with the distribution of correlations

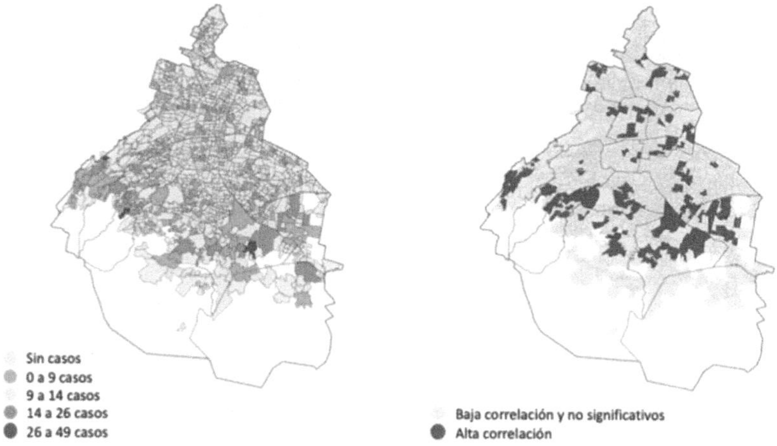

Fig. 3. Active cases by colony as of August 15, 2020 and clustering of colonies by spatial correlation of active cases. Source: Own elaboration based on daily active cases per colony for Mexico City, from the Sistema de Vigilancia de Enfermedades Respiratorias (SINAVE, 2020) of the Secretaría de Salud of Mexico City and Sistema para la Consulta de la Información Censal (SCINCE), INEGI (2016).

of neighborhoods with active cases, it can be seen that there is practically a negative correlation between the two.

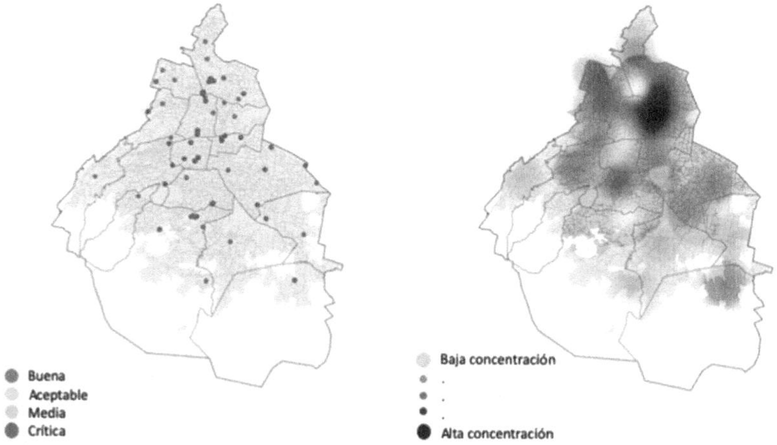

Fig. 4. Hospital capacity of Intensive Care Units (ICU) in health facilities and occupancy-weighted grouping of ICUs (heat map). Source: Own elaboration based on Mexico City health infrastructure (Salud, 2020) y Sistema para la Consulta de la Información Censal (SCINCE), INEGI (2016).

In parallel, to check and verify this observation, kernel density polygons were generated based on the centroids of daily active cases per colonia for Mexico City (SINAVE,

2020) (see Fig. 5). This new geo-spatial exploration shows a visual spatial segregation, in this case for the colonias with the highest frequency of cases. The reading of this cartographic representation shows that the location of the centroids with the highest cases of active COVID-19 infection does not constitute a territorial grouping, but a segregation.

This pattern of segregated active case location, not only from other areas with fewer cases but also from the largest health care areas of the city, allows us to infer a lack of coverage and poor accessibility to health services in the detected areas.

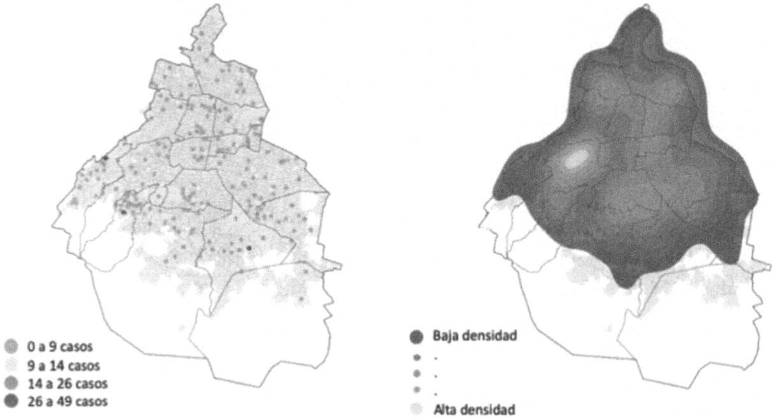

Fig. 5. Centroids of colonies with active cases and kernel densities for active cases. Source: Own elaboration based on daily active cases per colony for Mexico City, from the Sistema de Vigilancia de Enfermedades Respiratorias (SINAVE, 2020) of the Secretaría de Salud Mexico City and Sistema para la Consulta de la Informaci6n Censal (SCINCE), INEGI (2016)

3 Results

In order to be able to observe the results of the previous exploratory exercises in a cartographic manner, the core densities were incorporated as contours and mounted on the heat maps of the hospital units and neighborhood groupings according to their spatial correlation significance. With this methodology, we were able to obtain a map for Mexico City that identifies a clustering trend of neighborhoods with active cases of Covid-19 towards the south of the entity, coinciding with a strip of lower hospital coverage, accentuated by a low current capacity of intensive care units (see Fig. 6).

In other words, it is possible to visually identify a pattern that shows a greater clustering of neighborhoods with active cases where hospital coverage is lower. It can also be observed that the areas of the city with good coverage of health facilities show a low presence of clustering of cases, despite having it's hospital capacity close to critical levels.

Particularly noteworthy is the case of southern Mexico City, with a high concentration of cases precisely where the presence of health facilities, represented by a low density of nuclei, is low or non-existent.

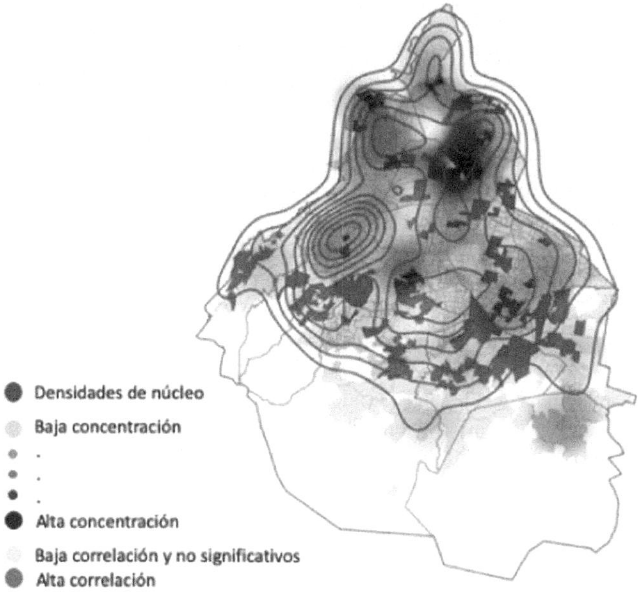

Fig. 6. Cartographic representation of results (data correlation). Source: Own elaboration based on daily active cases per colony for Mexico City, from the Sistema de Vigilancia de Enfermedades Respiratorias (SINAVE, 2020) of the Secretaría de Salud of Mexico City, health infrastructure of Mexico City (Salud, 2020) and Sistema para la Consulta de la Información Censal (SCINCE), INEGI (2016).

4 Conclusions

According to two key concepts of territorial analysis, the application of geographic information systems for urban planning allows making the intangible visible, and in the same vein, it fulfills the primacy of improving that which can be measured. Thus, it is possible to conclude that the perceived lack of health facilities in the peripheries of the city, specifically in the areas of irregular settlements, arises from a real deficiency in the location of health facilities. Therefore, this research proposes the integration of this methodology of analysis for a sustainable urban planning that promotes inclusive human settlements and affordable public health services for the population, from a locational perspective.

References

Anselin, L.: Local indicators of spatial association—LISA. Geogr. Anal. **27**(2), 93–115 (1995)

Camagni, R.: Economía urbana. Antoni Bosch Ed. Barcelona, España (2005).

CONAVI, Comisión Nacional de Vivienda: Perímetros de Contención Urbana. Secretaría de Desarrollo Agrario, Territorial y Urbano (SEDATU). México (2018)

Getis, A., Ord, J.K.: The analysis of spatial association by use of distance statistics. Geogr. Anal. **24**(3), 189–206 (1992)

INEGI, Instituto Nacional de Estadística y Geografía. Sistema para la Consulta de la Información Censal (SCINCE). 09 – Ciudad de México. Web. https://www.inegi.org.mx/contenidos/masiva/indicadores/inv/09_SCINCE_zip.zip (2016). Accessed 15 Aug 2020

Lefebvre, H.: El derecho a la ciudad. Península, Barcelona [1975] (1967)

Moran, P.A.P.: Notes on continuous stochastic phenomena. Biometrika **37**(1–2), 17–23 (1950)

ONU, Organización de las Naciones Unidas: Transformar nuestro mundo: la Agenda 2030 para el Desarrollo Sostenible. Asamblea General de las Naciones Unidas. Web. https://www.un.org/ga/search/view_doc.asp?symbol=A/RES/70/1&Lang=S (2015). Accessed 15 Aug 2020

ONU, Organización de las Naciones Unidas: Nueva Agenda Urbana. Programa de las Naciones Unidas para los Asentamientos Humanos (ONU-Hábitat). Web. http://habitat3.org/wp-content/uploads/NUA-Spanish.pdf (2017). Accessed 15 Aug 2020

SALUD, Secretaría de: Capacidad hospitalaria ZMVM. Web. https://datos.cdmx.gob.mx/explore/dataset/capacidad-hospitalaria/information/ (2020). Accessed 15 Aug 2020

SINAVE: Sistema Nacional de Vigilancia Epidemiológica. Casos activos diarios por colonia para la Ciudad de México. Sistema Nacional de Vigilancia de Enfermedades Respiratorias. Web (2020). Accessed 15 Aug 2020. https://datos.cdmx.gob.mx/explore/dataset/covid-19-sinave-ciudad-de-mexico-a-nivel-colonia/information/?disjunctive.colonia

Tobler, W.R.: A computer movie simulating urban growth in the Detroit region. Econ. Geogr. **46**, 234 (1970). https://doi.org/10.2307/143141

Indices and State of Vegetation Health, Obtained with Multispectral Cameras, in Two Thermal Springs of the Sierra Madre Oriental

Leonardo Uriel Arellano-Méndez[1](✉), Edgar Daniel Salmerón-Carreño[2], Víctor Hugo Velázquez-Fierro[2], Jerjes Rigoberto Pantoja-Irys[3], Edilia de la Rosa-Manzano[1], and José Guadalupe Martínez-Ávalos[1]

[1] Instituto de Ecología Aplicada, Universidad Autónoma de Tamaulipas, División del Golfo 356Ciudad Victoria, Colonia La Libertad 87019, Tamaulipas, México
luarellano@docentes.uat.edu.mx

[2] Corporación Ambiental de México, S.A. de C.V, Torre 2, Piso 6, Colonia Del ValleDelegación Benito Juárez, Patricio Sanz 03100 Ciudad de México, México
vvelazquez@cam-mx.com

[3] Corporación Ambiental de México, S.A. de C.V, Texcoco 100, Colonia Satélite Acueducto 64960, Monterrey, Nuevo León, México

Abstract. Multispectral cameras are a useful tool for evaluating cultivated areas, but their use in natural areas is limited. Using vegetation indices generated from multispectral images, obtained with an Unmanned Aerial Vehicle (UAV), the health of the vegetation surrounding the Taninul (mTa) and Mainero Azufroso (mMA) springs (San Luis Potosí and Tamaulipas respectively) was evaluated. Digital images were aligned and interpolated to generate a three-band model (RGB), a digital elevation model (DEM) and an orthomosaic, Normalized Difference Vegetation Index (NDVI), Soil-Adjusted Vegetation Index (SAVI) and Green Chlorophyll Index (GCI) was calculated. mTa showed a modified vegetation layer with very healthy vegetation values (0.66 to 1) at the top and dead plants or inanimate objects (-1 to 0) at the bottom and moderately healthy vegetation (0.66 to 0) was observed on the slope (0.33 to 0.66). mMA, located between two slopes, presented intact vegetation with values between moderately healthy (0.33 to 0.66) to healthy (0.66 to 1.00); SAVI presented some empty spaces due more to the reflectance of the images than to altered sites. GCI values were higher for mMA than for mTa ($\approx$1), indicating significant photosynthetic activity. Although it was expected that the presence of the springs would improve the health status of the vegetation, the mTa area showed diseased to moderately healthy vegetation and mMA exhibited dense vegetation and good health. mMA analysis presented more challenges due to slopes in light reflectance, this was moderately corrected by editing the light intensity due to underexposure in the images.

Keywords: Multispectral images · Unmanned Aerial Vehicles · Vegetation Indices · Normalized Difference Vegetation Index (NDVI) · Soil-Adjusted Vegetation Index (SAVI) · Green Chlorophyll Index (GCI), hot spring

This work was supported by the National Council for Humanity, Science and Technology (CONAHCYT) of Mexico (Grant No. FOP02-322161 to ERM).

M. F. Mata-Rivera et al. (Eds.): GIS-LATAM 2024, CCIS 2298, pp. 193–207, 2025.
https://doi.org/10.1007/978-3-031-80017-7_13

1 Introduction

The study of ecosystems and their biodiversity has evolved significantly. Traditional methods of collecting samples and data on-site can be costly, time-consuming, and sometimes challenging due to difficult access to certain locations [10]. However, the use of remote sensing technologies such as aircraft and satellites has made it possible to gather data much more quickly, particularly in areas with obstacles or in the aftermath of natural disasters like fires, landslides, and hurricanes [8, 17]. Additionally, the availability of unmanned aerial vehicles (UAVs or drones) for civilian purposes has lowered costs and improved spatial and temporal resolution for data collection [29].

UAV systems are composed of two main elements, an aerial platform equipped with a camera and navigation system, and the ground control center, where the flight is programmed and monitored. The great advantage that these systems offer (compared to traditional platforms, satellites and manned aircraft) is the obtaining of images with high spatial and temporal resolution, low acquisition and operation costs, use in environments that are difficult to access for the human being, the quick response and the few flight restrictions in most countries [2, 34, 39]. In some cases, UAVs present some drawbacks for use, such as inclement weather (mainly wind and rain), which prevents taking images of the site of interest [9]. Sometimes you must be careful with birds, as their space is invaded, and they tend to attack UAVs.

In recent years, there have been significant technological advancements in data acquisition techniques, particularly in the field of agriculture [7]. These techniques have also been applied to monitor natural resources. In addition to traditional RGB cameras, LiDAR and multispectral cameras have become valuable tools for evaluating crops. However, their application for understanding natural environments has seen less progress [8].

The use of cameras mounted on UAVs allows for the characterization of vegetation density, greenness, and overall health in areas affected by various factors such as water sources, human activity, droughts, accidents, and deforestation. This is achieved through the use of vegetation indices, which are derived from images captured at different wavelengths within the visible and infrared light spectrum [12]. These indices are generated using multispectral cameras and involve simple mathematical combinations or transformations of the reflectance of different spectral channels or bands, providing valuable insights into the state and condition of the vegetation in the area of concern [6].

The use of various vegetation indices from multispectral images allows the health status to be evaluated based on different characteristics such as chlorophyll content, water status, nutritional status or structural deficiencies [26, 30]. Various optical measurement equipment can provide this information, for example, foliar spectrometers allow measuring leaf vegetation indices, but there is a loss of spatial and spectral resolution [42]. This type of analysis allows us to improve the precision in the evaluation of the health status of the vegetation by generating a higher resolution of the area of interest.

In precision agronomy, vegetation indices are commonly used to assess the health of different crops [24, 33]. However, their application in non-damaged or human-influenced ecosystems, as well as in monitoring the impact of various factors on the ecosystem, is not widely practiced [42].

In this study, a multispectral camera mounted on a UAV was employed to evaluate the health of the vegetation near two thermal springs located on the Eastern Flank of the Sierra Madre Oriental in the states of San Luis Potosí and Tamaulipas, which are part of the stormwater network.

Thermal springs are water sources that emerge on the earth's surface due to geological phenomena such as faults, fractures, and thrusts (common in the Sierra Madre Oriental), or the weathering of geological layers. Depending on their surfacing temperature, these springs are classified [5]. The specific heat and solute characteristics of these water springs, influenced by the geological features of the site, have not been thoroughly documented regarding their impact on vegetation.

The purpose of this project is to utilize multispectral cameras mounted on a UAV and interpret the images using specific vegetation indices. This will allow us to assess the reliability of current commercial technologies. In addition, we aim to identify areas with high potential for providing environmental services, which may vary based on the type of vegetation, its density, and its level of development and conservation. The goal is to gather essential information to establish practical baselines for the implementation of forestry exploitation and restoration programs in natural areas. These programs will serve as effective and profitable compensation and mitigation measures for environmental impacts resulting from human activities or natural events.

2 Materials and Methodology

Two springs in the Sierra Madre Oriental, located in the states of San Luis Potosí and Tamaulipas, were surveyed. Unmanned Aerial Vehicle (UAV) flights were conducted at the Taninul spring (mTa) and the Mainero Azufroso spring (mMA), both at an altitude of 250 m. During these flights, a total of 482 (mTa) and 756 (mMA) photographs were captured using a multispectral camera. These photographs included images from the RGB camera as well as four different spectrums (blue, red, red edge, and infrared – B, R, RE, and NIR respectively).

These images were then processed using the Agisoft Metashape program to create a dense point cloud. Some photographs had issues with light intensity and overexposure due to shooting angles and times, so these were edited using professional photography software (Adobe Photoshop and Lightroom). After editing, the alignment process was repeated, and both the dense point cloud and Digital Elevation Model (DEM) were generated.

Each image has a series of metadata in it, one of the most important being navigation information. UAVs generally have an autonomous navigation system, which follows a flight path and altitude, which the user predefines from a ground control station. This navigation is given by an inertial system and a GPS system, which allows having a position (Lat-Long). The user defines a region of interest and enters the flight parameters, and the software calculates the flight lines and the overlap of the images, longitudinally and transversally, which are normally greater than 75%. With respect to the height of the flight or Ground Sample Distance (GSD), which is measured in cm/pixel, so at high altitudes it generates a large GSD (lower resolution) and low flight heights will generate a small GSD (higher resolution) [28]. Therefore, the alignment is given from the generation of the flight plan and the interpolation of the images will depend on the site and the degree of detail required.

The process that is carried out after data capture is characterized by three main stages: first, the configuration of the photogrammetric block, where the objective is to determine the information that recreates the scene at the time of capturing the images (exterior and interior orientation data of the camera and the points that relate the images to each other). This is carried out by extracting and correlating common points between the images. This allows knowing the relative orientation between images and the registered common areas of the terrain. Two other strategies at this stage correspond to determining the internal and external orientation data, through image calibration and orientation, respectively. The second stage is the reconstruction of the scene from the data extraction, where the terrain coordinates of each of the common points extracted from the images are determined and subsequently the terrain coordinates are determined for each of the pixels in images through what is called point cloud densification; and third, the generation of the digital surface model and the orthorectification of the images from it, which allows the elimination of the distortion in the images generated by the relief [22, 23].

Following this, the orthomosaic was produced, and vegetation indices were determined from the DEM.

$$NDVI = \frac{NIR - Red}{NIR + Red} \tag{1}$$

where:

NIR – Near Infrared value.
Red – Visible red light value.

The NDVI values range from −1 to 1. Sites with values from −1 to 0 represent dead plants or inanimate objects, 0 to 0.33 represent diseased plants, 0.33 to 0.66 represent moderately healthy plants, and 0.66 to 1 represent very healthy plants [35].

The Soil-Adjusted Vegetation Index (SAVI) is calculated using the following formula:

$$SAVI = \left(\frac{NIR - Red}{NIR + Red + L}\right) * (1 + L) \tag{2}$$

where:

NIR – Near Infrared value.
Red – Visible red light value.
L – Factor indicating the degree to which soil is buffered through the vegetation. It is 0 for areas with high plant density, 0.5 for moderately exposed soils, and 1 for areas with low plant density.

The scale value is the same as that used in the NDVI [16].

The Chlorophyll Index (GCI) was calculated out using the following formula:

$$GCI = \left(\frac{NIR}{Green}\right) - 1 \tag{3}$$

where:

NIR – Near Infrared value.
Green – Visible green light value.

Of this index, the highest values correspond to healthy vegetation with photosynthetic activity, while values close to zero indicate sick vegetation with little photosynthetic action [13].

3 Results

The vegetation study revealed that the mTa site had an 80% frontal connection and a 78% lateral connection. In comparison, the mMA site had a frontal connection of 78% and a lateral connection of 73%. The orthomosaic imagery (Figs. 1 and 2) provided a comprehensive overview of the vegetation due to the altitude at which the flights were conducted, resulting in a pixel size of 5.26 cm at mTa and 7.47 cm at mMA, as shown in Figs. 3 and 4.

Fig. 1. Orthomosaic of the Taninul spring.

The study also found that the mTa site is at a lower altitude (185 m) compared to the spring (207 m) at mMA. The mTa site is located in a recreational center and has a modified natural vegetation layer with constant irrigation, resulting in very healthy vegetation values (ranging from 0.66 to 1). The vegetation on the slope shows moderately healthy values (ranging from 0.33 to 0.66), while the lowest area contains values indicative of

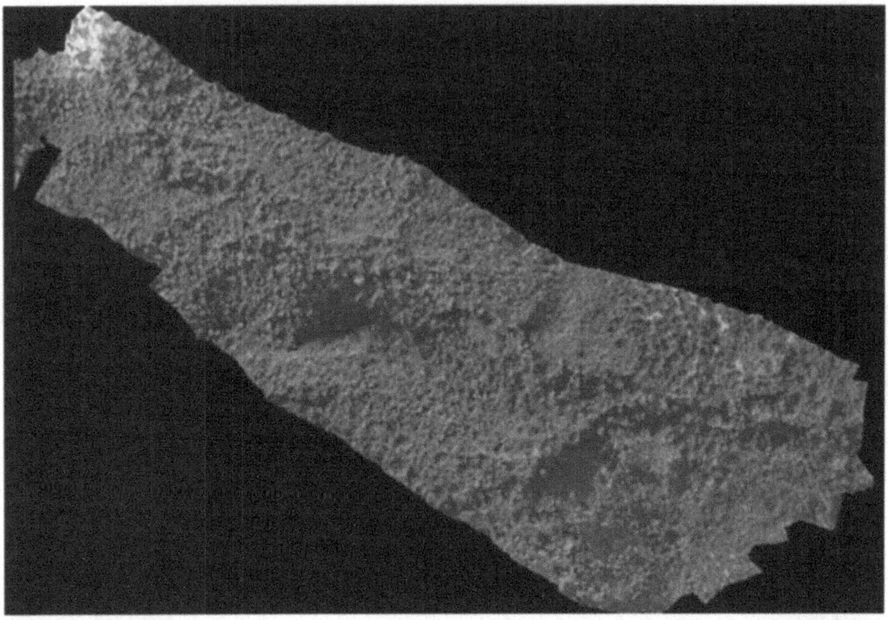

Fig. 2. Orthomosaic of the Mainero Azufroso spring.

Fig. 3. Digital Elevation Model of the Taninul spring.

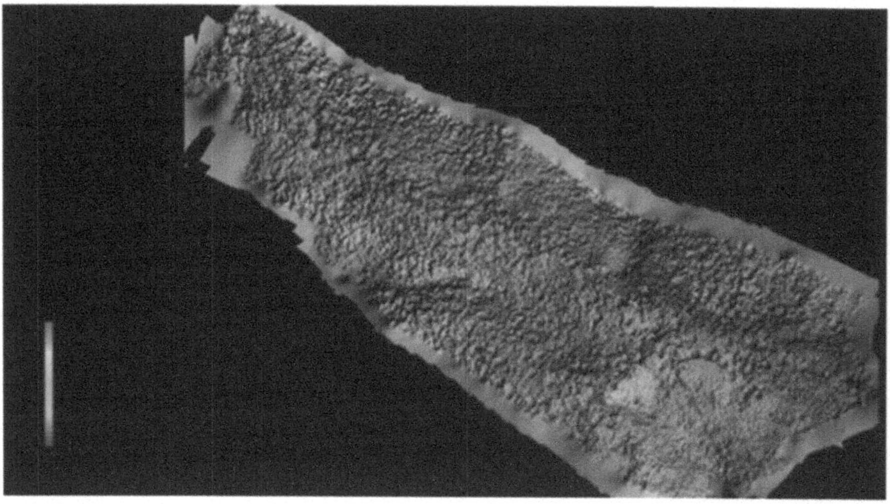

Fig. 4. Digital Elevation Model of the Mainero Azufroso spring.

dead plants or inanimate objects (ranging from −1 to 0), corresponding to the road, a hotel building, its parking lot, and a cleared area (Figs. 5 and 6).

When correlating these results with the SAVI and GCI, many red areas were observed, indicating bare soils related to paths used by hotel guests as nature trails. Overall, the vegetation around the hotel is very healthy (Figs. 7 and 8).

The mMA site is located in a ravine formed by a geological thrust and has unaltered vegetation. The vegetation at the site ranges from moderately healthy (0.33 to 0.66) to very healthy (0.66 to 1.00). When comparing with SAVI, there were gaps in information due to reflectance in the photographs, rather than sites altered by roads or human presence. The GCI values were the highest, approaching the maximum index value (1.00), indicating significant photosynthetic activity (Figs. 9 and 10).

The index values demonstrate that the vegetation at mTa ranges from diseased to moderately healthy, with lower reflectance in the red band. On the other hand, mMA shows areas of very healthy plants, with greater reflectance in the near infrared, resulting in dense vegetation and high photosynthetic activity. The study also revealed that areas of good health in vegetation and good photosynthetic activities exist in mMA despite the presence of dense vegetation in the higher areas, which is not the case in mTa due to a greater anthropogenic impact.

In both cases, the water flowing from the spring is creating a healthy ecosystem. However, it is evident that anthropogenic influence in mTa spring is creating pressure due to the influence of people doing activities nearby.

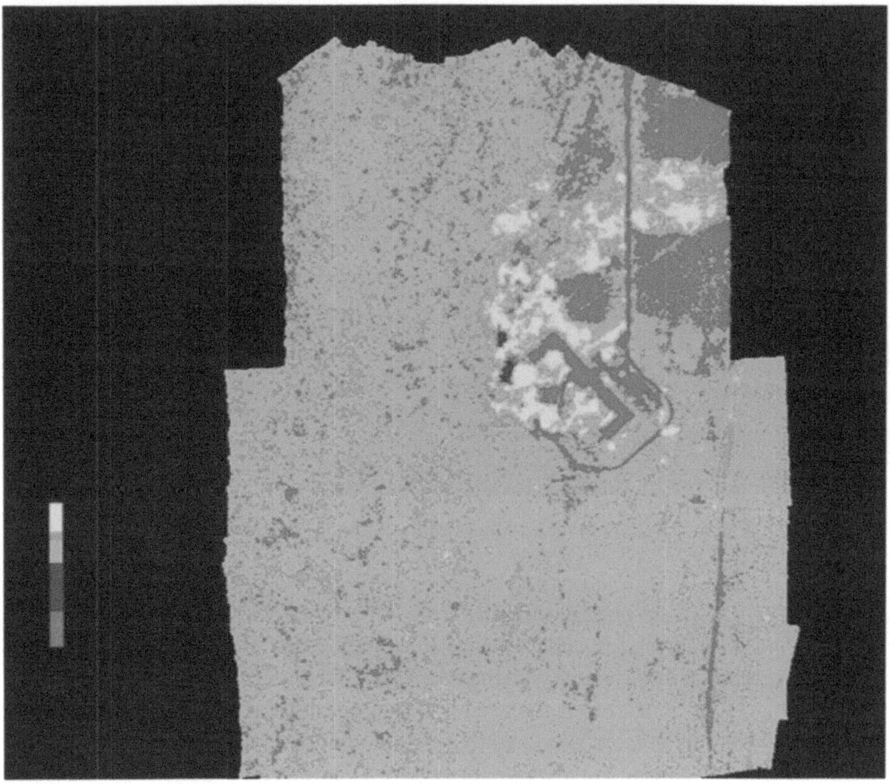

Fig. 5. Normalized Difference Vegetation Index (NDVI) of the Taninul spring.

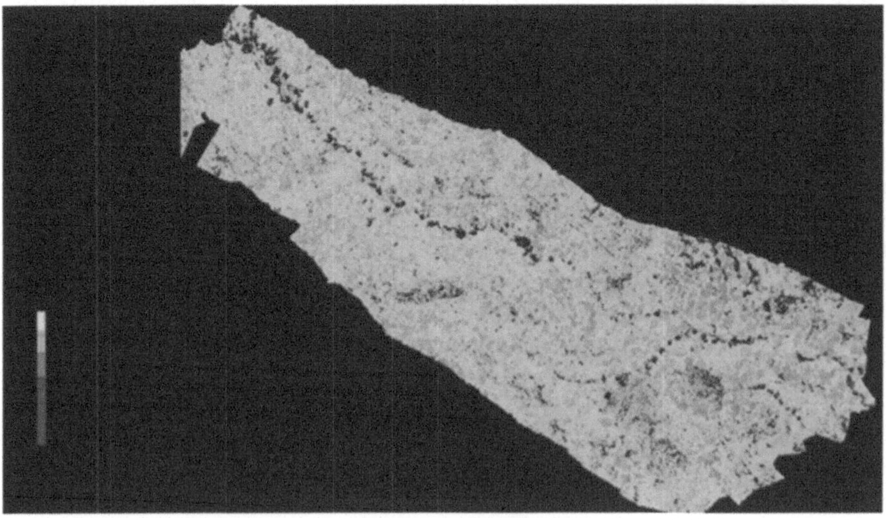

Fig. 6. Normalized Difference Vegetation Index (NDVI) of the Mainero Azufroso spring.

Fig. 7. Soil Adjusted Vegetation Index (SAVI) of the Taninul spring.

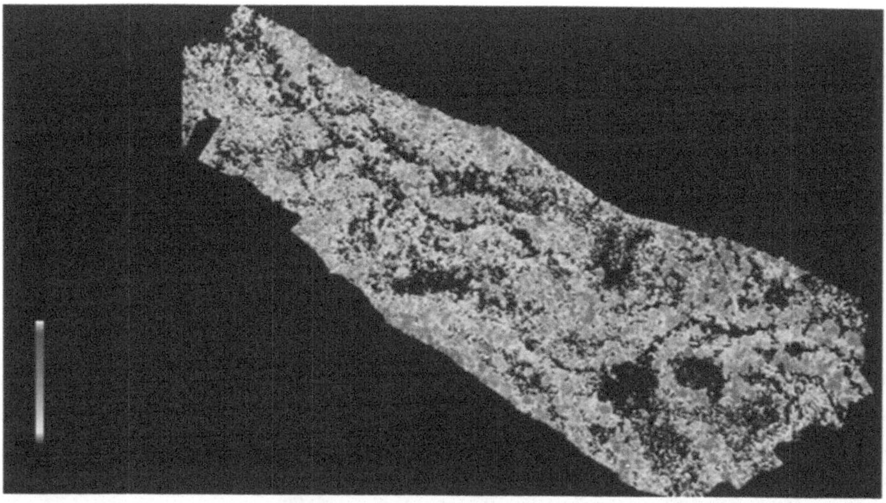

Fig. 8. Soil Adjusted Vegetation Index (SAVI) of the Mainero Azufroso spring.

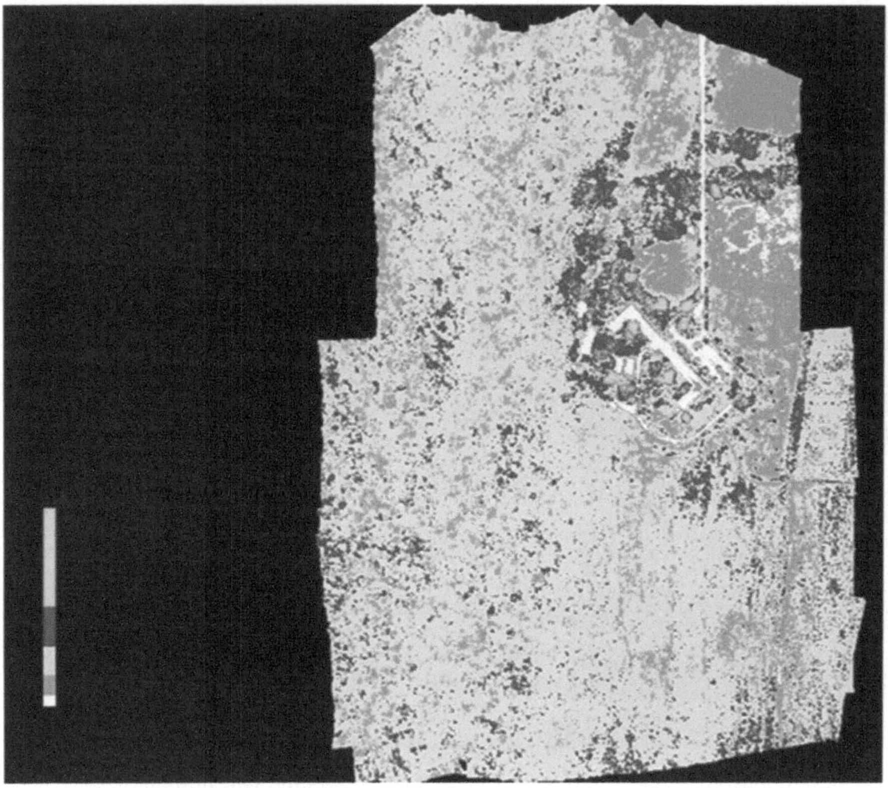

Fig. 9. Green Chlorophyll Index (GCI) from the Taninul spring.

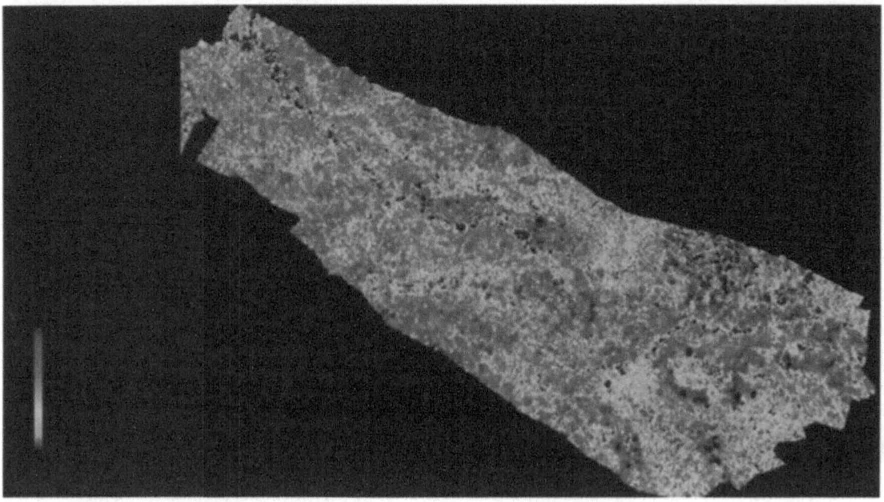

Fig. 10. Green Chlorophyll Index (GCI) from the Mainero Azufroso spring.

4 Discussion

Our research focuses on using a multispectral camera mounted on a UAV to analyze vegetation indices derived from the analysis of photographs. Although these photographs are easy to obtain and access, they come with some limitations and challenges. When analyzing a large area, it's important to delimit the specific area to be studied.

The photographic analysis from UAV flights allows for a cost-effective and efficient interpretation of the environments to be studied. Selecting the right flight altitude is crucial to create a good orthomosaic with a pixel size that enables the recognition of species, vegetation damage, and areas of disturbance. In long-term studies, this method helps in determining the resilience capacity of ecosystems [31]. Therefore, initial reconnaissance flights are necessary to properly identify geomorphological features and determine the optimal altitude for subsequent flights.

The difference in pixel size in the generated orthomosaic between the two sites is due to the angle of the slopes and the maximum height, despite both sites being flown over at the same altitude. The less steep slope of the mTa provides better definition of the vegetation, while the steeper slope of the mMA does not allow for clear definition of the vegetation, resulting in different spatial scales in both cases. These findings differ from those reported by Mallmann et al. [26], in the Quarta Colônia State Park in Río Grande do Sul, Brazil, where flights at the same altitude resulted in a higher resolution pixel (3.98 cm). However, this park is located in a flat area unlike the cultivation sites, where very fine spatial resolution can be achieved due to the flat terrain [11, 44, 45].

The different vegetation indices each have their own limitations. As a result, many authors suggest that they should be used in combination, depending on the specific analysis objectives [18–20, 27, 32]. The use of various indices provides a good interpretation of results in determining the health status of vegetation as presented in multispectral images. For instance, the quality of photosynthetic activity, indicated by GCI values in mMA, allows us to infer the good photosynthetic activity of the vegetation, which is observable in the vegetation canopy [3, 14, 15].

The use of vegetation indices from multispectral images allows the health status to be evaluated based on different characteristics such as chlorophyll content, water status, nutritional status or structural deficiencies, and although various optical measurement equipment can give this information (for example, foliar spectrometers allow measuring leaf vegetation indices), there is a loss of spatial and spectral resolution [1, 4, 36]. This type of analysis allows us to improve the precision in the evaluation of the health status of the vegetation by generating a higher resolution of the area of interest.

While this study focuses on the potential of vegetation indices to observe phenological variations due to thermal springs, it's important to note that factors such as plant species and topography should be considered in future research to obtain more accurate results [21].

The influence of water generates different responses with respect to the distance from the spring; the further the vegetation is from the discharge site; the vegetation shows a decrease in the value of the index. The presence of environments with slopes does not allow better absorption of water from runoff or the use of vegetation through its roots is less. Furthermore, it does not allow nutrients to be used in the upper and middle parts, only in the lower region. This type of response differs, for example, from agricultural sites where constant irrigation by the producer, as well as fertilization of the orchard, generates an optimal state of health in controlled environments [25, 43].

The photographs obtained through UAV have proven to be an effective tool for understanding how the phenological behaviors of plant communities relate to landscape phenology [37, 41]. In addition, these photographs provide an accurate representation of the phenology of a heterogeneous landscape around specific measurements of ecosystem-scale processes [38]. This can be a useful tool in calibrating and interpreting measurements of ecological processes depending on vegetation phenology, such as canopy-scale photosynthesis.

Vegetation indices are images that are calculated from algebraic operations between different spectral bands whose function is to highlight the vegetation cover (graphically highlighting certain pixels related to different parameters of the vegetation cover, such as density, leaf area index and chlorophyllic activity) based on its spectral response and attenuate the details of other components such as soil, lighting, etc., but each vegetation index has its limitations. The NDVI is sensitive to the effects of the soil and the atmosphere, which is why it is recommended to apply additional indices for a more precise analysis of the vegetation [4, 26, 40].

5 Conclusions

There is no single vegetation index that encompasses all the characteristics needed to evaluate the study. However, the combination of NDVI, SAVI, and GCI provides a good assessment of the vegetation health in the areas under examination. By integrating various vegetation indices and utilizing spectral information, we can complement and determine the health status characteristics in the areas surrounding the springs.

The analysis of the images captured by the UAV presented several challenges, particularly in the case of Mainero Azufroso. This was due to the angle of inclination of the slopes affecting light reflectance, which was a result of the flight schedule for taking photographs. The orthomosaic presents spaces without information (black), so carrying out flights at 3 different times a day could have helped to have fewer spaces without information. Due to the angle of the light and in order to mitigate the effect of those empty spaces, having carried out a flight in the morning, at noon and in the afternoon, would have been the best, to have the greatest amount of light possible and less shades.

However, these challenges can be moderately corrected with the use of photo editing programs. It's worth noting that correcting the light in the images through editing may lead to errors in sensor readings. This occurs because adjusting the brightness of the photograph can magnify or decrease details that are not visible in the original image. When making such corrections, the program determines a new light value and adjusts it with the sensor value, which may result in a different value than the rest of the photographs. This discrepancy can cause an alteration to the index value, leading to the omission of the photograph to avoid this corrected value, thereby resulting in gaps in the index images.

The selection of work areas and the altitude at which the images should be captured is a preliminary task that needs to be done at each specific site in order to determine the specific features required for subsequent analysis. Using multispectral images taken by cameras mounted on UAVs enables us to quickly assess the health status of natural vegetation in areas of concern, with better spatial resolution than that provided by satellite images. This can be further enhanced by considering the temporal scale, as sampling can be conducted at any time to analyze unaltered spaces or damaged areas, such as those impacted by deforestation or fires.

Utilizing various indices allows for a better identification of processes and the classification of ecosystems, thus prioritizing the implementation of short, medium, and long-term evaluation strategies. These strategies aim to facilitate future research on resilience in natural ecosystems experiencing moderate to severe impacts, or to develop plans for restoration in highly affected sites.

References

1. Alba, E., Mello, E., Marchesan, J., Silva, E.A., Tramontina, J., Pereira, R.S.: Spectral characterization of forest plantations with Landsat 8/OLI images for forest planning and management. Pesq. Agrop. Brasileira **52**(11), 1072–1079 (2017)
2. Anai, T., Sasaki, T., Osaragi, K., Yamada, M., Otomo, F., Otani, H.: Automatic exterior orientation procedure for low-cost UAV photogrammetry using video image tracking technique and GPS information. The International Archives of the Photogrammetry, Remote Sensing and Spatial Information Sciences **XXXIX-B7**, 469–474 (2012). https://doi.org/10.5194/isprsarchives-XXXIX-B7-469-2012
3. Berra, E.F., Gaulton, R., Barr, S.: Use of a digital camera onboard a UAV to monitor spring phenology at individual tree level. Forest Ecology Management. On IEEE International Geoscience and Remote Sensign Symposium (IGARS), pp. 3496–3499 (2016)
4. Bolin, F., et al.: Classifying vegetation communities karst wetland synergistic use of image fusion and object-based machine learning algorithm with Jilin-1 and UAV multispectral images. Ecol. Ind. **140**, 108989 (2022)
5. Camargo-Cruz, T., Núñez Benítez, J., Ángeles-Hernández, J.G.: Aguas Termales del Estado de Hidalgo. Universidad Autónoma del Estado de Hidalgo. Área de Investigaciones en Ciencias de la Tierra y Materiales. Fondo Editorial (2022)
6. Carmona, J.Á.S., Quirós, E., Mayoral, V., Charro, C.: Assessing the potential of multispectral and thermal UAV imagery from archaeological sites. A case study from the Iron Age Hillfort of Villasviejas del Tamuja (Cáceres, Spain). J. Archaeol. Sci.: Reports **31**, 102312 (2020)
7. Castaldo, J.H.: Revolutionizing agriculture from the skies: exploring the potential of spraying drones in precision farming. Cadernos de Ciência & Tecnologia **40**, 27284 (2023)
8. Chaves-Pabón, S.B.: Uso de drones y sensores remotos para el monitoreo de laderas: una revisión. Ingenierías USBMed **12**(2), 65–73 (2021)
9. Colomina, I., Molina, P.: Unmanned aerial systems for photogrammetry and remote sensing: a review. ISPRS J. Photogramm. Remote. Sens. **92**, 79–97 (2014)
10. Davidovich, B., Nassi, B., Elovici, Y.: Towards the detection of GPS spoofing attacks against drones by analyzing camera's video stream. Sensors **22**(7), 2608 (2022)
11. Ding, S.P., et al.: Discrete element modelling (DEM) of fertilizer dual-banding with adjustable rates. Comput. Electron. Agric. **152**, 32–39 (2018)
12. Fay, C., Wu, L.: Critical Importance of RGB Color space specificity for Colorimetric Bio/chemical sensing: a Comprehensive study. Talanta **266**, 124957 (2024)
13. Fernandes, M.R., Aguiar, F.C., Martins, M.J., Rico, N., Ferreira, M.T., Correia, A.C.: Carbon stock estimations in a Mediterranean riparian forest: a case study combining field data and UAV imagery. Forests **11**, 376–397 (2020)

14. Garcia-Garcia, D., Reynafarje de la R., X., Bedoya, D.G., Schrevens, E.: Linear mixed model analysis of NDVI-based canopy coverage, extracted from sequential UAV multispectral imagery of an open field tomato irrigation experiment. Comput. Electron. Agric. **189**, 106399 (2021)
15. Ge, W., Li, X., Jing, L., Han, J., Wang, F.: Monitoring canopy-scale autumn leaf phenology at fine-scale using unmanned aerial vehicle (UAV) photography. Agric. For. Meteorol. **332**, 109372 (2023)
16. Gonzaga-Aguilar, C.: Aplicación de índices de vegetación derivados de imágenes satelitales Landsat 7 ETM+ y ASTER, para la caracterización de la cobertura vegetal en la zona centro de la Provincia De Loja, Ecuador. Facultad de Ingeniería y Facultad de Ciencias Astronómicas y Geofísicas de la Universidad de La Plata. La Plata, Ecuador (2014)
17. González-Morgado, A., Álvarez-Cía, C., Benot, G.H., Baturone, A.O.: UAV Fully-actuated: modelo, control y comparación con configuración coplanaria. Revista Iberoamericana De Automatica E Informatica Industrial. **20**(4), 401–411 (2023)
18. González, M.A., Schwendenmann, L., Jiméne, J., Schulz, R.: Forest structure and woody plant species composition along a fire chronosequence in mixed pine-oak forest in the Sierra Madre Oriental, Northeast Mexico. Forest Ecol. Manag. **256**, 161–167 (2008)
19. Heredia, L.A., Martínez, S.S., Quintero, E., Piñeros, W., Chuvieco, E.: Comparación de distintas técnicas de análisis digital para la cartografía de áreas quemadas con imágenes landsat ETM+. Revista internacional de ciencia y tecnología de la información geográfica **3**, 216–234 (2003)
20. Key, C.H., Benson, N.C.: Landscape assessment sampling and analysis Methods. En: Lutes, D.C. (eds.), Firemon: Fire Effects Monitoring and Inventory System (pp. LA1 – LA51). Rocky Monuntain: USDA Forest Service Gen. Tech. Rep. RMRS-GTR-164-CD (2006)
21. Klosterman, S., et al.: Fine-Scale perspectives on landscape phenology from unmanned aerial vehicle (UAV) photography. Agric. Forestry Meteorol. **248**, 397–407 (2018)
22. Lingua, A., Marenchino, D., Nex, F.: Performance analysis of the SIFT operator for automatic feature extraction and matching in photogrammetric applications. Sensors **9**(5), 3745–3766 (2009)
23. Lingua, A., Marenchino, D., Nex, F.: Performance analysis of the SIFT operator for automatic feature extraction and matching in photogrammetric applications. Sensors **9**(5), 3745–3766 (2009). https://doi.org/10.3390/s90503745
24. Lira, J., Aguilar, R.: Edge enhancement in multispectral satellite images by means of vector operators. Geofisica Internacional **53**(3), 289–308 (2014)
25. Liu, S., et al.: UAV multispectral images for accurate estimation of the maize LAI considering the effect of soil background. Int. J. Appl. Earth Observ. Geoinform. **121**, 103383 (2023)
26. Mallmann, C.L., de Almeida Prado, D., Pereira Filho, W.: Normalized difference vegetation index for characterization of forest dynamic in parque estadual Quarta Colônia, Rio Grande do Sul State – Brazil. Revista Brasileira de Geografia Física **8**(5), 1454–1469 (2015)
27. Mas, J.F., Díaz-Gallegos, J.R., Vega, A.P.: Evaluación de la confiabilidad temática de mapas o de imágenes clasificadas: una revisión. Investigaciones Geográficas. **51**, 53–72 (2003)
28. Nex, F., Remondino, F.: UAV for 3D mapping applications: a review. Applied Geomatics **6**(1), 1–15 (2013)
29. Ochoa-Salinas, P. A., Morales-Díaz, A. B., Pérez-Villeda, H. M., De Jesús Villalobos-Salazar, R.: Implementación de controladores visuales en dron comercial: estudio comparativo. PÄDI boletín científico de ciencias básicas e ingenierías del ICBI **11**(Especial2), 86–93 (2023)
30. Ponzoni, F.J., Shimabukuro, Y.E., Kuplich, T.M.: Sensoriamento remoto aplicado ao estudo da vegetação, 2 edn. Saraiva, São José Dos Campos, p. 160 (2012)
31. Rodríguez, S.F., Molina, M.J.R., Castillo S.M.: Aproximación metodológica para la evaluación del impacto ecológico de los incendios forestales, mediante el uso de teledetección

especial, aplicación mediante el uso de imágenes Modis. En: Memorias del Cuarto Simposio Internacional Políticas, Planificación y Economía de los Incendios Forestales, pp. 305–319. General technical report PSW-GTR-245 (2012)
32. Rondeaux, G., Steven, M., Baret, F.: Optimization of soil-adjusted vegetation indices. Remote Sens. Env. **55**(2), 95–107 (1996). https://doi.org/10.1016/0034-4257(95)00186-7
33. Santillán, O., Rentería-Rodríguez, M.: Agricultura de precisión. Ciudad de México, México: Oficina de Información Científica y Tecnológica para el Congreso de la Unión (INCyTU) (2018)
34. Shi, J., Wang, J., Xu, Y.: Object-based change detection using georeferenced UAV images. Int. Arch. Photogramm. Remote Sens. Spatial Inf. Sci. **XXXVIII-1/C22**, 177–182 (2012)
35. Tran, B.N., Tanase, M.A., Bemmett, L.T., Aponte, C.: Evaluation of spectral indices for assessing fire severity in australian temperate forests. Remote sensing **10**, 1680 (2018)
36. Triana-Martinez, J.C., De Swaef, T., Bora-Serrano, I., Lootens, P., Barrero, O., Fernandez-Gallego, J.A.: Comparative leaf area index estimation using multiespectral and RGB images form a UAV platform. Auton. Air Ground Sens. Syst. Agr. Optim. Phenotyping VIII **12539**, 1253906 (2023)
37. Wingate, L., et al.: Interpreting canopy development and physiology using a European phenology camera network at flux sites. Biogeosciences **12**, 5995–6015 (2015)
38. Woodcock, C.E., Strahler, A.H.: The factor of scale in remote sensing. Remote Sens. Environ. **21**, 311–332 (1987)
39. Xiang, H., Tian, L.: Development of a low-cost agricultural remote sensing system based on an autonomous unmanned aerial vehicle (UAV). Biosys. Eng. **108**(2), 174–190 (2011)
40. Xue, J., Sun, S., Zhao H., Chen, W.: Vegetation classification of UAV multispectral remote sensing images based on deep learning. In: 3rd International Conference on Consumer Electronics and Computer Engineering (ICCECE), Guangzhou, China, pp. 768–771 (2023)
41. Yang, X., Tang, J., Mustard, J.: Beyond leaf color: comparing camera-based phenological metrics with leaf biochemical, biophysical and spectral properties throughout the growing season of a temperate deciduous forest. J. Geophys. Res. Biogeosci. **119**, 181–191 (2014)
42. Zeng, Y., et al.: Optical vegetation indices for monitoring terrestrial ecosystems globally. Nat. Rev. Earth Environ. **3**, 477–493 (2022)
43. Zeng, X., Tang, S., Peng, S., Xia, W., Chen, Y., Wang, C.: Estimation of Chlorophyll Content of Tea Tree Canopy using multispectral UAV images. In: 11th International Conference on Agro-Geoinformatics (Agro-Geoinformatics), pp. 1–6. Wuhan, China, 2023 (2023)
44. Zhang, X.Q., et al.: Effects of spray parameters of drone on the droplet deposition in sugarcane canopy. Sugar Tech. **22**(4), 583–588 (2020)
45. Zhou, H., et al.: Application of a centrifugal disc fertilizer spreading system for UAV's in rice fields. Heliyon. **10**, e29837 (2024)

Identifying Spatio-Temporal Patterns of COVID-19 Vaccination Effects in Social Networks of Mexico City

Erick Quintana Martínez[1], Moisés Arango León[1], Roberto Eswart Zagal Flores[1](✉), Elizabeth Montero[2], Miriam Pescador Rojas[1], and Rene Baltazar Jimenez Ruiz[1]

[1] Escuela Superior de Cómputo (ESCOM), Instituto Politécnico Nacional. Ciudad de México, Ciudad de México, Mexico
{quintanam1500,marangol1500}@alumno.ipn.mx, zagalmmx@gmail.com, {rzagalf,mpescadorr,rbjimenez}@ipn.mx

[2] Universidad Técnica Federico Santa María, Valparaíso, Chile

Abstract. During the early years of the COVID-19 pandemic in Mexico, the lack of a structured system for collecting data on vaccine side effects highlighted a critical gap in the national healthcare infrastructure. Today, social media has become a key platform where citizens share their post-vaccination experiences, often reporting physical and emotional discomforts following vaccine administration. Collecting and analyzing this information enables the visualization of the spatiotemporal impact of post-vaccination health across various regions of Mexico City. The main challenge lies in extracting this data in real time, understanding the dynamics of terms used to describe vaccination effects on social media, and subsequently identifying the known side effects of different COVID-19 vaccines. The most commonly reported side effects on Twitter, such as "headache," "fatigue," "fever," "muscle pain," and "chills," reflect consistency between public perceptions and clinical observations, particularly for vaccines like AstraZeneca and Sputnik-V. Notably, "fever" and "headache" were concentrated in the central and southern regions of Mexico City. Our study proposes a framework for analyzing narratives obtained from Twitter using Natural Language Processing (NLP), spatial analysis, and data mining techniques. This approach complements official vaccination campaign data and can help shape future strategies and health policies.

Keywords: Vaccination health effects · COVID-19 · Spatial Data Mining · Social networks · GIS

1 Introduction

In Mexico, vaccination campaigns began in late 2020 with healthcare workers, and subsequently continued with the rest of the Mexican population. Throughout the following year, Mexicans received the necessary doses of vaccines such as Sputnik V, AstraZeneca, Moderna, Pfizer, Johnson & Johnson, Cansino, and Sinovac. Most people experienced

M. F. Mata-Rivera et al. (Eds.): GIS-LATAM 2024, CCIS 2298, pp. 208–221, 2025.
https://doi.org/10.1007/978-3-031-80017-7_14

normal reactions within the first 24 h, such as arm pain, fatigue, headache, muscle pain, chills, fever, nausea, etc. However, some exhibited serious side effects in the following days, including fatigue, joint pain, fever, nausea, allergic reactions like rash, itching, or facial swelling, among others [1].

Various nations implemented specific tools for the registration and monitoring of secondary reactions that occurred in patients. These epidemiological and pharmacological surveillance systems obtained detailed statistics that allowed for evaluations of the side effects and effectiveness of their vaccines [2] and [3]. However, in Mexico, during the initial vaccination campaigns, no actions were taken to identify the effects of the different vaccines administered to the population.

In the realm of global public health, the dissemination of information through social networks regarding the side effects of COVID-19 vaccines has garnered substantial attention. This study in [7] explores the emotional responses of the Brazilian public towards the COVID-19 vaccine as expressed on Facebook. Using content analysis, the authors evaluated the sentiments surrounding vaccine-related posts and comments. The findings highlight a wide range of emotions, with a significant portion of the population expressing positive attitudes such as hope and relief. However, negative emotions such as fear and distrust were also prevalent, especially in response to misinformation about vaccine side effects and conspiracy theories circulating on the platform. The researchers suggest that effective communication strategies should consider the emotional landscape of social media discussions to address vaccine hesitancy and misinformation in a more targeted manner.

The authors report in [8] the side effects experienced by recipients of the CoronaVac COVID-19 vaccine in a province of Turkey. Conducted a cross-sectional survey, gathering data on common post-vaccination symptoms reported by individuals. The most frequently observed side effects were localized pain at the injection site, fatigue, and mild fever. These symptoms were generally transient and did not require medical intervention. The study emphasizes that while side effects were present, they were mild and manageable, reinforcing the overall safety of the vaccine. The authors conclude that continued monitoring of vaccine side effects is necessary to maintain public confidence and ensure the successful rollout of vaccination programs.

The work in [9] examines individual preferences for COVID-19 vaccination in China, using a survey-based study to analyze factors influencing vaccine uptake. The research identified several key drivers of vaccination intent, including trust in vaccine efficacy, perceptions of personal risk, and government recommendations. The study highlights the importance of transparent communication regarding vaccine safety and efficacy to foster higher acceptance rates. It also suggests that public health campaigns should address specific concerns related to vaccine side effects and efficacy, which play a critical role in shaping individuals' willingness to get vaccinated.

The study in [10] shows the relationship between social media exposure, peer discussions, and behavioral intentions to receive COVID-19 vaccination in China. The researchers used a cross-sectional survey to measure participants' vaccination intentions and how these were influenced by their engagement with social media content and discussions with peers. The results showed that frequent exposure to vaccine-related content on social media and positive peer discussions significantly increased the likelihood of individuals intending to get vaccinated.

The findings suggest that social media plays a crucial role in shaping public attitudes toward COVID-19 vaccination. The study calls for targeted interventions on social platforms to promote accurate information and positive discourse around vaccination to increase uptake rates, especially among groups exhibiting hesitancy.

In another study involving a cohort of 200 patients, the most common side effects of the Sputnik V vaccine were identified, including fever, headache, body aches, and injection site pain, with men reporting these symptoms more frequently than women [11]. The study underscores the importance of education and transparent communication in reducing vaccine hesitancy. It suggests that healthcare centers should actively engage with the community to address specific concerns about the vaccine, leveraging trusted sources of information to build confidence and increase uptake rates.

As a result, social media platforms have emerged as significant channels for public expression on health-related issues. Unlike official channels provided by governments or pharmaceutical companies, social networks offer an alternative space for users to share their experiences and concerns, including discussions about vaccine side effects. This unfiltered exchange of information creates valuable opportunities for real-time monitoring of public reactions and symptoms associated with COVID-19 vaccination.

2 Methodology

The architecture of the prototype is comprised of the following phases: (1) Iterative extraction of tweets based on location and keywords describing the effects of COVID-19 vaccinations across the 16 boroughs of Mexico City. (2) Data cleaning and preprocessing. (3) Detection of vaccination effect topics through Topic Modelling, a natural language processing (NLP) technique. (4) Trend detection using Spatial Data Mining, involving statistical analysis of variables across time and space based on the results of the topic modelling. (5) Spatial exploration of the processed data, enabling analysis and interpretation of the discovered topics in relation to the identified spatiotemporal trends.

2.1 Iterative Tweet Extraction Process

The extraction of tweets was conducted using the Snscrape library [4], employing up to three iterations. In the initial iteration, broad terms describing vaccination campaigns were used. For the subsequent iterations, the terms were refined following exploratory analysis of the data retrieved in the first iteration, allowing for the identification of relevant terms used by citizens to describe vaccination effects.

During the first phase, 87,047 tweets were retrieved from Mexico City between December 24, 2020, and September 25, 2022. The primary search vectors included vaccine names and hashtags promoted by the government, such as #vacuna, #AstraZeneca, and #Sputnik, as well as terms describing physical symptoms like 'headache,' 'sore throat,' 'pain vaccine,' 'vaccine effect,' 'vaccine reaction,' 'vaccine discomfort,' and 'vaccine symptom.'

Upon analyzing the tweets from the first iteration, the use of verb conjugations such as "poner" (put), "sentir" (feel), "recibir" (receive), "tocar" (touch), "aplicar" (apply), and "vacunar" (vaccinate) was observed. These verbs were combined with keywords like "vacuna" (vaccine) or "dosis" (dose) to generate new search terms, such as "dosis vacunar" (dose vaccinate), "aplicar vacuna" (apply vaccine), and "recibir dosis" (receive dose). Additionally, new terms associated with medications, spatiotemporal descriptors, and GPS coordinates were incorporated, such as "paracetamol vacuna" (paracetamol vaccine), "noche vacuna" (night vaccine), "dormir vacuna" (sleep vaccine), and location-specific terms like "vacuna en Iztapalapa" (vaccine in Iztapalapa) or "vacunación en Benito Juárez" (vaccination in Benito Juárez). This refinement in the search process yielded a total of 139,642 tweets from the 16 boroughs of Mexico City.

2.2 Data Cleaning and Preprocessing

In this phase, irrelevant information and duplicate content were removed, and processes such as text normalization and tokenization were applied, following the methods outlined in [5]. Spatial data was then identified in each tweet. The final output consisted of 128,292 tweets, following the data processing steps described below:

a) Removal of web hyperlinks.
b) Removal of mentions and hashtags.
c) Removal of emoticons.
d) Elimination of special characters and punctuation marks. The letter "ñ" was replaced with "n," and all punctuation (including periods, commas, semicolons, colons, quotes, parentheses, question marks, exclamation points, ellipses, hyphens, and dashes) was removed.
e) Conversion of words to lowercase.
f) Correction of abbreviations using a dictionary of common abbreviations used by Spanish-speaking Twitter users (e.g., "x" for "por" (for), "q" or "k" for "que" (that), and "xq" for "porque" (because)).
g) Tokenization: Separation of terms into individual words for spelling correction and vectorization.
h) Removal of stop words (articles, pronouns, and prepositions without lexical meaning).
i) Spelling correction: Applied to the tokenized tweet content.
j) Lemmatization: Reducing words to their base form (e.g., "trabajar" (to work) as the root for "trabaje" (I work) and "trabajaba" (I was working)).
k) Removal of duplicate tweets: Tweets with identical content were eliminated.

Following preprocessing, tweets were filtered to include only those containing spatial information. Using the Snscrape library, geolocation attributes (coordinates and places) were extracted when reference points were specified during the tweet search process. Only tweets from the 16 boroughs of Mexico City were selected. For tweets lacking geographic coordinates, a heuristic process using the GeoPy library was applied, which retrieves geographic coordinates based on addresses, cities, countries, and reference points mentioned in the text, helping to identify the relevant boroughs in Mexico City.

2.3 Spatial Distribution of Preprocessed Data

Mexico City is divided into 16 boroughs. The highest concentration of tweets was collected in the central boroughs of Benito Juárez and Cuauhtémoc, with 18,428 and 15,151 tweets, respectively. In the eastern boroughs, Iztapalapa and Gustavo A. Madero, which are the most densely populated, 14,771 and 7,686 tweets were gathered, respectively. The southern borough of Álvaro Obregón yielded 9,638 tweets. In the western borough of Miguel Hidalgo, known for its high socioeconomic status, 10,828 tweets were collected, surpassing the northern boroughs. In the southern boroughs of Coyoacán and Tlalpan, 12,424 and 8,723 tweets were recorded, respectively, areas with a higher socioeconomic profile compared to the northern boroughs. Figure 1 illustrates the concentration of tweets in the most densely populated and economically active areas of Mexico City, providing a robust data sample for further analysis.

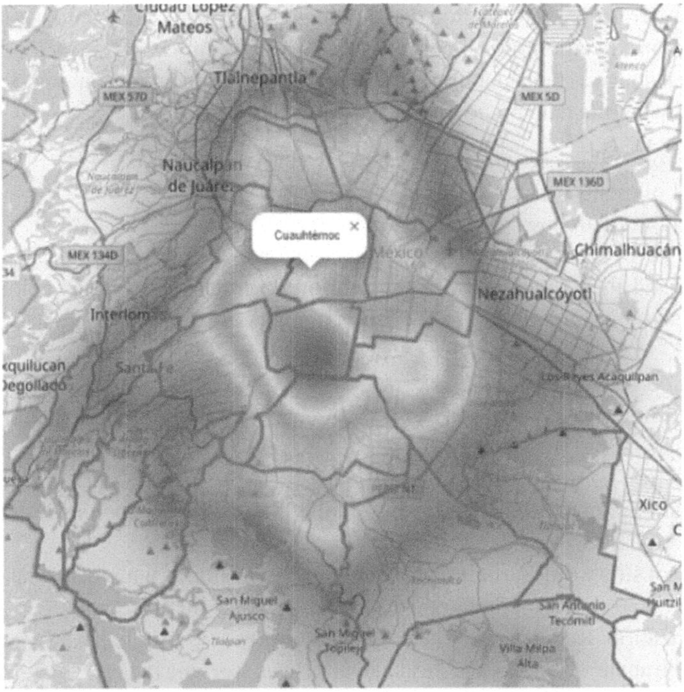

Fig. 1. Distribution of collected tweets in Mexico City (CDMX).

2.4 Detection of Vaccination Effect Topics

To numerically represent the collected text data, the Word Embeddings model was employed. This model effectively captures the syntax and semantics of each word within a tweet (which is treated as a 'document' in natural language processing). Additionally, the Doc2Vec model was implemented to capture the contextual relationship between tweets, assigning vectors to individual words and tweets. The combination of these models facilitates the identification of semantically similar tweets.

The Doc2Vec model incorporates two neural network architectures: the Paragraph Vector-Distributed Memory (PV-DM) model and the Distributed Bag of Words version of the Paragraph Vector (PV-DBOW). The PV-DM model captures the local context of each word within a tweet, effectively analyzing its placement in relation to surrounding words. On the other hand, PV-DBOW uses the document identifier as input and generates a vector representing the entire document, but it does not account for the document's internal context or word-level semantics. PV-DBOW predicts word contexts based on a predominant word or central term, without considering syntactic or grammatical sentence structure.

2.5 Semantic Correspondence Between Secondary Effect Topics

In this phase, both architectures were tested to determine the model with the best performance. To validate the learning accuracy of the Doc2Vec model, two methods were used: one based on Word Embeddings, and the other utilizing cosine similarity. These methods helped analyze the semantic proximity between words and the overall context derived from the input set of tweets.

The vector space, sized at 100 dimensions, was visualized in a two-dimensional space for improved interpretability, following the criteria outlined in [6]. To reduce the dimensionality, the Principal Component Analysis (PCA) statistical method was applied, which allowed for better representation of the relationships between word vectors. For instance, in Fig. 2, the vector representation of the PV-DBOW model shows that the terms "síntoma" (symptom), "secundario" (secondary), and "reacción" (reaction) cluster closely together within the same partial vector space. Additionally, topics related to health effects, such as "fiebre" (fever), "temperatura" (temperature), "cuerpo" (body), "brazo" (arm), "cabeza" (head), "dolor" (pain), "sueño" (sleep), and "cansancio" (fatigue), also form clusters, indicating strong semantic correspondence between them. This clustering reflects the narratives on Twitter expressing side effects related to the COVID-19 vaccines.

Moreover, it was observed that the words "efecto" (effect), "secundario" (secondary), "reacción" (reaction), and "síntoma" (symptom) exhibit a strong semantic relationship. Other terms, such as "sentir" (feel), "noche" (night), "pasar" (pass), and "recibir" (receive), also share significant semantic proximity, further reinforcing that the discovered topics accurately represent the semantics of side effects described in the collected tweets. Notably, vaccine names, such as "cansino," were also identified within these clusters.

On the other hand, using the PV-DM ("Paragraph Vector-Distributed Memory") algorithm, a semantic representation is generated between the words "cuerpo" ("body"), "brazo" ("arm"), "sueño" ("sleep"), and "temperatura" ("temperature"), which describe common side effects. This relationship is illustrated in Fig. 3. Additionally, terms such as "reacción" ("reaction"), "efecto" ("effect"), and "astrazeneca" also form meaningful connections within the model. Notably, the topic "noche" ("night") stands out, though it is not as closely associated with symptoms as observed in the PV-DBOW model. The

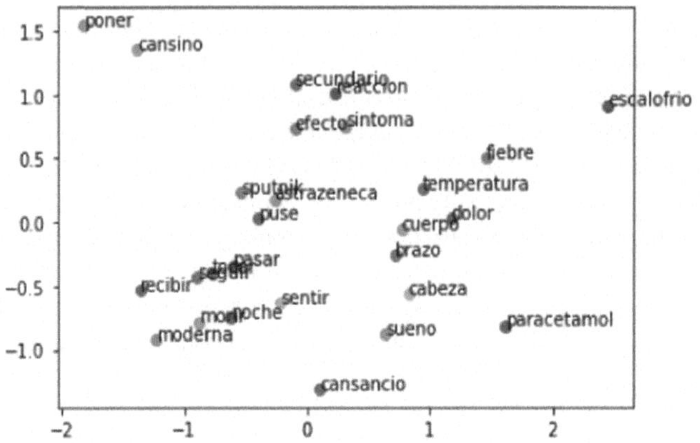

Fig. 2. Word embeddings, Distributed Bag of Words version of the Paragraph Vector (PV-DBOW)

relevance of the term "noche" lies in its ability to capture the temporal aspect, indicating that many citizens reported experiencing vaccine side effects during the night.

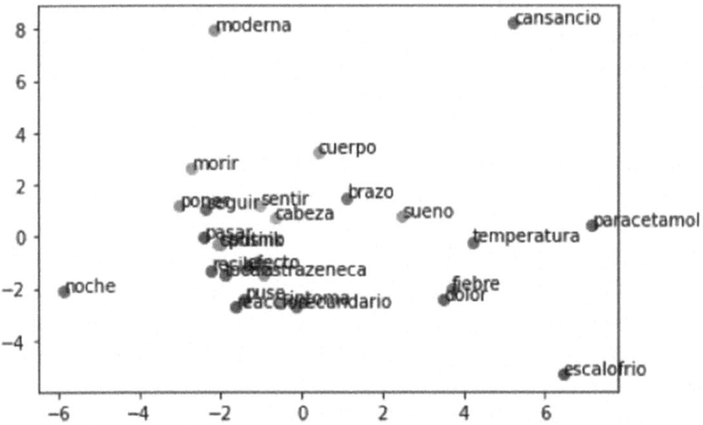

Fig. 3. Word Embeddings, Paragraph Vector-Distributed Memory (PV-DM) model

Although Figs. 2 and 3 offer a visual representation of the relationships between topics, it is recommended to use cosine similarity for a numerical evaluation to confirm these relationships. For instance, when calculating the similarity between the topics "noche" ("night") and "fiebre" ("fever"), the PV-DBOW model yields a value of 0.20, whereas the PV-DM model gives -0.0016. This indicates that PV-DBOW identifies a stronger relationship between these topics, as its similarity score is closer to 1. Similarly, for the topics "dolor" ("pain") and "brazo" ("arm"), PV-DBOW produces a score of 0.3389, while PV-DM results in 0.1961. In contrast, for the topics "sentir" ("feel") and "AstraZeneca vaccine," PV-DBOW achieves a similarity of 0.4293, while PV-DM gives a higher value of 0.574; in this case, PV-DM performs better, although this does not necessarily indicate the most accurate result. To further validate the PV-DBOW and

PV-DM architectures, it is crucial to evaluate the cosine similarity between tweets. In this regard, Table 1 presents a sample of cosine similarity values, demonstrating that the PV-DBOW architecture consistently performs better for smaller text datasets.

Table 1. Cosine Similarity Evaluation of the Doc2Vec Architectures

Tweets (English / Spanish)	**Architecture**	Cosine similarity
Tweet 1 Just getting over the vaccine 💉 reaction, only sleepiness remains because I couldn't sleep with such a headache and fever, let's go! / Ya saliendo de la reacción de la vacuna 💉 solo quedaba el sueño porque no pude dormir con semejante dolor de cabeza,fiebre. A darle! **Tweet 2** You can't take much, can you? I'm the most squeamish about injections and it honestly hurt, I got a little fever with the first doze. But the second one was like nothing #AstraZeneca / Como que no aguantan nada ¿no creen? Soy la más chillona para las inyecciones y la neta ni dolió, si un poco de fiebre la primera dosis. Pero la segunda me hizo los mandados #AstraZeneca	PV-DBOW	0.2328
	PV-DM	0.0094

2.6 Text Clustering and Word Clouds for Topic Visualization

After generating the vector representation of the tweet set, the K-Means clustering algorithm can be applied to identify groups of similar topics. Using the elbow method and the silhouette coefficient, it was determined that six clusters provide the optimal number of groups for K-Means.

For topic analysis, several attributes were considered, including URL, tweet content, tokens, day, month, year, latitude, longitude, and borough. Each tweet is assigned a cluster label, which is associated with these attributes, enabling the classification of tweets into distinct topic groups.

To visualize the topic clusters, word clouds were employed. Word clouds offer a straightforward way to identify and interpret key words based on their frequency within the dataset—the larger a word appears in the cloud, the more frequently it occurs in the associated tweets. This visual representation helps to quickly grasp the main themes discussed in a set of tweets.

For example, Fig. 6 highlights prominent words such as "efecto" ("effect"), "dolor cabeza" ("headache"), "reacción" ("reaction"), "brazo" ("arm"), and "potente" ("potent"). These words suggest that the corresponding cluster is predominantly related to side effects from vaccination.

While the word cloud in Fig. 6 provides a broad overview, generating smaller, more specific clusters is recommended for a more detailed analysis and accurate interpretation of the topics. To achieve this, the Topic Modeling technique using Latent Dirichlet Allocation (LDA) was employed.

Figures 4 and 5 present topics that range from discussions about the benefits of vaccination to the vaccination of teachers. However, one particular cluster focuses more on the side effects experienced after vaccination, with words such as "dolor brazo" ("arm pain"), "dolor cabeza" ("headache"), and "fiebre" ("fever") being prominent. Other side effects mentioned in this cluster include "dolor" ("pain"), "muscular" ("muscular"), "temperatura" ("temperature"), "cansado" ("tired"), "dolor cuerpo" ("body pain"), "dolor articular" ("joint pain"), "mareo" ("dizziness"), "náusea" ("nausea"), "escalofrío" ("chill"), "frío" ("cold"), and "fatiga" ("fatigue"). These terms are considered significant topics as they are directly related to the subject of vaccination side effects.

Fig. 4. General Terms

Fig. 5. Side Effects Report Theme

Finally, 606 tweets were obtained that comment on their possible effects due to vaccination. Subsequently, data cubes were designed to statistically analyze the side effects of the COVID-19 vaccine: 2 spatial dimensions (Borough and Coordinate) to identify the location of the most important topics, 1 temporal dimension (date) to determine when certain topics occurred, 2 categorical dimensions (COVID vaccine effect, COVID vaccine brand) showing the different types of topics found, and 1 metadata dimension (Tweet) corresponding to the attributes associated with the tweets.

3 Results

A total of 21 different types of potential side effects were identified, as detailed in Table 2. The highest number of reported side effects occurred in July 2021. Common symptoms included headache, fatigue, fever, body aches, and chills, which manifested within hours after vaccination, both during the day and night, and in some cases, even days after receiving the dose. During this period, many individuals also reported experiencing sleepiness and nausea. Notably, in August 2021, five women reported experiencing cramps following vaccination, potentially indicating changes in their menstrual cycles.

Table 2. Identified Secondary Effects

Topic	#
Fever/fiebre	86
Arm pain/dolor de brazo	109
Headache/dolor de cabeza	97
Joint pain/dolor articular	8
Body pain/dolor de cuerpo	35
Sleepiness/sueño	40
Drowsiness/mareo	17
Cut body/cuerpo cortado	18
Temperature/temperatura	29
Fatigue/fatiga	11
Chill/escalofrío	34
Cold/frío	9
Tiredness/cansancio	38
Sore throat/dolor de garganta	4
Flu/gripe	8
Tired/cansado	14
Nausea/nausea	14
Muscle pain/dolor muscular	11
Colic/cólico	9
Sweat/sudor	2
Menstrual cycle/ciclo menstrual	13

In 2022, comments on potential side effects primarily focused on booster doses, with February being the month with the most mentions. The vaccines most frequently discussed by citizens were AstraZeneca and Sputnik-V. For AstraZeneca, the predominant side effects included headache, fever, arm pain, chills, and body aches. In contrast, the most reported symptoms for Sputnik-V were headache, fever, arm pain, and sleepiness.

Geographically, the boroughs of Cuauhtémoc, Benito Juárez, Tlalpan, and Iztapalapa reported headaches as the most common effect associated with AstraZeneca. Meanwhile, in Coyoacán and Cuauhtémoc, arm pain was more frequently mentioned. In Coyoacán, headaches were more commonly reported following the Sputnik-V vaccine.

Figure 6 shows that the central boroughs of Benito Juárez and Cuauhtémoc recorded the highest tweet density, similar to the initial tweet extraction phase. In the southern boroughs of Coyoacán and Tlalpan, a high concentration of tweets was also observed, as well as in the western borough of Miguel Hidalgo. This can be attributed, as noted during the data exploration, to these boroughs being either densely populated or having a large number of residents who actively use Twitter to communicate and express themselves more freely (particularly in Benito Juárez, Cuauhtémoc, and Miguel Hidalgo).

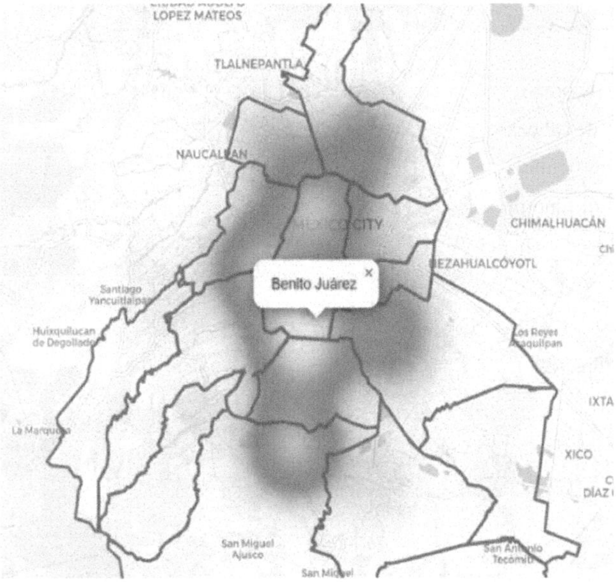

Fig. 6. Heat Map: Secondary effects in Mexico City (CDMX)

Figure 7 illustrates the geographical distribution of "fever," which is concentrated in Benito Juárez. The boroughs with the highest incidence of reported side effects were Benito Juárez, Cuauhtémoc, Coyoacán, Tlalpan, and Miguel Hidalgo. The most frequently mentioned symptoms in these areas were headache, arm pain, and fever.

Finally, Fig. 8 shows that "headache" effects are primarily reported in the central and southern areas of Mexico City.

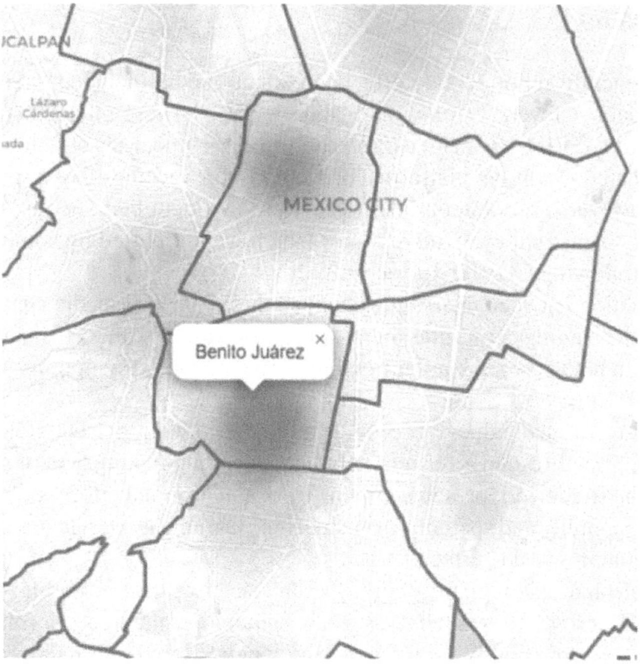

Fig. 7. Heat Map: Distribution of "fever" effect in Mexico City (CDMX)

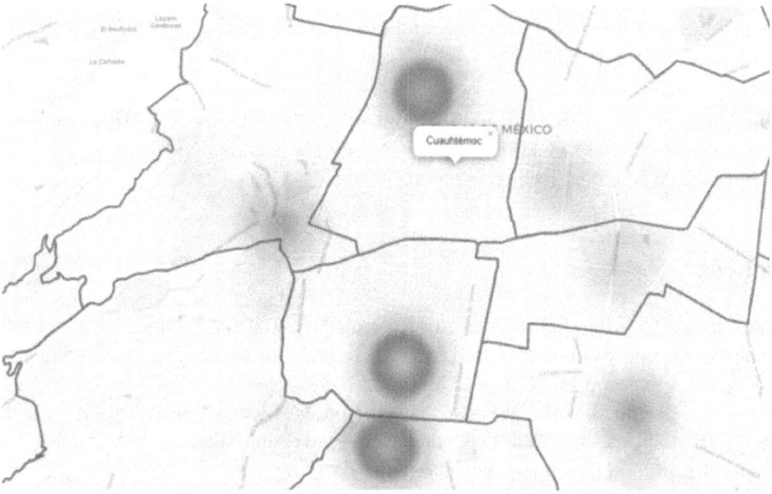

Fig. 8. Heat Map: Distribution of secondary of "headache" effects

4 Conclusions

The most frequently reported side effects on social media included "headache," "fatigue," "arm pain," "fever," "chills," and "muscle pain." These reflect a consistency in the response to COVID-19 vaccines, as seen in both clinical observations and public perceptions shared on digital platforms, particularly for vaccines like AstraZeneca and Sputnik-V. However, less common side effects were also identified, such as "drowsiness," "nausea," and "menstrual cycle disruption," which were reported by some residents of Mexico City following COVID-19 vaccination.

The correlation between the results obtained through social media analysis in Mexico City and the findings from the literature review supports the consistency of these observations. In both cases, a similar trend in post-vaccination symptoms was observed throughout 2021.

Although social media does not provide a fully accurate representation of reality, it has become a crucial resource for remotely understanding the impacts of public health campaigns. The framework presented in this work can leverage information from social media, both temporally and spatially, using machine learning models to identify potential or previously unknown side effects.

Traditional pharmacovigilance could be enhanced by incorporating social media monitoring, as these platforms serve as a raw source of unfiltered information. Social networks have become highly informative and beneficial tools for uncovering medical concerns, such as tracking adverse effects.

This work could set a precedent in the design of pharmacovigilance systems, improving the monitoring of the effects of emergency vaccines. At the same time, it aims to increase public trust by sharing the experiences of individuals, thereby fostering greater confidence in COVID-19 vaccines.

Acknowledgments. The authors would like to thank to projects SIP-20240707 and 20242869, IPN, and Conahcyt CF-2023-G-1170 and ESCOM-IPN, Secretaría de Investigación y Posgrado, Instituto Politécnico Nacional for their support.

References

1. Centros para el Control y la Prevención de Enfermedades (CDC): Posibles efectos secundarios después de vacunarse contra el COVID-19 (2022). https://espanol.cdc.gov/coronavirus/2019-ncov/vaccines/expect/after.html
2. Encabo, I.: El precio del "milagro" israelí con la vacuna: pagar más y dar datos a Pfizer (2021). https://www.elindependiente.com/vida-sana/salud/2021/01/21/el-precio-del-milagro-israeli-con-la-vacuna-pagar-mas-y-dar-datos-a-pfizer/
3. Salud. H.: Nuevos efectos secundarios de las vacunas de Pfizer, AstraZeneca, Moderna y Janssen (2021). https://www.heraldo.es/noticias/salud/2021/03/10/nuevos-efectos-secundarios-vacuna-pfizer-moderna-1476559.html
4. Beck, M.: How to scrape tweets with snscrape (2020). https://betterprogramming.pub/how-to-scrape-tweets-with-snscrape-90124ed006af
5. Garcia, J., Martinez, J., Garcia, E., Reyna, O.: Revisión de técnicas de pre-procesamiento de textos para la clasificación automática de tweets en español. Revista de Cómputo Aplicado **1**(2), 4–7 (2017)

6. Stack Overflow: How should I interpret "size" parameter in Doc2Vec function of gensim? (2016). https://stackoverflow.com/questions/34948650/how-should-i-interpret-size-parameter-in-doc2vec-function-of-gensim. Accessed 25 Nov 2022
7. Fernandes-de-Oliveira, G., Massarani, L., Oliveira, T., Scalfi, G., Alves-dos-Santos, M.: The COVID-19 vaccine on Facebook: a study of emotions expressed by the Brazilian public. Comunicar (2023). https://doi.org/10.3916/C76-2023-10
8. Güven, O., Kaşikeman, O., Selçuk, H., Demireller, M., Kurt, B.F.: The side-effects of Covid-19 vaccine (Coronavac): a study in a province of Turkey. Turkish J. Family Med. Primary Care **17**(1), 87–93 (2023). https://doi.org/10.21763/tjfmpc.1151226
9. Leng, A., Maitland, E., Wang, S., Nicholas, S., Liu, R., Wang, J.: Individual preferences for COVID-19 vaccination in China. Vaccine **39**(2), 247–254 (2021). https://doi.org/10.1016/j.vaccine.2020.12.009
10. Luo, S., et al.: Behavioural intention of receiving COVID-19 vaccination, social media exposures and peer discussions in China. Epidemiol. Infect. (2021). https://doi.org/10.1017/S0950268821000947
11. Priyadharshini, A., Begum, J., Ali, S., Pattnaik, S., Sharma, D., Lalitha, D.: Sputnik V vaccine perception and hesitancy in a tertiary health care centre transformed to COVID-19 vaccine centre: a case study. J. Educ. Health Promot. **12**(1), 366 (2023). https://doi.org/10.4103/jehp.jehp_322_23

Author Index

M. F. Mata-Rivera et al. (Eds.): GIS-LATAM 2024, CCIS 2298, pp. 223–224, 2025.
https://doi.org/10.1007/978-3-031-80017-7